A LITTLE
ANTHROPOLOGY

Third Edition

A LITTLE ANTHROPOLOGY

Dennison Nash

Prentice Hall
Upper Saddle River, New Jersey 07458

Library of Congress Cataloging-in-Publication Data
NASH, DENNISON.
    A little anthropology / DENNISON NASH.—3rd ed.
        p.   cm.
    Includes bibliographical references and index.
    ISBN 0-13-906736-1
    1. Anthropology.   I. Title.
GN25.N37   1999
    306—dc21   98-30166

Editorial director: *Charlyce Jones Owen*
Editor in chief: *Nancy Roberts*
Managing editor: *Sharon Chambliss*
Production editor: *Edie Riker*
Cover art director: *Jayne Conte*
Cover design: *Kiwi Design*
Cover image: *French Government Tourist Office*
Buyer: *Lynn Pearlman*
Marketing manager: *Christopher DeJohn*

This book was set in 10/12 Palatino by East End Publishing Services
and was printed and bound by Courier Companies, Inc. The cover was
printed by Phoenix Color Corp.

 © 1999, 1993, 1989 by Prentice-Hall, Inc.
Simon & Schuster / A Viacom Company
Upper Saddle River, New Jersey 07458

Printed in the United States of America

10   9   8   7   6   5   4   3   2   1

ISBN 0-13-906736-1

Prentice-Hall International (UK) Limited, *London*
Prentice-Hall of Australia Pty. Limited, *Sydney*
Prentice-Hall Canada Inc., *Toronto*
Prentice-Hall Hispanoamericana, S.A., *Mexico*
Prentice-Hall of India Private Limited, *New Delhi*
Prentice-Hall of Japan, Inc., *Tokyo*
Simon & Schuster Asia Pte. Ltd., *Singapore*
Editora Prentice-Hall do Brasil, Ltda., *Rio de Janeiro*

Contents

Preface
to the
First Edition

This book is my own attempt to interest a new generation of American college students, and others, in what the subject of anthropology has to offer them. When it was written, anthropologists in many American colleges and universities were struggling with the realization that theirs, like other "impractical" disciplines, was a subject of declining demand. Enrollments were down. Anthropology majors and graduate students had drifted away to more vocationally viable disciplines. The job market for anthropologists was tough and money for field research was hard to find. Finally, in their classrooms, anthropologists were having to come to terms with an indifference and even aversion to what they had thought was an intrinsically fascinating subject.

There had been a time in the 1960s and earlier when student interest in anthropology was strong; at that time our courses were full and at times even overcrowded. Except in the more privileged corners of academia, that time was obviously past. This came as a shock to old hands who remembered the earlier Golden Age, when even mediocre teachers had no difficulty in finding a respectable audience. Some of those old hands were unaware of what was going on in their classrooms or, if aware, preferred to concentrate on their research interests. Others recognized a decline in anthropology's fortunes, but did little more than curse the students, wring their hands, and hope for better days. Still others considered the drift of anthropology toward the academic periphery as something that might be addressed in a variety of adaptive ways. The production of new, more interesting reading matter about the subject was one of them.

A Little Anthropology is my own response to the challenge of dealing with the new, tough audiences that we anthropologists are faced with—audiences that must be engaged as well as instructed in the essentials of our discipline and its subject matter. These essentials, it seems to me, revolve around a number of general pedagogical questions: What do anthropologists study? How do they go about it? What perspective do they bring to their work? What have they found out about the subject? And finally, what is the relevance of all of this for them and for those whose interest they are trying to stimulate and satisfy? In my view, one of the reasons for the decline in anthropological fortunes was that many of us, for whatever reasons, had lost track of these essential pedagogical questions and the need to communicate what we knew about them to the *general* reader. That is what I have attempted to do here.

Most of the writing of this book took place during a sabbatical leave from the University of Connecticut, where I have passed most of my professional career. It would be hard to imagine more auspicious circumstances. Supportive and stimulating environments included a study made available by the Graduate School of my university; a lovely apartment in the center of Beaune (Burgundy), France, where I also engaged in some research; and an office in the Department of Anthropology at Vassar College, where I was a visiting professor during a part of my leave.

A number of individuals helped by reading and criticizing portions of the manuscript. I am indebted for this to Arthur Abrahmson, James Barnett, Robert Bee, Carole Berman, Scott Cook, James Faris, Jean Fuschillo, Bernard Magubane, Ronald Rohner, and Benjamin Wiesel. A special burden of critical assistance was taken on by E. J. R. Booth and Seth Leacock. Finally, many students in my large 1986 introductory course (Anthropology 106) at the University of Connecticut kindly offered their comments on three chapters that they had read in class. To all of these people, and to Rita Govern and Deborah Crary of the University of Connecticut Research Foundation who typed the manuscript, I would like to express my appreciation.

The challenge provided by the new, tough generation of college students and the best possible outside assistance and support contributed greatly to the writing of this book, certainly, but it never could have been made without a deep and lively acquaintance with anthropology and its subject matter. It is a privilege for me now to share that acquaintance with students and others who would like to know what anthropology has to tell them about their world. If they find something of value in this work, it will add a bonus to the pleasure I've had in writing it.

Dennison Nash
Storrs, Connecticut

Preface
to the
Third Edition

Now, a decade after its first appearance, *A Little Anthropology* continues to be a modest success, thus confirming my belief that there is an audience for an introductory work in anthropology that is written simply, engagingly, directly, and with as little academic paraphernalia as possible. The audience I've had in mind consists mainly of American college students with whom I've been involved for many years. Experience has shown that the book appeals to intelligent laypeople as well.

The First Edition of the book, written at a time when I was still teaching large groups of introductory students, most of whom needed to be "turned on," practically wrote itself. Not so this time around. Perhaps my formal retirement has had something to do with it (I continue to teach only a small advanced course in fieldwork). Great changes in anthropology and the world since I first entertained the idea of writing this book—changes that only the most myopic would not recognize—certainly have posed problems in preparing this revision. Even as I put down these words, the changes threaten to make them obsolete, and it would be unconscionable not to try to take them into account. As a result, it may be that this Third Edition has been written with less of a feeling of assurance than the First Edition. I have noted no decline in my enthusiasm, however.

How have I kept up with all the changes? First, I've used informants who are currently teaching introductory students. The gist of their comments is that the students haven't changed much in a decade. They are not for the most part the "romantic adventurers" who once added zest to our classrooms, but, rather, the "hard headed," practical-minded types who I originally set out to seduce. Above all, they still want to know what they need to know for the exam. I know that these students and I continue to inhabit different worlds, but I, at least, seem to have to make a greater effort to reach them with my writing, and I am sure now that it is important to have a sympathetic and dedicated teacher assist me in this process.

Secondly, I've tried to keep up with developments in the field, which have not been trivial. Anthropology has always had its humanistic and scientific wings. Once I moved easily back and forth between them. Now as a new generation of humanistic types crowds onto center stage, this is not so readily accomplished. I'm not entirely unsympathetic to their "agenda," but for one reason or another, I find myself increasingly siding with those who feel that ultimately anthropology should be a generalizing, empirically based science of humanity. Still, I hope that in this edition I have not shut the door on humanistic inclinations and that those who like to think of anthropology as a humanistic science will be comfortable with my approach. In this regard, my views come close to those of Lawrence Kuznar in his *Reclaiming a Scientific Anthropology*.

As far as the world is concerned, anyone who attends to national and international events ought to be aware that the reality of change and attendant social problems are hard to ignore. As an introductory work, *A Little Anthropology* is more concerned with current events than most other "texts." The subject matter of anthropology is no longer far away but on our doorsteps, so to speak, making it impossible not to ruffle some feathers as we go about our anthropological business. Even those anthropologists who follow an ideal of neutrality will stir up people who are committed to this or that social arrangement; and since most sociocultural anthropologists these days take positions that tend to be critical of establishments and the people in them, we have reason to believe that there will be students who don't want to hear what we have to say.

My informants tell me that we have a problem here. Most students, they say, don't want to hear about the downtrodden and the role of the West in bringing about the current inequities of the world. These students may not want to have someone add to whatever burden of guilt they already have to bear. Already in adolescence, many of them seem to be committed believers in a system that is being questioned in the anthropological classroom. Perhaps they are like those early students in my classes who complained to a local priest about what they were learning. But I've also found that there are other students who have found something of value in course material that is both sympathetically and objectively presented. Hopefully, a "quorum" of such students remain who can be—if not convinced—at least touched by this little book, which it is my privilege to offer in this Third Edition.

ACKNOWLEDGMENTS

A number of people have helped me with this edition. Let me thank, first of all, colleagues of many years, Seth Leacock, Arthur Abrahmson, Scott Cook, Robert Bee, and new ones on board, Norman Chance and Mark Mansperger, who have given me the benefit of their criticism. Further, my assistant, Michael Gelfand, who handles word processors adroitly and who now knows today's introductory students better than I, has made an indispensable contribution to the production of this book (his critical reading of the manuscript was especially valuable). I would also like to thank the Prentice Hall reviewers: Eric J. Bailey, Indiana University; Lee Cronk, Texas A&M University; and Edwin S. Segal, University of Louisville for their comments and my corporate "handlers" at Prentice Hall for helping me to get the manuscript into publishable shape. Finally, I would like to express my appreciation to the University of Connecticut where I have spent most of my academic career. Now, even after retirement, I maintain strong ties to this institution and make use of its resources in various ways. With all of this assistance, I hope I have once again produced something of value.

As always, I appreciate your comments.

Dennison Nash
Storrs, Connecticut

REFERENCE

KUZNAR, LAWRENCE, *Reclaiming a Scientific Anthropology*. Walnut Creek, CA.: AltaMira Press, 1997.

To Begin

The ancient Chinese philosopher, Lao Tzu, said that a journey of a thousand miles begins with a single step. The reader of these words has just taken a few steps into the field of anthropology.

What does this field of study involve? Some people have never heard about it. Others have certain ideas that reflect what they've seen in newspapers or on television. Still others may have read some of the anthropological literature. Some people think that anthropologists are scientists who are interested in ruins—that they dig up old things like foundations of dwellings, pieces of pottery, and stone tools. Then they try to make sense out of them. Another view associates anthropologists with the theory of evolution, which leaves aside the work of a creator in accounting for the emergence and development of human beings. Parents who have a strict creationist viewpoint may want to protect their children from anthropologists and their doctrines. Still another view puts anthropologists in contact with strange or exotic people who may live on the edge of survival or carry on interesting sexual activities. All of these notions about anthropology contain a degree of truth. Like the views formed by those blind men clustered around an elephant, however, each is only partially correct.

Some anthropologists are interested in historic or prehistoric ways of life. Others are concerned with human origins and biological evolution; and a good many have studied strange or exotic peoples in faraway places. But anthropologists now also investigate the behavior of people in modern restaurants, in hospitals, in businesses, in urban ghettoes, or on tours. They may be concerned with modern nation-states as well as those of ancient times; and the behavior of the people next door can be just as interesting to them as that of an exotic people living far away. Taken in its broadest sense, anthropology investigates all aspects of all the people who have ever lived in all times and places. As far as we know, these creatures have only been found on the planet Earth for a rather brief period of time. They represent a comparatively recent form of life, one that began to emerge on this planet more than four billion years ago. Humans have certain physical qualities that set them apart from other animals, but these differences are, with certain crucial exceptions, comparatively slight and mostly a matter of degree. Humans and chimpanzees, for example, share more than 99 percent of the same biological heritage.

Anthropologists are not the only scientists interested in human beings. Political scientists deal with humans' political life, economists with their economies, psychologists with their psyches, physiologists with their bodies, and so on. But these other scientists do not view humans in the comprehensive way that anthropologists do. Moreover, they tend to confine themselves to certain kinds of human beings, such as the ones who live in present-day Western society, or as is sometimes the case with psychologists, the students in their classrooms.

Anthropologists, in contrast, consider all aspects of human beings in all times and places. What do these subjects have in common? In what ways are they different? Why are they the way they are? These are some of the grand anthropological questions that will be raised throughout this book.

Like other scientists, anthropologists, who are committed to the comprehensive study of human beings, have their specialties, which sometimes can take on a life of their own. In the United States, where I happen to be based, there are three or four major areas of specialization, each of which has its particular view of humans: physical anthropology, archeology, and sociocultural anthropology, which, in my view, also includes anthropological linguistics. Physical anthropologists are interested in variabilities and commonalities of the physical nature of human beings, including the genes that determine body structure. They see humans evolving along different paths from the time they first emerged on earth. Some of these anthropologists, like the Leakey family, have become famous in the course of discovering fossils that shed light on the emergence and development of early humans. Other physical anthropologists are well-known forensic specialists who help lawyers draw conclusions about sometimes fragmentary human remains that may have been discovered after some murder or massacre.

Archeologists search for things that humans leave behind. They dig a lot and sometimes even go under water. The remains of tools and weapons, hearths, pottery, foundations of dwellings, and art objects concern them. The aim of these scientists is to use such evidence in order to reconstruct the way people once behaved. It is surprising how many scientifically defensible conclusions can be drawn from only a few material remains.

This book is based mostly on the work of sociocultural anthropologists, myself included. This branch of anthropology corresponds to what others may call ethnology, ethnography, or even sociology. It deals primarily with the behavior of contemporary peoples who have been studied directly by these anthropologists. I use the word *behavior* here in its broadest possible sense; that is, to include not only observable actions, but also what goes on in the human body and a mind full of meanings. Such behavior can be viewed as a property of an individual, a group, or even larger collectivities that may ultimately embrace all of humankind. In humans, behavior is heavily dependent on learning and profoundly meaningful to the parties involved—qualities that have caused anthropologists to use the special term *culture*. It is to the cultures of different groups of human beings that sociocultural anthropologists direct their attention.

For those who like to pigeonhole, this little book is an introduction to sociocultural anthropology from an American point of view. It doesn't cover the whole of that field, however. People who have had the opportunity to look at one of the many introductory texts will see that it includes subject areas that are not dealt with here. However, I don't think it is necessary to be exhaustive in order to give people the feel for our subject matter and the way we approach it. Later on, readers will be able to peruse more extensive or specialized books. Furthermore, I believe that it would be a mistake to insist that what is included here pertains only to the field of sociocultural anthropology. Any anthropologist ought to have an overview of human beings that derives not only from a specialized area, but from other areas as well. It is this overview that makes anthropology so valuable. The important thing is never to lose sight of complete human beings and always to be willing to entertain what others have to say about them. Nothing about humans should be considered foreign to any anthropological undertaking. Accordingly, in this book I refer not only to the work of sociocultural anthropologists, but also to other anthropological specialists, social scientists, writers, and even some proverbial "men in the street."

A Little Anthropology has not been written to be studied. There are definitions in it. There are summaries. There also are names. For some students, these all cry out for underlining and for later regurgitation to some teacher. So it may be. But I had no intention of activating this almost reflex student mechanism when I began to write this book. I had thought, rather, to produce something that might be bought at an airport bookstall and read on what otherwise might have been a long, boring flight to somewhere. What I wanted to do was acquaint—even engage—a reader with the subject matter of anthropology. Being human, I thought readers ought to be fascinated by a discussion of the human condition as we know it. And being fascinated, they would continue their inquiries on their own, not only as students, but as people who must make a life for themselves. "Who am I?" "Where do I fit in?" "How should I live my life?" These are grand questions that can emerge on reading this book.

Anthropology is, then, about all of us human beings, and it is the charge of the anthropologist to tell our story. That story should try to give as understanding and objective an account of people as possible. It should include not just one group of people, but many. It should not confine itself to just one aspect of human life, but consider all aspects as areas of possible interest. As Miles Richardson has pointed out, anthropologists are modern myth tellers who try, as accurately and as sympathetically as they can, to describe the human condition. Because they are the first to have access to information about all the peoples who have ever lived, humans today are the first to be able to witness this condition in its entirety and to see themselves as a part of the vast sweep of it all. The anthropologist speaks directly to them.

The reader may ask, "What, then, is in it for me?" That, as they say, is a good question. Certainly, anthropology will not fulfill some narrow vocational interest. Though it does have a practical, or applied, side, as reference to the work of applied anthropologists will demonstrate, it seems at the outset to offer little that is of practical value. (Indeed, a colleague of mine once said that he became an anthropologist because it was his habit to pursue useless knowledge.) However, appearances can be deceiving. The habit of looking at things anthropologically can reveal misunderstood or overlooked workings of the world around us. Suppose we have problems in school or the workplace. Anthropologically viewed, those problems become an aspect of some human enterprise in which we are all involved and which may be understood and possibly changed for the benefit of ourselves and others. Further, as we delve more and more deeply into the study of other human beings, we may begin to see ourselves reflected in them. The reflection may be real, reversed, or distorted, and it may undercut some cherished notions about who we are and where we stand, but it should give one a firmer foundation for acting in a complex, changing world. In the end, anthropology will help us know something about the whole human condition and where we fit into it. In the contemporary world, where solid ground is more and more difficult to find, this would seem to be precious knowledge indeed.

For some people, the study of anthropology will open up new vistas and turn out to be something of a conversion experience. It will cause them to see everything in a new light. Others may be more modestly enlightened. Whatever turns out to be the case, I hope that the reader will find something valuable in *A Little Anthropology*. Enough said. So much for preliminaries. It is time to begin.

REFERENCE

RICHARDSON, MILES, "Anthropologist—The Myth Teller," *American Ethnologist*, 2 (August) 1975, 517–33.

Culture

WHAT IS CULTURE?

This word is something that has long been associated with anthropology. To be sure, anthropology does not have exclusive rights to this concept. Biologists deal with cultures in their laboratories. A government may have its department or ministry of culture. And sociologists, historians, and literary critics may use the term in their work. But especially in America, a good case can be made for anthropological ownership. The concept seems to be pervasive, spilling over into the public domain where people often use it to refer to the customs of some group of people. Common usage, however, does not necessarily mean a shared—or full—understanding. Even anthropologists may be fuzzy in their comprehension of the term, and they may differ in their views about what it means. But there does appear to be considerable agreement on the meaning of the term *culture* in anthropology. What is this meaning, and how is it used in anthropological work?

Like all scientific concepts, the concept of culture refers to some aspect of the world "out there," that is the reality that scientists are committed to study. It helps anthropologists to single out from this reality certain things that help them in their work. Consider behavior, taken in its broadest sense to include all aspects of action including ideas. One anthropological line of investigation concerns the behavior of human beings as compared with that of other animals, particularly nonhuman primates such as chimpanzees and gorillas, which are most like humans in their physical makeup. Anthropologists are also interested in the behavior of particular groups of people in comparison with others. Do humans everywhere tend to behave in the same ways or do they differ by population? If, as seems likely, the answer is "all of the above," what is the extent of their similarities and differences? The concept of culture helps to further both of these anthropological lines of investigation.

How does the concept of culture help in the comparison of humans with other animals? The crucial issue here concerns how behavior is acquired. Bees go on about their business day after day, year in and year out, in the same inflexible fashion. Each type of bee is specialized for a particular kind of activity, and it continues (or tries to continue) this activity regardless of changes around it. Thus a worker bee "works" to collect pollen, which contributes to the survival of the hive. This behavior is mostly programmed by genetic mechanisms that change comparatively slowly in a manner independent of changes in the environment. Behavioral change, then, tends to await a change in bee genes. As a result, the behavior of bees is comparatively inflexible. Chimpanzee or gorilla behavior is more flexible, but humans have a vast advantage over all other animals.

The flexibility of human behavior is the result of an enormously increased capacity to learn and remember not only from their own, but (with the aid of language) from others' experiences as well. So even though it is true that humans are not unique among animals in their ability to acquire and recall what they and others have acquired through learning, so great is their capacity that some kind of special marker seems to be called for. That label, as used by anthropologists, is the term *culture*. Sometimes, in order to keep things neater, anthropologists may use the word *protoculture* to distinguish the comparatively small amount of behavior acquired and retained from experience in other animals. But whether this distinction is made or not, the term culture is used to refer to what is considered to be an outstanding quality of humankind.

In addition to the comparison of humans and nonhumans, anthropologists are interested in the differences and similarities between human groups or populations, each of which works out, largely through learning, its behavioral adaptations to conditions of life. The cluster of these adaptations is called *a culture*, as, for example, the culture of the Cheyenne Indians of the North American plains, of a refugee camp in Thailand, or of the board of directors of a multinational corporation. When used in this way, the term is localized in a more or less well-defined group of human beings. Observations are made about common behavioral patterns that members of the group have developed, and accordingly, one often sees in anthropological writings some statement about culture being shared. This does not mean that all people in the group behave exactly alike, but that they refer to certain agreed-upon norms or standards of conduct. While recognizing that each individual has his or her own way of relating to social norms, anthropologists see in each group certain standards that provide direction for its members. Thus, group X may be characterized as being aggressive, monotheistic nomads even though there are some not-so-aggressive, atheistic, and possibly sedentary people among them. This type of general description helps anthropologists to identify a culture and to make comparisons with others.

A final comment about the concept of culture is made necessary by its association in the minds of many anthropologists with the greatly advanced, if not also unique, capacity of humans to think about their actions. So, in the consideration of the behavior of a human group, one may find its standards of conduct—that is, its culture—phrased in terms of mental representations such as values, ideas, symbols, and so forth. Certainly, such things are learned and qualify as culture according to the point of view of this book. But this narrower view of human actions does not do full justice to a science that is charged with the full-scale, comprehensive study of humankind, to which most anthropologists subscribe.

THE REALITY OF CULTURE

Culture then, like any other scientific concept, refers to an aspect of the world "out there,"—that is, the real world as we know it. A particularly good way to come to terms with this reality is to spend some time in a foreign country. For example, consider the case of an American I knew who set out to do business in Spain some years ago. This businessman gradually became aware that there was a human behavioral reality in this unfamiliar place and that he would have to adapt to it if he hoped to be successful. The native people with whom he dealt on a day-to-day basis in Spain tended to behave differently than people in the United States. The American wanted to be able to count on his host counterpart to fulfill his promises. For example, would the construction of a factory be completed by the date agreed upon? It became clear that this was unlikely. Delay tended to follow delay, and things that were promised for mañana might appear weeks later, or possibly never. As he gained experience, the American learned that this was not the exception, but the rule among the people he dealt with. For these people, mañana usually did not mean tomorrow, and more generally, a close fit between promises and deeds was not expected. It also became increasingly clear to the visitor that considerations of family and friendship often entered into business dealings. In this less-businesslike atmosphere, the American sputtered and fumed until he finally began to learn (usually the hard way) that the people he was dealing with were not wrong or crazy, only different. They had their own customs.

Perhaps the American also began to reflect on his own American ways of behaving, recognizing that these ways, too, were special. This may have led to the revelation that each group of people has its own standards of conduct that it considers natural or right and that individuals within the group are guided by these standards. From personal experience, then, the American had come to accept one aspect of the reality that anthropologists call culture. Having understood that, he could then use this understanding to advantage in his business activities.

An anthropologist might say that the transformed American had acquired a cross-cultural or transcultural perspective and that he was beginning to think like an anthropologist who makes comparisons between cultures. At first the businessman would have criticized the Spaniards by referring to their lack of reliability or even modernity. At that point, the "States" would have provided the benchmark for making judgments about other cultures. Such observations—as any anthropologist would be delighted to tell him—were *ethnocentric* because they were based on the assumption that his own culture was the center of the universe and that everything should be measured against it. The American, however, lacked the power to make his ethnocentric views prevail in Spain. Accordingly, he acquired, however reluctantly, something like the anthropological viewpoint that any culture (including one's own) is simply one of a number of ways in which people have worked out their adaptation to specific life conditions.

If he were particularly perceptive, the American might have had another revelation at this point: that, for better or worse, one is, more or less, a creature of one's culture. Each culture's norms have a hold over its people, and it is just as difficult to change norms as it is to change who someone is. People *can* change through learning, but it is not so easy to go against the norms or rules of one's group. Our culture becomes an inextricable part of our lives and sets limits on who we can reasonably be. Such a revelation points to a paradox. The capacity to create what has been called culture has liberated humans from the dictates of their biological heritage (referred to as "nature" by some anthropologists). But in each culture the weight of social custom or opinion limits people's outlook and their ability to change. James Baldwin, an African American writer, said that he did not realize how much of an American he was until he went abroad. The fact that Baldwin was not exactly in the mainstream of American society suggests how powerful a hold a culture can have on its people.

THE STUDY OF A CULTURE

All anthropologists deal with culturally constituted or constructed facts of human life, but it is, perhaps, those sociocultural anthropologists who study the lifeways of contemporary peoples, for whom the reality of culture is most evident. In their role as ethnographer-fieldworker, these anthropologists are bent on describing particular cultures and attempting to explain why they are as they are. In order to do this they prefer to associate intimately with a people for an extended period of time (studies of "cultures at a distance," as in historical research, are not ruled out, but they do not have quite the special cachet of fieldwork). During this period, in which ethnographic fieldworkers come face to face with their subjects in often difficult conditions, they seek to acquire an understanding of a particular way of life from both inside and out. Such an immersion into an alien life, which may begin with learning a sometimes very difficult language, is generally considered indispensable for the proper study of a culture in depth. Unlike biologists or geologists who study their subjects from outside only, the anthropologist, like the psychiatrist, has to get at the subjective dimension of meaning in human subjects as well, a task that is considerably aided by an intimate association with them.

There are many examples of anthropologists and others who, by virtue of special capacities or circumstances, have managed to delve deeply into the lives of particular peoples. An outstanding example is found in the account of Jan Yoors in *The Gypsies*. As a boy, Yoors was able to enter into the life of a band of European gypsy wanderers, normally not known for hospitality to outsiders. His account of that life, written from the point of view of an outsider who came to be fully accepted by these people, comes across as particularly authentic.

Anyone who has been abroad knows that there are problems in adapting to, and living among an alien people. Anthropologists are not immune to these problems, which sometimes can be severe. Among these are life-threatening circumstances, of which the disappearance of Michael Rockefeller (an art enthusiast from a wealthy American family) on a field trip in New Guinea is a haunting reminder. And usually there is some threat of culture shock, a kind of situational neurosis that comes about when one loses one's cultural bearings. In one case, this was so severe for me that I developed mild psychosomatic symptoms and attempted to "hide" from the natives I was studying. There also may be problems in establishing rapport or maintaining the interest of informants. This is illustrated in E.E. Evans-Pritchard's humorous introduction to a book on the East African cattle-keeping Nuer. After detailing a particularly frustrating conversation with an informant, this anthropologist speaks of the "Nuer-osis" that can afflict an outsider who has to deal with these Africans. Difficulties of this nature appear to have increased recently as native peoples have become more independent and assertive. Anthropologists these days may have to engage in long negotiations before they can begin their study and submit to surveillance of their work by various parties in the field.

Today, our world is changing rapidly and is filled with conflict. Anthropologists should know that events can overtake their work, and they must be prepared to encounter revolutions, terrorism, and ambiguous political authority. With increasing frequency, they are being forced to take sides and make moral choices that can have wrenching consequences. Imagine the difficulties in trying to conduct a firsthand, politically oriented study in a totalitarian country such as Iraq or an investigation of local conflict between, say, Serbs and Muslims in what was once Yugoslavia.

In addition to such "objective" hazards, there is always the threat of enthnocentrism, which can limit access to information and skew anthropologists' observations and interpretations. No matter their adaptability, in some corner of an anthropologist's mind is a tendency to think that the way things are at home is the way they ought to be. A notorious example of this occurred during Colin Turnbull's sojourn with the Ik, which he recounts in *The Mountain People*. Prevented from pursuing their traditional hunting and gathering way of life in eastern Africa, the Ik are depicted by Turnbull as disintegrating into a condition where collective interests have practically disappeared. In this condition, where individuals tended to think about themselves only, the stronger took from the weaker and even families fell apart. As Turnbull became immersed in this situation, he found himself being treated in the same way that the Ik treated each other and was so repelled by this "war of each against all" that he was unable to continue his role as an understanding and objective fieldworker. As a result, Turnbull's book is, perhaps, a better analysis of his ethnocentric problems in the field than of Ik culture.

This is an extreme example, surely, but it does illustrate the importance of reporting on personal facts that could subvert scientific ideals. No longer is the anthropologist considered to be some kind of superhuman, cross-cultural reporting machine. It is now widely recognized that anthropologists may experience problems like those of any overseas venturer. For many years, the experiences of Bronislaw Malinowski during his fieldwork in the Trobriand Islands (reported in *Argonauts of the Western Pacific* and other works) were taken as a model for the fieldworker. It came as a sensation, therefore, when Malinowski's *A Diary in the Strict Sense of the Term* revealed his personal turmoil and hostility—even prejudice—toward the Trobrianders. Having read this diary, one is in a better position to see where Malinowski was coming from when he wrote about Trobriand culture.

Two anthropologists who approach a people from the same point of view, who have equal access, and who look at the same things should come away with similar descriptions. If not, it could be that there are personal factors distorting the picture they develop. By telling the reader about themselves and their work in the field, as well as the research procedures they employed, anthropologists can help a reader to better evaluate their report. Further, it is increasingly expected that they will discuss their political position and personal background as well as their theoretical orientation. Finally, in keeping with an increasing awareness of rhetorical devices for giving particular "slants" to their descriptions, they might even suggest to the reader possible ways in which their writing style affects the picture they have drawn of a particular people. If they are not open about these matters, someone else almost certainly will be.

The discussion of factors that have the potential to bias an ethnographic report is increasingly expected of an ethnographer these days as anthropologists come round to the notion that they are affected by the same kinds of forces that shape their subjects. This is not to say that anthropological views should not be considered "privileged." Anthropologists, after all, do have systematic research procedures that presumably promote accuracy, and they are showing a greater awareness of biasing factors affecting their observations, interpretations, and methods of communication. Moreover, as they become increasingly above-board with others they can help those others to approach their work with a healthier critical acumen.

A particularly acute series of analyses of this type is found in the volume *Arab Women in the Field*, edited by Soraya Altorki and Camilla Fawzi El-Solh. The contributors, who are all women of Middle Eastern Arab origin, but with Western higher education, explore how such factors as the gender and foreign or indigenous status of the researcher interact with the Arab culture being studied to affect choice of topic, gathering of information, and the analysis and interpretation of that information. Several of the authors stress that being female usually restricts the amount of information they can get from Arab men who feel that certain topics are for men only. I am reminded here of how I was blocked from using participant observation to study certain "social" activities of American women in Spain. Such restrictions may not be final, however, as I demonstrated by the use of special informants and as one Arab woman ethnographer showed by playing up her role as an upper-class professional woman; and if they are indeed final, there may be compensating advantages in working with one's own gender. In any case, there is no substitute for being fully aware of oneself and the creative possibilities for using that self in the field.

Therefore, for the anthropological fieldworker (as well as the sensitive traveler), the reality of the thing called culture is indisputable. One gets in touch with this reality by engaging with people whose lives are directed by cultural norms. This process no longer can be considered as something that happens almost automatically for the reasonable and adaptable fieldworker; rather, it involves an often complex give-and-take between representatives of different cultures, which some anthropologists recognize and treat as a collaboration between natives and themselves.

THE LOOK OF A CULTURE

Anthropologists have a variety of theoretical orientations that they bring to their studies, and their descriptions inevitably take on the look of their theory. Beyond theories, though, there is a common perspective that anthropologists tend to share. This perspective gives each ethnography or field report a distinctive anthropological look that distinguishes it from, say, the look provided by a political scientist or travel writer. One of the dimensions of this look has to do with the normative aspect of a culture. It was pointed out earlier that each group has certain standards of conduct and that people's actual behavior tends to be guided by these standards. Most American drivers, for example, slow down or stop at a stop sign. A description of the behavior of individual motorists and interviews with them can give one some idea of the cultural norm involved in "stopping" and the actual nature of compliance with it. So when Beatrix Le Wita, in *French Bourgeois Culture*, says that the central tenets of that culture (specifically that of the *haut bourgeoisie*, whose status is roughly comparable to what Americans refer to as the upper middle class) involve the art of detail, self-control, and the ritualization of everyday existence, we have to assume this as a shorthand statement about standards or norms of conduct around which there exist ranges of behavior in the upper reaches of that great middling category of the French people.

Some anthropologists, perhaps because they are bent on the study of sociocultural change, may pay more attention to variation in people's behavior away from the norm. So Peta Henderson and Ann Bryn Houghton, in their exploratory study of the life histories of a number of women of a village in what was once British Honduras (*Rising Up: Life Stories of Belizean Women*), make it clear that these women interpret the cultural norm that "the man rules" (*el hombre manda*) in different ways. Although the standard still is for women to get married in their teens or early twenties and bear children, some women have made other choices in this regard, such as getting a job and living alone, living in common-law unions, or becoming nuns.

One would expect to find among every people certain deviants whose extreme behavior puts them beyond the cultural pale, so to speak. A consideration of these deviants has been an important line of anthropological inquiry and has thrown light not only on deviation, but also on cultural norms and the way they operate. Thus, in their study of a famous American example of witchcraft (*Salem Possessed*), Paul Boyer and Steven Nissenbaum suggest that accusations of witchcraft in the Salem witchhunt were used by the farming-oriented population of Salem Village against an advancing commercially oriented class with values that threatened their traditional, agriculturally oriented way of life. Similarly, a student of mine studying a group of sexually active college women found that her subjects were beginning to gossip and show other forms of social disapproval toward a member of their group who they felt was sleeping around too much. All peoples act to limit behavioral variability and so to reinforce the cultural norms on which an orderly social life depends. However, no people, however collectivized, has managed to eliminate behavioral variability. For this reason, a true picture of a culture should give us not only some idea of the standards or norms of conduct, but also of the permitted and prohibited variability from those standards. As in the case of Salem, it also may give us some idea of things to come.

Another dimension of the look that anthropologists have given to a culture has been called holistic. In the anthropological view, the various behaviors of a group of people should not be thought of as existing in isolation, but as fitting together in some way. For example, anthropologists have found that witchcraft tends to be associated with a kind of social structure that, in fact, prevailed in Salem at the time of its witch hunt. This view, which in the light of the current fragmentation and changes in contemporary ways of life, can be overdone and is better taken as a hypothesis rather than an assumption. Indeed, the parts of a culture may reinforce or concur with one another, as in the case of capitalism and individualism, or they may conflict with or contradict one another, as in the interests of different social classes in a particular population. They may, in fact, have no enduring relationship to each other, but many anthropologists have assumed that they do.

There are some obvious examples where the holistic view has been overdone, as in some anthropological references to the capitalist system and Ruth Benedict's famous formulations in *Patterns of Culture*. Benedict thought that single principles could be found to underly the cultures of three peoples who had been studied firsthand by other anthropologists: the Dobuans in the southwestern Pacific, the Pueblo Indians of the southwestern United States, and the Indians of the northwestern coast of America. For example, the fundamental principle underlying various aspects of the Dobuan way of life, according to Benedict, was an extreme suspiciousness bordering on what we might call paranoia. This formulation, at once simple and comprehensive, exaggerated the idea of cultural integration even in more tradition-oriented societies. These days, most anthropologists would be more cautious about tying things together. Nevertheless, they continue to search for more essential elements on which other components of a culture depend. In their studies of kinship, for example, they might refer back to George Murdock who in *Social Structure* argued that the rule of residence (where the newly married couple lives in relation to their relatives) tends to act as a shaping influence on other aspects of kinship, such as kinship terminology or family form (discussed more fully in Chapter Four). Others might profit from the work of Maurice Godelier who, in a number of sophisticated works (including *Perspectives in Marxist Anthropology*), has asserted the primary influence of relations of production (that is, social relations involved in the production of commodities) over other facets of a culture.

Yet another dimension of the look that anthropologists give to a culture is contextual. They tend to see a culture as fitting into some natural or social setting. A culture is seen to be the way it is, in part, because of the setting in which it is embedded. Though this explanatory device has been overworked, it has become an essential part of most ethnographies, which often begin with a discussion of the natural habitat and surrounding peoples. The trick here is to get at the *relevant* setting. Not all aspects of the surrounding world are equally important for understanding a culture. For example, to understand American culture today, Canada, which is close by, may be less relevant than, say, Western Europe, which is across the Atlantic. And different aspects of a culture's setting may be more or less relevant depending on the focus of the research.

The San (Bushmen) of the Kalahari Desert in southern Africa provide a good example of a culture that was, until recently, finely adjusted to its natural setting. In that existence, before the San adopted a more settled way of life on reservations or farms, they practiced hunting and gathering, which involved moving about and stopping for longer or shorter periods according to the availability of water, game, and vegetation. Possessing only a simple technology, they had to pay close attention to nature's requirements in order to survive. The size of their bands, the length of their stay in a given spot, and the need to keep moving around were all dictated by the availability of naturally occurring food and water. And because substantial accumulation of belongings was impossible, the San worked only long enough and hard enough to provide for present satisfaction. This way of life, which Marshall Sahlins has described (in *Stone Age Economics*) as the "original affluent society," existed in what some might consider an inhospitable desert. Yet it was well enough adapted to produce levels of health and longevity that even a modern people might value. Other hunters and gatherers, living in harsher habitats, have not made out as well, but all have had to be attentive to the dictates of their natural environment in order to survive.

The natural environment is not always the first thing to be considered in analyzing a culture. Sometimes the social environment is more important, as in the case of the San today. Currently, they are more dependent on governments or local farmers for support. Hunting and gathering ways are rapidly disappearing as the San are forced to adopt a more sedentary existence. Increasing rates of illness, signs of demoralization, and political protests indicate that this adaptation has not been entirely successful; nonetheless, the present culture of the San cannot be comprehended without reference to the generally more powerful peoples with whom they are increasingly involved.

The pattern of sociocultural change just described has turned up often in recent anthropological literature dealing with questions of development or acculturation. Change now is so obvious that many anthropologists have sought to capture and explain it. It reminds us that every culture has a history that is continually being made and remade through time—a history that needs to be depicted in one way or another. This adds a further dimension to the look that the anthropologist must give to a culture—the historical. By knowing the historical trends in a culture, the anthropologist is better able to understand the present and perhaps the future. Sometimes the picture the anthropologist offers freezes change at a particular point in time. This would be most appropriate for tradition-bound societies such as the San around the turn of this century. In other cases, the picture emphasizes change and attempts to give some idea of events through time, as in studies of recent San "development." Obviously, what is happening "out there" dictates what kind of picture should be presented, but sometimes change and stability are so intertwined that scientific interests will dictate which perspective is dominant. The dimension of history must be dealt with in some way, however.

To recapitulate, although anthropologists approach cultures from different points of view, there are certain common anthropological dimensions in the pictures that these scientists offer of the cultures they have studied. A culture is seen as normative, that is, as having certain standards of conduct or norms that direct and limit people's behavior. It also tends to be thought of as composed of different kinds of conduct, which may be related to each other in some way. It exists in some natural-social setting to which it is more or less adapted. And finally, it has a history that can be frozen in time or captured from the point of view of change. Every ethnography has a particular point of view, but it usually is cast in terms of these dimensions.

The degree of accuracy or validity of an ethnography may not be easy to determine, as debates about some famous anthropological studies have demonstrated. Consider the claim by Margaret Mead (in *Coming of Age in Samoa*) that adolescents in American Samoa in the southwestern Pacific had much sexual freedom and a consequent lack of emotional conflict. This claim is disputed by Derek Freeman (in *Margaret Mead and Samoa: The Making and Unmaking of an Anthropological Myth*), who argues that adolescents everywhere experience such conflict. Though some progress has been made in resolving this dispute, which is of some importance because of implications concerning the effect of existing sociocultural arrangements on the developing individual, the issue is still being debated. In this case and others, the more open ethnographers are about themselves and their work the easier it will be to evaluate their studies.

WHAT'S THE POINT?

Thousands of more or less adequate anthropological monographs have been written about particular cultures. What is the point of all this work? One goal has been simple description: to describe the immense variety of human customs even as the naturalist describes the variety of living things that have inhabited our globe. It is possible to look at the panorama of cultures and to classify them in various ways. For example, the manner in which food is obtained, the system of political organization, or the beliefs about supernatural beings are readily classifiable. Then, the anthropologist can begin to define the limits of the famously flexible human behavior and discover cultural universals; that is, the elements that all cultures have in common. Thus, it will be possible to sort out pan-human from culture-specific traits, as in the case of the charges by Freeman against Mead about sexual troubles in adolescence. Are adolescents everywhere troubled by sex regardless of their upbringing? Is a certain kind of culturally constituted upbringing responsible? Perhaps the answer lies somewhere in between.

A second goal of all this study is explanatory. Why the variety and why the sameness of all these cultures? A simple answer that has been proposed repeatedly is that behavior is biologically based, or controlled, and that people behave the way they do because of the genes they inherit. Thus, common biology accounts for the sameness in behavior and biological differences (racial differences, for example) account for variety. Are some peoples inherently more creative than others, as Adolph Hitler maintained? Are they the way they are because of differences in their inherited physical makeup? This kind of thinking and other more sophisticated attempts to account for variability in human behavior in terms of biology have not been welcome in anthropology, where the stress on humans' culture-making ability has tended to downgrade biological explanations. Where behavioral differences between human groups are concerned, some kind of learned adaptation has been the preferred explanation. The things that all cultures have in common (for example, sociability) are more likely to have a biological basis, but even here one has to be careful. All humans are biological creatures. They have bodies with biologically dictated impulses, without which there can be no behavior, and they share a common biological heritage, as, for example, being born in a relatively helpless state. But in the course of their evolution humans have developed a capacity for acquiring a broad range of behavior which promote great flexibility in their adaptation. There are common problems that all peoples face, such as caring for relatively helpless infants. But humans could just as easily learn to handle these problems in common ways as to have them dictated by biology. Therefore, in accounting for both behavioral differences and similarities between peoples, it would seem perilous, to downgrade the cultural mode of adaptation.

Another goal of anthropologists is to find out whether different elements of a culture are related to each other, and if so, how. Are there, for example, certain sociocultural conditions that regularly go together with warlike tendencies? Might such tendencies have something to do with population pressure? Is it possible to find the keys to the direction of sociocultural change? Might they be found, for example, in certain "contradictions" that develop in a culture, as in the opposing interests of different social classes? These kinds of questions continue to concern anthropologists, and it is appropriate that those most familiar with the workings of cultures should try to answer them.

One could argue that it is enough to know about the myriad cultural worlds that humans have created, to have this story told by scientific story-tellers, and to try to explain why they are as they are. But some would like to hear of the more practical implications of all of this scientific activity. ("What's in it for the average householder?" is a question I often asked of an astronomer colleague in a radio series we were doing together.) So far in this chapter the argument has been that all humans (including the writer and reader of this little book) are creatures of their cultures, which may be thought of as centering about standards of conduct that groups of people have created to deal with particular life conditions. Those who have really acquired such an understanding will have an advantage in transcultural work because they have learned to take different customs seriously. This is what the astute American businessman working in Spain, discussed earlier, had learned to do. In a world where intercultural mobility is increasing dramatically and national, corporate, and personal interests can extend around the globe, the ability to transcend one's own culture appears to have become a necessary skill. Surprisingly, it is something that is still not taken seriously in some quarters. Some American firms, for example, continue to deal with overseas problems by dispatching technically specialized troubleshooters who have little or no knowledge of the host culture, including its native language. One wonders how such a disregard of the culture of what anthropologists like to call "the other" can contribute to the competitive advantage these firms say they are seeking.

The study of cultures can also heighten an individual's self-awareness and speak to the problems of personal identity that multiply in a world where change and social fragmentation are on the march. It is not easy to know who you are and who you can be in such a world. For example, consider an average American young woman who is reasonably sensitive, open-minded, and intelligent, and who is struggling to work out her own line of personal identity. By learning about the various cultures of the world she becomes aware of the greater possibilities in life. She learns that cultures are the creations of groups of humans in response to the dictates of particular life circumstances. It becomes increasingly clear that there is no right or natural way to live or be—only different ways. This realization may add to her growing awareness that a life is not something that has been pretty much laid out for her from the beginning. Now she sees that there are many possibilities, and she must ask herself what she will make of them all. Questions such as this may have intrigued the many students who made Benedict's *Patterns of Culture* one of the most popular anthropological works. The Pueblo Indians, whose culture is one of the three discussed by Benedict in that book, are portrayed as living a measured, harmonious, and cooperative existence. Benedict pictures them as not asserting themselves and as not engaging in the excesses exhibited by the Indians of the northwestern coast of America, for example. The variety of lifestyles presented in the book opens up additional alternatives for self-seekers and conveys a sense of freedom beyond one's dreams. Those reading Benedict's work for the first time could get the feeling that they could be anything they wanted to be and feel justified in doing so. Anthropological studies of different cultures have always cultivated this feeling.

However, further study of the cultures of the world may show that one does not have quite so much freedom in working out a personal identity. Consider the average American who attends a State Department orientation for people about to travel abroad. The lecturer suddenly asks how many of her listeners are touching the people next to them. From the benefit of her experience, and perhaps from having read some of the works of the anthropologist Edward T. Hall, the lecturer knows that even though the people in her American audience are seated close together, they will not touch each other. She uses this understanding to begin a digression about the personal "bubble" that Americans carry around with them. Each culture, she says, has a different notion of personal space that comes to be accepted as natural. For Americans, that space is rather large, but for others, like the San who once lived virtually on top of one another in their little bands, it may be hard to find any personal "bubble" at all.

What is the upshot of this lecture on cross-cultural differences in personal space and others like it? One effect may be a realization that if culture can exert such an influence on an almost unconscious area of our lives, it must be a powerful determining force indeed. At this stage of her cultural awareness our average American might be forgiven for taking the opposite tack, which leads her to believe that, even if there are many other possibilities in life, they may not actually be realizable. By some means, the standards of conduct of a culture take hold of us, a hold that extends even into the unconscious domain. In this process of internalization we become creatures of our culture.

But the realization that our own personal identity is inextricably tied up with our own culture is not the whole truth either. A culture can have a strong influence over its members, but it can never be an all-determining influence (to quote a colleague, "culture isn't *everything*"). In the first place, in order to survive, a people must work with certain biologically dictated universals that emerge out of human evolution and seem to be responsible for many behavioral commonalities across cultures (which are treated by Donald Brown in his book *Human Universals*). In the second place, there are group and individual differences in all societies. Even in totalitarian societies where deviation is treated harshly, such variability still exists. No society has eliminated them. What it does is set up certain socially desirable lines of conduct (ideal norms) and put limits on social deviation. Beyond these limits one takes one's chances, but within them there can be a good deal of acceptable space for maneuver. For more timid individuals, the possibility of some socially acceptable freedom exists. It merely requires knowledge of cultural norms and their limits for one to realize the available alternatives. For the more heroic or daring—the revolutionaries, the great innovators, the rejecters, and all other major deviators—cultural limitations are less of a problem. Driven by powerful individual needs, they may succeed eventually in changing others' lives—as was the case with Jesus of Nazareth or Karl Marx—or their deviations may satisfy no one but themselves and they will fall into oblivion.

In the course of her odyssey of cultural awareness, our average American has come to grips with the concept of culture and its implications for her own life. And because she is reasonably sensitive and intelligent, it may have some consequence for her own self-realization. Instead of being merely a creature of culture, then, she will have become one who is culturally aware and able to use that awareness to chart her own, and perhaps even some collective, destiny. In a rapidly changing, open society such as our own where one's fate is not predetermined, but must be achieved—often painfully—this is quite an achievement.

SELECTED REFERENCES

ALTORKI, SORAYA, and CAMILLIA FAWZI EL-SOLH, eds., *Arab Women in the Field: Studying Your Own Society*. Syracuse: Syracuse University Press, 1988.

BENEDICT, RUTH, *Patterns of Culture*. Boston: Houghton Mifflin Co., 1980.

BOYER, PAUL, and STEVEN NISSENBAUM, *Salem Possessed*. Cambridge, MA: Harvard University Press, 1974.

BRIGGS, CHARLES, *Learning How to Ask: A Sociolinguistic Appraisal of the Role of the Interview in Social Science Research*. Cambridge: Cambridge University Press, 1986.

BROWN, DONALD, *Human Universals*. Philadelphia: Temple University Press, 1991.

EVANS-PRITCHARD, E.E., *The Nuer*. Oxford: Clarendon Press, 1940.

FREEMAN, DEREK, *Margaret Mead and Samoa: The Making and Unmaking of an Anthropological Myth*. Cambridge, MA: Harvard University Press, 1983.

GEERTZ, CLIFFORD, *The Interpretation of Cultures*. New York: Basic Books, 1973.

GODELIER, MAURICE, *Perspectives in Marxist Anthropology*. Cambridge and New York: Cambridge University Press, 1977.

HALL, EDWARD T., *The Hidden Dimension*. Garden City, NY: Doubleday and Co., 1966.

HAMMERSLEY, MARTIN, and PAUL ATKINSON, *Ethnography*, 2nd ed. London: Routledge, 1995.

HENDERSON, PETA, and ANN BRYN HOUGHTON, eds., *Rising Up: Life Stories of Belizean Women*. Toronto: Sister Vision Press, 1993.

LE WITA, BEATRIX, *French Bourgeois Culture*. Cambridge: Cambridge University Press, 1994.

MALINOWSKI, BRONISLAW, *A Diary in the Strict Sense of the Term*. New York: Harcourt Brace and World, 1977.

MEAD, MARGARET, *Coming of Age in Samoa*, 3rd ed. New York: Morrow, 1961 (1928).

MURDOCK, GEORGE P., *Social Structure*. New York: Macmillan, 1949.

NASH, DENNISON, *A Community in Limbo: An Anthropological Study of an American Community Abroad*. Bloomington: Indiana University, 1970.

TURNBULL, COLIN M., *The Mountain People*. New York: Simon and Schuster, 1972.

YOORS, JAN, *The Gypsies*. New York: Simon and Schuster, 1967.

3

The Individual
In Culture

"Cogito ergo sum." ("I think; therefore I am.") This was an important conclusion of the French philosopher René Descartes who began his philosophical inquires by doubting everything, including the existence of the individual.

Any American adolescent could have told the philosopher that he was wasting his time worrying about the existence of the individual. That is something Americans generally take for granted. Anthropologists, on the other hand, are suspicious of such assumptions. Too many things that are considered "natural" or "right" by a people turn out to be culturally specific. Is it possible that somewhere (possibly in some Buddhist society in the Far East) there are people who might not recognize the human individual? The answer is *no*. All peoples do recognize the individual among the objects they discriminate. The first, second, and third person singular exist in all languages, and, as Melford Spiro has reminded us in a number of recent works, some concept of what we take to be the individual person or self is found in all cultures. But that concept may not always be like the one most Americans take for granted. The anthropologist would like to know how it varies from culture to culture and what, if any, regularities exist. How may such differences and similarities be explained? What is the nature of the relationship between individual and culture? These are the main questions that will be addressed in this chapter.

We in the West tend to think of the person or self as independent or autonomous. In this view, there are recognizable boundaries between the individual and the rest of the world. This conception has developed in a culture where individualism has been on the march for centuries and where an individuating capitalism currently reigns. Other cultures with different histories have different conceptions of the person. This poses a problem for the psychologically oriented who may want to apply, say, the Western notion of personality (referring to the system of psychological dispositions in the individual) cross culturally. This concept does not need to be rejected totally, but it has to be tried on with a good deal of trial and error in other cultures. Also, it should not be forgotten that the individual and his or her actions may be more consequential in one society than another. Finally, it should be remembered that anthropologists may be more inclined to think of a culture as the life-ways of a group or simply of a bunch of individuals (the forest or trees issue). Depending on their orientation, the individual will be a more or less important element in its description and analysis.

Keeping all of these cautions in mind, it is nevertheless possible to assert that something like what Western psychologists refer to as personality can be seen to exist in all cultures. One aspect of this personality is the self or self-image, which refers to an individual's conception or his or her own person. This subjective side of the person, which is derived from the advanced capacity of humans for conceptual thought, has, along with culture, evolved through the ages and is currently considerably removed from the prehuman condition that studies of apes help us to comprehend. In his various writings on the subject, a number of which are collected in his *Culture and Experience,* A.I. Hallowell traces the evolution of this self and lays out a number of its universal characteristics. Following George Herbert Mead, Hallowell argues that individuals everywhere constantly look at themselves from others' perspectives, as well as their own, and evaluate the resulting self-image. All human behavior is self-oriented in this fashion, which is to say that it attends to both individual and social requirements. It would seem that, in order to survive, every population must develop a culture that satisfies *both* of these requirements, but some have generated selves that lean more in one direction than another.

JAPANESE AND AMERICANS

Although the Japanese seem to be becoming more and more Westernized, they still tend to differ as individuals from Americans in a number of ways. Many Americans these days would like to better comprehend the differences they encounter in dealing with Japanese businesspeople in the international marketplace. An understanding of the typical Japanese citizen can help to explain not only the suicide-prone *kamikaze* pilots of World War II, but also the remarkable productivity of Japanese industrial firms today. To know how the Japanese tend to think of themselves is to know something about what makes them "tick." There is no lack of literature on this subject. Looking over this literature, one finds a preoccupation with the collective orientation of the Japanese in contrast, say, to the greater individualism of Americans. Recent studies suggest that the Japanese are less group oriented than originally supposed and that they are becoming more individuated; but for an American who has just begun to work with them, the difference still can be impressive. For a Japanese employee, an enormous firm like Mitsubishi still may be thought of as a kind of giant family with paternal obligations to its employees, something that tends to be the exception, rather than the rule, among American corporations. Though harder times for Japanese business have prevented its full realization, the cultural ideal is that a firm will try to take care of its employees throughout their lives, in good times as well as bad. To further one's career by taking a job elsewhere is not so easy an option in Japan as it is in America. Rather, Japanese employees tend to develop a sense of obligation to the firm, to stay put, and to do whatever is asked of them. What kind of self tends to be found in a culture with this more collective orientation?

Looking at the Japanese in terms of their self-image, one sees that they tend to be less willing than Americans to put themselves forward or to stand out. They seem to be, in Takie Sugiyama Lebra's words, more "exposure sensitive." Eye-to-eye contact, which is idealized in American business circles, is anathema in Japan. The Japanese seem bent on keeping as much of themselves as possible hidden. Such reticence suggests to Lebra (in "Shame and Guilt: A Psychocultural View of the Japanese Self") that, compared with Americans, the Japanese keep a larger part of their total self hidden or unexpressed. In contrast, typical Americans these days are encouraged to "put all their cards on the table," "tell it like it is," or "let it all hang out" as on a confessional talk show.

What happens when, for some reason, a Japanese person stands out from others? He or she may then begin to experience *haji*, which is a kind of shame derived from self-exposure. It is not the shame that comes from acting improperly, but just from being conspicuous. Because such shame can be a painful experience, it must be avoided. This results in a reticent individual who prefers to blend into a group. But not always. There are times when the Japanese let their hair down with intimates at a bar where heavy drinking is the norm or at a hotspring bath where semi-public nudity is practiced. In this special type of setting, it is possible for them to put aside their covering-up operations and possibly compensate for the stress of ordinary life.

The intense shame orientation of the Japanese indicates that they keep themselves under considerable scrutiny from what they take to be others' points of view; and because they are very concerned with what they believe to be others' views of them, the selves of the Japanese appear to be rather other-oriented. A further indication of this is found in the Japanese tendency to blame themselves for their real or imagined transgressions against others. It is no empty gesture when the president of Japan Airlines apologizes publicly to the families of victims of an air crash. The Japanese bear a heavy burden of guilt (*sumanai* or *mōshiwakenai*), which is strongly other-oriented. When other people do things for you it is not possible to rest until they are repaid, possibly many times over. One is supposed to gladly shoulder the blame for others' misfortunes. One offers endless apologies for what an American would like to think is beyond the area of responsibility. Of course, Americans also suffer other-oriented guilt, but in America it is something to get rid of—in therapy, perhaps. In Japan, one form of therapy actually involves promoting guilt consciousness through self-reflection.

This little cross-cultural excursion is not intended to be an exhaustive comparison of Japanese and Americans, but it does suggest some dimensions in which they tend to differ as individuals. First, in regard to exposure, it has been suggested that, in contrast to Americans, the Japanese try to minimize self-exposure. Second, in regard to their orientation toward others, the Japanese self appears to be more other-oriented than that of Americans. In Japan, the burden of collective concerns imposed on the individual through the self would appear to require some kind of relaxation. One way is to provide culturally sanctioned get-togethers with intimates in certain locales. Here, the individual side of the Japanese self may be given greater room for expression.

Although this analysis may have given the reader a deeper understanding of the Japanese orientation toward the group, it does contain some rather sweeping generalizations. Is it legitimate to describe whole nations as having a single personality? There are many different kinds of Japanese and Americans, as anyone who has associated with them intimately will confirm. At one time, some psychologically oriented anthropologists spoke of the national character, or basic personality, of a society, which was said to exist—more or less—in all of the people in that nation. An analogy might be a picture of a group of individuals who had all been dipped in the same pot of paint. More careful investigations, though, have shown that such a view is difficult to sustain. There may be a number of "basic" personality types in a culture—how many depending on the culture and the viewpoint of the analyst. Even in some supposedly primitive cultures where people were expected to be more alike, it became apparent that it was hazardous to say that most people in a culture come in the same few basic colors. Close scrutiny revealed too many individual exceptions.

Having given up their tendency for easy generalizations about whole societies, psychologically oriented anthropologists these days may present frequency distributions of personality types or traits. For example, Lebra, whose work has contributed importantly to this discussion of Japanese and American selves, details the frequency of shame- and guilt-type responses on the psychological tests she administered in a Japanese city. Such distributions are, of course, entirely consistent with the notion of individual variability around cultural norms discussed earlier. Some authors try to tie down their generalization to a specific social location or subculture. Thus, they might refer to young, male, urban, middle-class Japanese or similarly located Americans. Or they might dwell on gender differences, as does Brian McVeigh in his study of a Japanese womens' junior college ("Cultivating Femininity and 'Internationalism': Rituals and Routine at a Japanese Womens' College"). Such specification is more and more the expected thing in a discipline with any scientific pretensions. Thus, the above excursion into the psychological qualities of Japanese and Americans individuals should be considered only an exploratory operation with finer and finer analyses expected to follow.

THE FORMATION OF THE INDIVIDUAL

It *is* possible, then—in contrast to speculations suggesting otherwise—to begin with the assumption that in every culture there are recognizable individual persons, each of whom can be thought of as having a personality that includes a self. This is a general way of conceiving the various images people hold of themselves as individuals. Every culture has norms for how these personalities ought to be—or are—constituted. Hallowell calls them "culturally constituted" personalities, which means they have been shaped in terms of the cultural conventions around them. How this process occurs has been a major consideration for psychological anthropologists. Research in this area has proceeded by fits and starts. It should be mentioned at the outset that there have been ebbs and flows of anthropological concern with individual as opposed to the group. Still, there have been real advances in our understanding of the psychological aspect of social life.

Consider first, the individual at birth—not just in American culture, but in all cultures. This individual is an organism with the potential for becoming a full-fledged human being. We may think of this organism as a bundle of biologically dictated behavioral impulses. These impulses, which ultimately are genetically determined, are not inflexible. The human infant is neither a "full organism" nor "hard-wired" at birth. On the contrary, it takes growth and experience in some group to form a human individual. There has been a good deal of debate about how great a role experience plays in this process, but if we take humans to be cultured creatures (as discussed in Chapter One), it would appear to play a considerable role.

Through birth, the infant organism appears in some human population somewhere—a population that has a culture. The infant arrives with certain qualities that include the capacity to elicit care from caregivers, who respond to dependent children in terms of whatever culturally induced expectations the caregivers themselves have acquired. Thus mothers from North Indian communities, as reported by Beatrice Whiting and Carolyn Edwards in their cross-cultural study, *Children of Different Worlds*, tend to be inconsistent in their care, which is said to encourage a more assertive dependency in their children. So, it may be said that through the agency of caregivers, a culture shapes the growing child. The child, of course, makes something of himself or herself on the basis of specific needs, but a good deal of what the child becomes is dictated by its experience with the representatives of a culture. To the extent that a person is formed by this experience, anthropologists say that he or she is *socialized* (or *enculturated*). Anthropologically viewed, the formation of the human individual takes place through this process.

Take a typical anthropological problem: Are the individuals in culture *A* more intelligent on the average than those in culture *B*, and if so, how may the difference be explained? Consider an example close to home. American blacks and whites, however designated, have been tested repeatedly for intelligence with results that indicate that blacks generally score lower than whites on intelligence tests. This general difference, however, is narrowed (but usually not eliminated) when the individuals being tested come from similar cultural backgrounds that include, for example, the important factor of nutrition. Is the remaining difference to be attributed to biology or culture? With the 1994 publication of *The Bell Curve*, Richard Herrnstein and Charles Murray have reignited a virulent controversy on this issue. Using a vast array of statistical data of varying quality, these authors argue that, even though the experience of the growing individual (that is, culture) is a factor to be considered, a major part of the difference must be attributed to the different biological makeups of the two populations. Their critics, on the other hand (including most anthropologists), have said that people should not be taken in by all the statistics, which are of an uneven quality. They have argued that, among other things, intelligence (IQ, for example) is not a single unitary trait, but an amalgam of various intellectual skills; that tests of intelligence, which have been constructed and standardized for certain white populations, are unfair to American and other blacks; and that inasmuch as racial discrimination still exists in American society, blacks—even those with comparable socioeconomic status—will not have an equivalent cultural background, and consequently their test scores will continue to be inferior to those of American whites.

The issue is socially important because acceptance of one or the other position can justify doing something (or nothing) about racial inequality and its social and individual consequences. The issue is so complex, and the claims and counterclaims so strident, however, that one might easily give up trying to come to a rational conclusion and instead go on gut feeling. (The edited collection by Russell Jacoby and Naomi Glauberman, *The Bell Curve Debate*, gives a good idea of the nature of the controversy.) Even a superficial glance through the literature reveals that there is a wide variety of opinion as to the value of the hereditary (biologically dictated) component of intelligence. The truth appears to be that heredity and environment interact in different ways in different populations. Thus, any attempt to fix a universal value on the weight of the component for making comparisons between populations is inevitably fraught with difficulties. Herrnstein and Murray and others before them have been banking on a comparatively high value derived from sometimes inadequate twin studies in the same culture. However, studies of different populations have suggested that environment plays a greater role in the intelligence test performance of American blacks than whites. In addition, other studies have found little or no relationship between degree of African and European ancestry and intelligence test performance (see, for example, Sandra Scarr et al.'s "The Absence of a Relationship..."). This suggests that *all* of the differences between average black and white scores could, indeed, be the result of environmental factors. Given a fair test, adequate nutrition before and after birth, enough psychic and emotional nurturance, and equal educational, economic, and social opportunities, the average American black would have a good chance of doing as well as the average American white. Earl Hunt's "The Role of Intelligence in Modern Society" gives a good idea of the work that still needs to be done in resolving this issue scientifically, but one is entitled to have severe doubts about the the biological explanation and to wonder whether it is not just another instance of "blaming the victim" (of social inequities).

Does this mean that biology should be discounted as a factor in explaining psychological differences between populations? Unfortunately, no cut-and-dried answer is possible. It would appear to depend not only on the populations being investigated, but also on the psychological traits involved. For example, consider behavior that might indicate something like temperament. Are some populations more emotionally volatile than others, as in the oft-noted comparison between northern and southern Europeans? If so, can this difference be attributed to biological or racial differences? Daniel Freedman was an early investigator of the responses of different "ethnic" groups. In "Personality Development in Infancy," he reports that Caucasian (in this case, white American) infants tested shortly after birth tend to respond more readily, excitedly, and over a longer duration to a series of provocations (for example, holding a cloth over the nose) than do infants of Asian origin. His experiments, which appear to support the idea that the alleged Asian "inscrutability" or lack of emotional expressivity is to some extent inborn, have raised storms of protest from some readers of his work. Their first reaction is to attack the methodology of these experiments. But Freedman had anticipated most, if not all, of these objections by employing a fairly sophisticated series of controls. The fact that his Chinese wife assisted him in his experiments also tends to counter any accusations of racism that may come his way. Some additional controls are needed to verify his findings, but it now seems to be a fair inference that Asian and Caucasian newborns do indeed tend to differ in their reactions to various provocative stimuli and that this difference probably is biologically dictated.

Does this mean that Caucasian Americans and, say, Japanese individuals will exhibit what some might call racially determined differences in temperament? Yes and no. Freedman also analyzed studies of communication between Japanese American mothers and their infants in the United States. First-generation mothers and their infants tended to behave as would be expected from the experiments; there was very little verbalization between them. However, the principal anthropologist involved in this particular investigation reported that third-generation Japanese American mothers and their progeny were chattering away at a "super-American" rate. Since their biology had not changed (that is, there had been no gene flow with Caucasian Americans through intermarriage), some kind of environmental influence must have been responsible. That influence would seem to have been the result of being raised and functioning in a culture with a higher value on emotional expressiveness. It would seem, therefore, that however they differ from Americans at birth in their level of ebullience, Japanese Americans are capable of changing more than enough to wipe out the difference in a lifetime. Freedman recognizes this in his concept of "reaction range," which specifies the range of possibilities for development of a particular behavioral trait. Some traits, he suggests, have broad ranges, others narrow. The particular course of development a growing individual takes within a range will be determined by the special nature of his or her life experiences.

To illustrate how all of this would look on a broader canvas, consider aggression in human males and females. The evidence suggests that males tend to be born with a greater disposition to aggressive behavior than females. There are individual females who show more aggression than males from the same society, but the general tendency is toward greater aggression in males. The difference has been noted in early childhood not only in American culture, but also in many cultures for which there are adequate data. (There are a few cultures in which there is no apparent difference, but none in which females, generally, are more aggressive than males.) Moreover, the same pattern is found in nonhuman primates. This suggests that the difference in aggressive disposition is likely to be evolutionarily based and biologically dictated. But in humans, levels of aggressiveness may change considerably throughout life. In his cross-cultural study "Sex Differences in Aggression," Ronald Rohner notes that the difference in aggressiveness between females and males tends to disappear as the child grows into adulthood. There are exceptions, notably in American culture, but in most cases socialization appears to diminish, if not eliminate, the differences that were noted in early childhood. From Freedman's perspective, this would mean that males and females in a society generally differ in aggressive disposition at birth. However, the reaction range for the trait appears to be broad enough to permit environmental influences, acting through the process of socialization, to eliminate the difference completely. There seem to be no grounds, therefore, for any argument that suggests that women are *biologically* incapable of generating the kind of aggression needed to function effectively in, for example, military combat. They may have other drawbacks in assuming combat roles, but this is not one of them.

You can't make a silk purse out of a sow's ear, but possibly some other object can be fashioned. Using Freedman's concept of reaction range, we can say that individuals cannot be turned into something beyond the limits of their range. Environmentalists used to argue that if you took a child from another culture and raised it from infancy as an American, it would become an American. Putting aside the possibility of prejudice, discrimination, and their consequences, it would seem judicious to be more cautious these days about the plasticity of human nature. Inborn dispositions cannot be entirely dismissed in accounting for differences and similarities in the psychological qualities of different peoples but the overall impression of human plasticity remains.

Now consider another way in which biology may affect personality development. Jean Piaget, the Swiss psychologist, and others have suggested that there are stages in modes of thinking through which individuals generally pass as they grow up. For example, there is a progressive differentiation and specialization of psychological functions from earlier to later stages. Culturally constituted experience and practice may delay or advance the times of these changes, but individuals nevertheless tend to pass through the same sequence of stages. Attempts to validate this hypothesis cross-culturally have run into a number of problems familiar to the psychological anthropologist, but some encouraging results have been obtained— especially for the early stages proposed by Piaget. However, there are enough discrepancies to warrant caution about accepting the hypothesis in too specific a form.

Yet, another way in which biology may affect personality development is by making the individual more or less receptive to environmental influences at different stages of development. Rohner, for example, has found that, except for the infantile stage where his data are unclear, an attitude of parental acceptance or rejection can have greater consequences if it occurs earlier rather than later. Also, students of foreign languages may have become aware of the early "critical period" for better language learning and retention (up to age fourteen or so). Generally, early socializing experiences seem to be of greater importance in personality development. However, no psychological anthropologist these days would exclude later experiences— even those of middle and old age—from consideration.

All of this suggests that biological nature helps to make the individual an active agent in the socializing process. At birth, environmental influences do not fall on some *tabula rasa* on which anything can be written. The infant organism is more sensitive to certain influences than others, and with growth new biologically based sensitivities appear. As the capacity for conceptual thought emerges, the child begins to put him- or herself imaginatively in the place of others and to respond to their views. In addition, the child has his or her own views on what line to take. Out of this interactive process, the human individual is formed.

The give-and-take is not always easy. Cultures differ in the harshness of their socializing practices. For example, some early New England Calvinists seem to have had a very rough upbringing, but one present-day study in a community outside of Boston shows little of the old-time Calvinist severity in the raising of children. However, no group of people has managed to do away with the frustrations of socialization entirely. This is because individual and social needs or requirements never can be completely compatible. Inevitably, in order to get along with others, the growing child must do some things that he or she does not want to do. Here it is important to keep in mind that the degree of individuation encouraged in the growing individuals varies considerably around the world and that what a more individualistic American would regard as a humiliating submission to the group might be viewed otherwise by a more "collectivized" Japanese. But socialization always requires some self-sacrifice. When this is severe, some initiation ceremony involving group support may be developed to mark the transition into group membership. Thus, in Tikopia in the southwestern Pacific, a little boy's kinsmen help him to pass through a painful circumcision ceremony marking an important passage in life by exhorting him not to cry out, but to suffer in silence as becomes a man.

The inevitable frustrations of socialization leave a residue of conflict in the individual between social and personal demands. What a clinical psychologist or psychiatrist may refer to as psychodynamic mechanisms are the means an individual uses to deal with these more or less painful conflicts. Culturally standardized "ways out" may help in this regard. So, in societies with a strong tabu on interpersonal aggression, as among the aboriginal Ojibwa of the Lake Winnipeg region of Canada studied by Hallowell, unconscious aggressive impulses are seen to be transformed (through the mechanism of psychological projection) into threatening culturally constituted supernatural beings, thus resolving the internal conflict and safeguarding the society from the direct release of aggressive impulses.

HOW DOES IT ALL HAPPEN?

Human socialization always takes place in some group that has a more or less coherent culture. The actions of the socializers of each group tend to shape growing individuals along socially desirable lines. How does this shaping take place? Psychologists may speak of such mechanisms as reinforcement, modeling, or identification. Sociologists may talk about role taking. These are all specific ways of comprehending the process whereby the growing individual acquires new behavior through experience. But the child's development is always culturally directed by people who have power over the child. The most important socializing agents of the society are usually members of the child's family of orientation—that is, the family in which he or she grows up. Such people have the greatest access to the child when he or she is in a highly malleable state, and they act as a shaping environment even before birth, as, for example, when a pregnant mother is a heroin addict. Any action by the mother or other socializer has potential significance for the child's socialization. The action might not even be directed at the child, as in the cases of the working mother whose absence may be experienced as a kind of rejection, the amorous mother whose lovemaking might be observed, or the mother having problems with someone else in or outside of the family. Psychological anthropologists are slowly acquiring a scientifically based, cross-cultural understanding of the consequences of socializers' actions. Ronald Rohner's continuing work, mentioned earlier, is one example of careful, systematic research in this area. His enumeration of the universal consequences of parental acceptance or rejection, discussed in "Patterns of Parenting . . . ," illustrates the depth and breadth of a long-term anthropological commitment to one subject.

Taking his cue from a variety of psychological investigations, including those which have noted care-seeking behavior in infants, Rohner argues that children everywhere have a need for acceptance (some more than others); that is, they need warmth and affection from significant others such as their parents. If that need is not well satisfied (or if it is rejected), children are likely to develop psychological maladjustments such as, lowered emotional responsiveness and stability; greater aggression, dependency, or defensive independence; and lowered self-esteem—in degrees reflecting the magnitude of the rejection. Such dispositions will tend to continue on into adulthood unless later, more positive experiences turn them around.

Rohner has drawn cross-cultural data from over a hundred societies, and recently from his own and others' intensive investigations in a number of particular societies. One of the peoples in his cross-cultural sample are the Alorese of the southwestern Pacific who were studied by the anthropologist Cora Dubois. Using her reports, Rohner predicts that the Alorese, who are portrayed as possessing weak self-esteem, having difficulty sustaining emotional relationships, and being often angry, suspicious, and fearful, will have been rejected in childhood. This prediction appears to be correct. Alorese mothers view children as a great burden, often leaving them at home while they work the fields. Siblings who take care of the children during this time do not take up the slack. They often become impatient with their charges and sometimes abandon them. They and other socializers frequently tease and frighten the children. Such rejecting socializing practices, not overcome by later acceptance, appear to turn the typical Alorese into the kind of personality that is to be expected from Rohner's theory.

Abraham Kardiner once referred to a society's whole body of socializing and related behavior as primary institutions. Like other aspects of a culture, they are affected by the context in which they are embedded. American mothers who follow the advice of a popular book on child rearing are acting in what amount to institutionalized ways suggested by the author. But the author's views on child rearing and the mothers' acceptance of these views are conditioned by their cultural context. What are the immediate forces that shape socializers' actions? Anthropologists have identified a number of these: household arrangements, family forms, and economic activities, for example. Thus African mothers in the cross-cultural study of Whiting and Edwards have heavier workloads and recruit their children, especially daughters, to help them out. This may be why they tend to take a "commanding" posture toward their children. Some American mothers who lament their decline of authority over their children might envy them. Still other factors in the cultural context may turn out to be involved in this.

HOW DOES IT ALL WORK OUT?

A writer on socialization may say that its aim is to produce individuals who will carry on a culture. Thus, Erich Fromm, in a famous statement, said that children must be made to want to act in the way they have to act if the culture is to continue on. Though their degree of authority differs by culture, people everywhere probably do have enough power to turn those of the next generation—most of them, anyway—into something resembling themselves. Thus, the culture will be (to use a little anthropological jargon) internalized or recapitulated. But this does not inevitably lead to adaptive success either for the individual or for the society. Every society has collective prerequisites that must be met—the need for some system of authority, for example. If it is to survive, a society must socialize individuals who help to meet these prerequisites. But individuals, no matter how much they are shaped for collective tasks, have their own personal needs to satisfy and they require some leeway to accomplish this. If they do not get it, frustrations could pile up to an intolerable level and threaten to undermine the social order. This means that people in all continuing cultures must allow for some accommodation between the needs of the individual and collective requirements. In looking over the cultures of humankind, it is possible to see a great variety of ways in which at least a minimal accommodation has been accomplished. One example was envisaged by the American founding fathers, who sought to create a political society for individuals with certain inalienable rights. Though recognizing the need for some system of authority in the society, they also sought to put limits on the sacrifices individuals would be expected to make in helping to satisfy this need.

It is important to remember, finally, that though there are norms for socialization in any culture, there is also variability around the norms, a variability that can become more significant with sociocultural change. All of this variability, combining with the genetic variability of the upcoming generation, produces a range of socializing tracks and, hence, personalities. All of these personalities are recognizable individuals who work out their destiny in a complex process of give-and-take between their notions of what others want of them and what they want for themselves. Every culture offers more or less well-defined selves as models to help people in this task. For example, for an American kid, Michael Jordan, the great basketball player, might provide such a model.

Although anthropologists have tended to concentrate on the early, formative years of life in analyzing the relationship between culture and the individual, we should keep in mind that this relationship continues throughout the life course and that it results in both changes and stability in a culture and the individuals in it. Sometimes there even may be extraordinary individuals who manage to bring about profound changes in their culture. We should not forget that socialization is a two-way street that continues throughout an individual's life course and that there is an ebb and flow of power between a culture and the individual from beginning to end. In referring to socialization, Margaret Mead at one point spoke of the "triumph of the adults." There certainly is more than a germ of truth in this observation, but we ought to be careful about assuming it in complex, disrupted, or rapidly changing societies.

CASE STUDY

Scheper-Hughes on Socialization Gone Awry:
An Irish Example

In order to bring this discussion of socialization down to earth, consider a specific anthropological study, *Saints, Scholars, and Schizophrenics*, conducted in Ireland in the late 1970s by Nancy Scheper-Hughes. In this work, this anthropologist shows an early indication of her commitment to a politically and ethically based anthropology. Carried out in western Ireland, in an area that has interested scholars and artists over the years, her study shows how certain culturally patterned socializing practices can lead in the direction of mental illness. Though the author deals with other matters in this early study, her principal concern, which should be of interest to anyone concerned with the cultural aspects of mental disorder, is with variation in mental illness (or mental health) in a particular population.

Scheper-Hughes, who together with her husband and children had settled into the little village of Ballybran for her fieldwork, was aware of the decline of the small family farm that had been the economic mainstay of the region. Becoming a more and more marginal economic operation, this farm was increasingly run by what might be called "leftovers," that is, aging parents and a son (often the last-born) who had not emigrated in search of a more promising career. It is among these sons that the greatest rate of diagnosed psychosis is to be found. What is it about the socialization of this son that makes him turn out psychotic more frequently than his siblings?

The author is aware that schizophrenia has a hereditary component, but that is unlikely to be the cause of the systematic *difference* in rates within a family (genetic differences are randomized hereditarily). More likely responsible, she thinks, is a difference in the ways different children are normally socialized. Is there something about the last-born male's socialization in this culture that would tend to push him along the road to mental illness? Scheper-Hughes notes that Irish children generally are raised by cold, rejecting mothers who manage to make their boys, especially, quite dependent on them. However, it is the custom among these people to favor some children more than others. In particular, it is the "runt" of the family—the last-born son usually—who experiences the worst side of Irish socialization. Normally he becomes a scapegoat for family difficulties and is made to feel the most inadequate of all. "Desperate," "hopeless," and "the bottom of the barrel" are expressions that Scheper-Hughes heard parents using in public to refer to these boys who grow up (the word may not be the most appropriate one to use here) anxious about sex and all other forms of self-assertion and who are constantly reminded how inadequate they are.

The rural Irish family investigated by Nancy Scheper-Hughes is faced with the problem of who will remain on the farm to take care of the aging parents and run what is increasingly a failing proposition. This thankless task is likely to fall to the last-born son who, bound by ties of guilt to his mother and unable to assert himself enough to marry or emigrate, remains caught in a situation of trying to please others who are giving him a very hard time. At home and in the community he must accept his parents' denigrating views of him and still try to please. But deep down some kernel of self-respect asserts itself. What to do? Overt rebellion and escape would seem to be almost out of the question. They are made very difficult by his feelings of inadequacy and guilt toward his parents. Another "adaptive" alternative would seem to be some kind of psychological withdrawal, which, in a person with the appropriate genetic constitution, could lead toward schizophrenia or some other form of mental illness. The higher rate of mental illness in last-born sons, therefore, appears to be the result of one variant of the primary institutions of this developing culture, that is, the way last-born sons are treated.

This brief summary hardly does justice to a rich and sensitive, prize-winning ethnographic study, which, as might be expected, generated a good

deal of controversy in Ireland. It is not possible here to delve into the theoretical matters that are treated by Scheper-Hughes. Nor can we say very
much about the fascinating field of culture and mental disorder, which considers the nature of psychological pathologies, their distribution in and
between populations, and their causes and treatments. But it does make one
process of socialization come alive and does illuminate the anthropological
perspective that has been presented in this chapter.

First, Nancy Scheper-Hughes assumes that people are born with certain
hereditary tendencies (in this case, toward mental health or illness). Second,
she emphasizes the importance of experience, particularly within the family,
in shaping these tendencies. Third, this experience is seen to be culturally
patterned, that is, there are conventional socializing procedures that are
shaped by the overall culture and what is happening to it. Fourth, individuals are seen to acquire a residue of conflict from their socializing experiences.
This is something that all humans share, but in this case it is exacerbated by
culturally patterned circumstances. Finally, individuals (last-born sons) are
portrayed as actively adapting creatures who cope as best they can with (in
this case) difficult socializing circumstances. One might say that the adaptation of these individuals is not very successful; but neither is that of this particular culture at this point in its history.

This brief visit to rural Ireland demonstrates once again the problemat-
ic nature of any cultural arrangement, including socialization. Working out a
path that meets individual needs and social requirements at the same time is
no small accomplishment. The fact that so many cultures have attained at
least a minimum successful accommodation in this regard can be attributed
to humans' social proclivities as well as their considerable ability to profit
from experience. It is important to keep in mind, however, that individuals,
no matter how socialized they become, can never be entirely creatures of their
sociocultural world and sometimes can be very much at odds with it.

SOCIALIZATION IN AMERICA

How does all of the foregoing illuminate what is going on in present-day
America as far as socialization is concerned? Like any other culture,
American culture has its primary institutions, which tend to shape developing individuals in a certain way. However, growing up in America these days
poses special problems not encountered in most of the cultures that have
been investigated by anthropologists in the past. America is a complex,
rapidly changing society in which a good deal of individual mobility is the
rule. Here, socialization pressures come at the individual from a variety of
directions. Thus, a child raised in a small-town family will be brought up in
certain ways. If the family moves to another town in another region of the
country, new (sub-) cultural norms will be encountered and new tracks of

socialization will open up. Will the individual go to a college or university? If so, still other paths appear. Upon graduation a job may be found in which career mobility is the norm. Still further lines of socialization now become a possibility. All of this takes place in a society where long-term, stable expectations about the transition to adulthood are becoming more and more difficult to maintain and the demands of adulthood itself are more open and varied. This condition of life, which no longer can be seen as something that happens only to exceptional others in and outside of this society, is so institutionalized as to justify the American playwright William Saroyan's observation that "there is no foundation all the way down the line."

How does all of this affect the socialization of a more or less typical American? As compared with growing individuals in less complex and more stable societies, Americans tend to find themselves in a more destructured socializing environment. American socializers are less certain about how to raise children, and even if certain, they are more likely to be contradicted by others, including those on television whose influence over children continues to be the subject of a lively dispute. As a result, American adults lose authority over their children, which creates a lack of certainty for children that is noteworthy in the range of contemporary cultures. (There may be more uncertain socializing venues, as, for example, those involving immigrants or refugees, but these do not involve the mainstream of a well-established society.) Not being able to rely so much on the external world for guidance, the typical American is forced back on himself or herself for direction. This means that the growing individual is faced with a greater responsibility for his or her own socialization, and accordingly, is less likely to fit into the culture of the preceding generation. Some people may flee from this responsibility and take their cues from the mass media or bureaucratic regulations without really believing what they have to say. Some others will welcome it. But it is the rare American who can escape the fact that what one makes of oneself is increasingly up to each individual. This would appear to be one reason why Descartes' problem with the existence of the self, mentioned at the beginning of this chapter, would be considered a false problem by most Americans.

SELECTED REFERENCES

ALLAND, ALEXANDER, JR., MICHAEL BLAKEY, C. C. LORING BRACE, ALAN GOODMAN, STEPHEN MOLNAR, and J. PHILLIPPE RUSHTON, "The Eternal Triangle: Race, Class and IQ," *Current Anthropology*, 37, suppl., 1996, 143–181.

BUCHMAN, MARLIS, *The Script of Life in Modern Society: Entry into Adulthood in a Changing World*. Chicago: University of Chicago Press, 1989.

COHEN, ANTHONY, *Self Consciousness*. London and New York: Routledge, 1994.

COHEN, MARK, "Anthropology and Race: The Bell Curve Phenomenon," *General Anthropology* 2(1), 1994, 1-4.

FREEDMAN, DANIEL, "Personality Development in Infancy: A Biological Approach," in *Perspectives on Human Evolution*, ed., S. L. Washburn and Phyllis Jap, pp. 258–87. New York: Holt, Rinehart, and Winston, 1968.

HALLOWELL, A. IRVING, *Culture and Experience*. Philadelphia: University of Pennsylvania Press, 1955.

HERRNSTEIN, RICHARD, and CHARLES MURRAY, *The Bell Curve*. New York: Free Press, 1994.

HUNT, EARL, "The Role of Intelligence in Modern Society," *American Scientist*, 83, 1995, 356–68.

JACOBY, RUSSELL, and NAOMI GLAUBERMAN, eds., *The Bell Curve Debate*. New York: Times Books, 1995.

KIRMAYER, LAURENCE, *Research in Cultural Psychiatry: History and Prospects*. Paper prepared for the annual meeting of the Society for the Study of Psychiatry and Culture. Montreal: Dept. of Psychiatry, McGill University, 1994.

LEBRA, TAKIE S., "Shame and Guilt: A Psychocultural View of the Japanese Self," *Ethos*, 11, 1983, 192–209.

LEVINE, ROBERT, *Culture, Behavior and Personality*, 2nd ed. New York: Aldine, 1982.

LEVY, ROBERT, *Tahitians: Mind and Experience in the Society Islands*. Chicago: University of Chicago Press, 1973.

McVEIGH, BRIAN, "Cultivating Femininity and 'Internationalism': Rituals and Routine at a Japanese Womens' College," *Ethos*, 24, 1996, 314-49.

ROHNER, RONALD, "Patterns of Parenting: The Warmth Dimension in Worldwide Perspective," in *Readings in Psychology and Culture*, ed. W.J. Lonner and R.S. Malpass, pp. 113–120. Needham Heights, MA: Allyn and Bacon, 1994.

————, "Sex Differences in Aggression," *Ethos*, 4, 1976, 57–72.

SCARR, SANDRA, A. PAKTIS, S. KATZ, and W. BARKER, "The Absence of a Relationship between Degree of White Ancestry and Intellectual Skills within the Black Population," *Human Genetics*, 39, 1977, 69–86.

SCHEPER-HUGHES, NANCY, *Saints, Scholars, and Schizophrenics: Mental Illness in Rural Ireland*. Berkeley: University of California Press, 1979.

SPIRO, MELFORD, "Is the Western Conception of Self 'Peculiar' within the Context of World Cultures?" *Ethos*, 21, 1993, 107–53.

WHITING, BEATRICE, and CAROLYN EDWARDS, *Children of Different Worlds*. London and Cambridge, MA: Harvard University Press, 1988.

Societies

HOW IS SOCIETY POSSIBLE?

Some philosophers once believed that before humans became social they lived alone in a state of nature. Their life often was not very pleasant, and there were times when they fought each other. But they were rational creatures and eventually figured out that life might be better if they lived together. The society that resulted was thus a rational creation of individual human beings who wanted to get out of an unpleasant state of nature.

Anyone who knows even a little about the human past will recognize that this is one of those just-so stories about human origins that cannot possibly be true. From what we know now, there was never a state of nature in which human beings or any other related creatures lived alone. If living apes can be taken as rough models for the prehuman way of life, it would seem that some form of association existed among our ancient ancestors. Indeed, the existence of loose social groupings among chimpanzees, other apes, and monkeys suggests that the essentials of human society were established long before humans came on the scene.

A good deal of ape or monkey association seems to be due to inborn nature, and undoubtedly there is some carryover of this nature into humans. The particular form that an ape or monkey society takes appears to vary with biological type. However, different populations of the same species tend to behave differently according to the nature of their environment. But these variations are comparatively small. Among humans, on the other hand, variation in behavior between groups is comparatively great and seems to be independent of the relatively insignificant biological differences between them. So, while some thrust to human association and its nature is given by biology, the specific manner in which different human populations group and carry on collective activities appears to be more of a cultural matter.

In considering any human population, one deals with people who are interacting with each other not only in an observable, but also subjectively meaningful way. To understand such interaction, one has to find out what the parties are up to, that is, what meanings they attach to their actions. One also has to keep in mind that all interaction combines both associative and dissociative tendencies, with one or the other dominating in a particular situation. A certain amount of harmony is found everywhere in all societies, but sometimes the amount of dissociation can seem extraordinary. This is the case, among the Qalander, gypsy entertainers of northern India and Pakistan, who, as pointed out by Joseph Berland, "travel together and fight a lot." Living in a fluid situation where disengagement from their traveling group is always a possibility, these people have developed a culture where "disputing" is expected and social fission and fusion are the order of the day (see Berland's "Qalander").

Over time, the interactions of people in a given population give rise to the norms or standards of conduct that, in turn, regulate their actions and interactions. In any group there is some kind of ordered arrangement of social roles, groups, and categories that constitutes its social organization. In a society such as the United States, this organization is extremely complex; among wandering hunters and gatherers or people like the Qalander, it is a simpler matter.

Although it may look like an inanimate object when viewed on some organizational chart, social organization actually involves real live human beings who may be seen as acting out certain parts or roles in some culturally informed social arrangment. How do they come to play these roles? In America, people like to think that choice and individual effort count a lot. Although there are positions in this society that are beyond a person's reach, choice and individual initiative do play a greater role in assigning people to their places in the social structure than in more tradition-oriented societies. When the position that one occupies has been attained by choice and individual effort, an anthropologist may say that it has been *achieved*. If, on the other hand, the attainment of a position is determined by factors that tend to be beyond one's control, such as being born with black skin in America, it may be said to be *ascribed*. Traditionally, anthropologists have tended to work in societies where ascription has played a greater role in sorting people out for the parts they play in social life. Now, this is less often so.

The particular criteria for this social sorting vary from society to society. Thus, different universities may use different mixes of criteria for choosing a freshman class. One institution may weigh academic excellence more heavily while another puts more emphasis on well-rounded types. Depending on the part one is to play in a society, the principal criteria for selection could be physical strength and aggressiveness, the ability to enter trance states, or having the "right" connections. There are certain criteria that all peoples use, however. Among the more important of these are age, gender, and kinship, which are matters that individuals can do relatively little about and may therefore be considered as ascribing factors. All of these will be discussed in this chapter.

Those Americans who believe that what they become in the world is up to them may be impatient with so much discussion of ascription and the attention it has been given by anthropologists. Once again they need to be reminded that the United States is not the world and that in many societies ascription still plays a large role in sorting people out; and, contrary to what some people think, ascription is not insignificant in the United States either. An African American or member of any other ethnic group who has been subject to discrimination from early in life can testify to that.

GENDER

The existence of two sexes or genders is taken by people of the Western world as a fact of life. Though we may be increasingly aware that there are some people who do not fit easily (even on the basis of chromosomal tests such as those used in the Olympics) into one or the other category, it still may come as a surprise that in some societies other genders are recognized and accepted. Among the alternate genders described in the literature is the *alyha* of the Mohave Indians, a group of Native Americans who were once established in southern California. The *alyha* is one variant of the *berdache*, a general term used to refer to alternate genders of many North American Indian tribes. Such people were born with male genitals, but acted in female ways. Before they reached puberty, a ceremony was held to test their inclinations. If they danced the way a normal girl was supposed to dance, they were confirmed as an *alyha*. Later on, they would choose men as sexual partners, take husbands, perform domestic duties, dress like women, and sometimes act as if they were giving birth.

There are children in all societies that display androgynous physical and behavioral characteristics and who do not fit easily into the category of male or female. For them, the existence of an alternate or intermediate gender spells some relief. But not all societies provide it. For the United States, it would be difficult to maintain that the category of bisexual has become a socially recognized alternate gender. For better or worse, most Americans are socialized to become unambiguously male or female.

Whether they have alternate gender categories or not, all societies have the categories of what Westerners refer to as male and female. Though the extent and nature of the difference varies, all peoples recognize the difference between male and female genders and assign them different roles to play. For example, in their study of women of Belize, mentioned in Chapter 2, Henderson and Houghton point out that the traditional norm is for the man to be head of the household, to give orders, and to have ultimate control over all decisions. Further, cross-cultural studies have shown that males rarely, if ever, have the primary responsibility for child care, while females seldom, if ever, hunt, trap, or herd large animals. Though there may be some modern women who believe that eventually they will be able to do everything a man can do, and vice versa, the odds would seem to be seriously against it. Men in some societies may actively participate in the birth of their child, but they will never be able to bear children.

Even so, the variation in gender-type roles in the cultures of humankind is enormous. Some anthropologists were once so carried away by the possibilities of such cultural variability as to suggest that temperamental differences between the sexes in Western society could be almost completely reversed with the right upbringing. That is what Margaret Mead suggests about the Tchambuli, one of three New Guinea peoples she reports on in *Sex and Temperament in Three Primitive Societies*. In this society, according to Mead, the women played the major role in the economy by fishing and trading and had the temperament to match these activities. Also, the rapidly changing roles of men and women in America, as well as in other countries such as Sweden, tend to support the notion of very great plasticity as far as the sexes are concerned. These days, anthropologists may be a little less enthusiastic about the power of culture over gender, but the debate continues.

A number of developments in the contemporary world tend to undermine ascription by gender, and they demonstrate that both men and women are capable of becoming far more alike than has been supposed. Such developments can rile male chauvinists, who may feel that the natural order of things is somehow upset if women try to be something other than a wife and mother. Divorce, abortion, and inadequate parenting are only some of the bad things envisaged by the American chauvinists when women try to go beyond what men think is a woman's "true nature." Similarly, in *Women of the Forest*, Robert and Yolanda Murphy report an origin story of the Mundurucú Indians of South America. According to this story, women once dominated men; but because they could not hunt nor make ritual offerings of meat to certain spirits, women lost their power and men have dominated ever since. Therefore, any attempt to reverse the position of the sexes in this male-dominated society is thought to work against the natural order of things and is doomed to fail. The chauvinist may be entitled to his opinions about gender, but when he invokes "nature" in support of his view, he comes onto anthropological turf where he must contend with anthropologists' findings on the subject.

In their work, anthropologists themselves have not been entirely free of bias where gender is concerned. It is true that early anthropological considerations of the subject were mostly undertaken by men, some of whom may have had a male-oriented axe to grind. The extremely popular books of Margaret Mead, though, seem to have done a good deal to make up for the anthropological tilt in the male direction. It would be difficult these days to argue that the study of gender is now dominated by males, though accusations of male bias continue. The subject remains emotionally charged, and one has to pick one's way carefully through the claims and counterclaims.

To illustrate some of the issues involved, I have chosen to summarize two recent anthropological studies in the area of gender. The first study concerns gender differences in a *kibbutz*, a collective settlement in Israel. The other investigates the relative power of women in a supposed bastion of male supremacy, namely Andalusia in southern Spain.

CASE STUDIES

Spiro on the Counterrevolution In a Kibbutz

Kibbutzim are small collective settlements in Israel. Melford Spiro is one of the leading authorities on kibbutz life. He first studied Kiryat Yedidim, then a utopian agricultural community, in the 1950s, and has returned to this developing kibbutz from time to time since then. The young European-born founders of this little community dreamed of getting rid of many of the evils associated with industrial capitalism. They thought that by developing a certain collective, agricultural way of life and passing it on to their children they would eliminate or at least minimize such things as individualism and gender differences in work and other roles. Their plan involved abolishing private property and setting up collective routines that included communal dining rooms and children's houses. Males and females would be treated as equally as possible. For example, they would circulate through all of the community's jobs (thus helping to minimize the division of labor by sex as an ascribing factor). Children would be raised in mixed nurseries and dormitories and would see their parents only a couple of hours each day. The essentials of this regime had been established when Spiro first studied this *kibbutz* in the early 1950s. Some of the developments that the founders hoped for had yet to occur, but they felt that the new social changes they had instituted would eventually bring about significant changes in the character of the people involved in them. All of this is reported by Spiro in *Kibbutz: Venture in Utopia*.

After further field work in the 1970s, Spiro reported (in *Gender and Culture: Kibbutz Women Revisited*) that though some of the founders' dreams had been realized, the attempt to minimize gender differences had been only partially successful. There continues to be marked differences in work roles. Women, who had been concentrated in certain service occupations—in the kitchen, nursery, and dormitories—at the time of the first study, continue to be concentrated there. Men, who had been the principal handlers of heavy farm machinery, continued to monopolize this kind of work. Not only were men and women still concentrated in certain occupations, but they had come to regard this as normal, not something that was expected to change. Other differences between the sexes that the founders had attempted to downplay were also being accepted and even emphasized. Spiro, in this re-study, found women, who earlier had disdained such things, marking their femininity by wearing jewelry, cosmetics, and "feminine" clothing. Meanwhile in the dormitories, adolescent girls, who had been raised in a presumably gender-blind environment, had made good a rebellion against mixed showers and bedrooms. These now had been almost entirely abandoned.

The founders had thought that they could reduce the family to its bare essentials by collectivizing community life, but Spiro now found a renewed emphasis on family ties. People continued to follow the socialist design of the community, which reduced private concerns and promoted communal preoccupations, but now they were having increasingly elaborate (private) family affairs in their collectively owned apartments. In the early days of the community, parents and children got together daily for an hour or two after work. Now children were spending more time at home with obviously devoted parents. So, instead of withering away, family relationships were flourishing.

Reporting on the situation in the mid-1990s in a revised *Gender and Culture,* Spiro notes that these "counterrevolutionary" trends continue in Kiryat Yedidim and other similar *kibbutzim.* The most dramatic example, perhaps, of a general movement away from the collective goals that were so crucial to the founders is the almost complete transformation from communal sleeping (of children) to family sleeping. The division of labor by sex is no less noticeable, but an important goal of the founders, namely full-fledged social equality of the sexes, seems to have been achieved. Overall, there seems to be an acceptance by *kibbutz* members that though the sexes are fairly equal, there are certain irreducible differences between them that cannot be eliminated.

Apologists for the utopian dreams of the founders have pointed out that their scheme never had a fair chance. Any *kibbutz,* they say, has to contend with outside influences from a bourgeois, capitalist order as well as traditional Judaic influences. They also maintain that differences between the sexes had not been completely eliminated at the outset and so have been experienced by the first generation of growing children. Thus, the "counterrevolution" was the result of social factors stemming from outside and inside the kibbutz. Spiro does not share this "cultural" argument. He feels, rather, that the founders' attempt to remake human nature by creating a new culture had collided with certain unchanging facts of that nature. The most important evidence for this argument comes from a series of studies of preschool infants and children in the kibbutz, in which the preschoolers demonstrated (through play at the communal nursury, for example) significantly different behavioral dispositions, which Spiro describes as "precultural," that is, unaffacted by the kibbutz culture. Subsequent differences in behavior by gender, could not, therefore, be the result of role modeling or other socializing experiences unique to the kibbutz. Spiro also thinks that the attempt to minimize the special relationship between mother and child by reducing contact between parents and children and turning over child rearing to nurses and teachers failed because the connection between a mother and child has a deep-seated evolutionary basis. And the counterrevolution by the adolescent girls against mixed showers and sleeping arrangements (which, significantly, was not shared by boys who had been raised in the same gender-neutral conditions) reflects a specifically female reaction against surging sexuality in an emotionally charged living arrangement.

Spiro's argument (which now continues against feminist critics) that the rebellion of women and girls *was not* due to cultural influences is hard to dismiss. He points out, for example, that the adolescent girls could not have taken their cues from outside the kibbutz because their rebellion occurred before they had any significant contact with city people or their culture. Moreover, the adults and boys with whom they were in regular contact appear to have generally favored continuing unisex arrangements in the dormitories. By adding to this the "counterrevolt" of mothers, whose ties to children would appear to have an evolutionary basis, and the inclinations of both men and women, whose different natures (physical strength, for example) seem to be responsible for a number of universal features of the division of labor by gender (certainly evident in this kibbutz), one can better appreciate the strength of Spiro's argument.

Melford Spiro is careful about specifying the factors that he believes are responsible for the persistence of gender-related differences in a culture that had been specifically created to minimize or stamp them out. He refers to such factors as precultural because they reflect either biological nature or the way that nature is shaped very early in life (before local socializing factors begin to assert themselves). Besides, he is at pains to point out that whatever pan-human differences between the sexes do exist, they are not of kind, but of degree only. Human beings, Spiro argues, are born with more or less androgynous qualities with some clearly female infants having male tendencies and vice versa. A society may socialize its children in a variety of ways, but must contend with an infant's gender-related and other potentials. Whether these are genetically determined or acquired through experience with their own male and female bodies still is difficult to determine. The limits for shaping male and female children through socialization also remain unclear.

So as a result of precultural and cultural factors, genders tend to differ in some ways. Vive la difference! But the existence of such differences does not automatically imply that they must differ in social status. The founders of the kibbutz, also had hoped to create real equality between the sexes. Spiro points out that, though they have not managed to eliminate gender differences in behavior, they have, in contrast to the outside world, created a society in which men and women are considered to be fairly equal. This would suggest that culture plays an important role in determining the social status of men and women.

Gilmore on Women's Power in Andalusia

The social standing of women and men and their relative power in social affairs are important issues for us all. Spiro's study suggests that gender status can be changed, and those of us who have witnessed the movement toward greater rights for women in the United States can confirm this. Martin Whyte's ambitious cross-cultural investigation (*The Status of Women in Preindustrial Societies*) also suggests that the social standing of the sexes is a cultural matter that varies with social complexity. In the simplest societies generally (the San, for example), he notes men and women to be of equal or nearly equal status, while in societies practicing intensive agriculture (such as in pre-revolutionary China) women's status hit bottom. Though Whyte has adequate data only for preindustrial societies, he does speculate that the status of women has been rising and will continue to rise with industrialization. Whyte recognizes a number of different dimensions of status, one of which is power, that is, the ability to prevail in collective decisions.

David Gilmore, an anthropologist whose name has become associated with the people of Andalusia, considers the matter of female power in "Men and Women in Southern Spain: 'Domestic Power' Revisited." Since Andalusia has long been regarded as a bastion of male supremacy, it would be expected that his work would chronicle the many ways in which women give way to men in their lives together. But Gilmore's study shows that not only are some women not dominated by men in the domestic sphere, they *are* the dominators.

In an article filled with sometimes hilarious references to actual events and local folklore, this anthropologist acquaints us with the battle of the sexes among the working classes (peasants and agricultural workers) of two small agro-towns in the Guadalquivir River Basin, where the staple crops include olives, wheat, and sunflowers. At the time of the field research in the 1970s, neither of the towns had much in the way of industry, being largely dependent on agriculture. In these towns men and women live a segregated existence. Women's place is in the home and men's is outside, either at work or in bars where the men carry on a lively social life filled with banter and storytelling. In the home, the men usually allow their wives to prevail in domestic matters such as the location and nature of residence, how many children to have, and how to raise them. Gilmore claims that the typical Andalusian woman tends to dominate in all domestic matters including when to have sex. One thing she wants to do is live near *her* mother, so she and her husband usually move in with or reside near her parents (in anthropological terms, a *matrilocal* or *uxorilocal* rule of residence). This means that the husband is a stranger or outsider among women having well-established ties to each other.

Why does the wife prevail so often in domestic matters? Gilmore believes that the residential arrangement of these Andalusians maintains an alliance between the wife and her mother. Together they are in a position to gang up on the residentially unaffiliated husband and, in those few instances where he enters into a dispute, they can wear him down. For example, the author cites the case of a man who fits all of the specifications for manliness in this part of the world, being athletic, gregarious, assertive, and so forth. He wants to put off his marriage for another year and tells his buddies at the bar that the matter is decided. But the matter is not in fact decided. To the consternation of his friends, he agrees to an earlier date. In cases like this, the men often see the sinister hand of the mother-in-law and have a host of songs and stories that deal with this powerful female scourge.

Thus, the wife tends to prevail in the domestic sphere, and she is seen to do this with the aid of her mother. But this is only one area of social life. What about the public domain in which men are supposed to dominate? Gilmore argues that in these towns men of the working classes have very little political power and that their relations with their friends are mostly ones of equality, which means that they don't have much power generally. Not so among the men of the upper classes, who have servants and who tend to live near the husband's blood relatives after marriage. They have real power to shape public events, and as it turns out, the nature of their domestic life.

The issue of men's and women's relative power is an important one. Seen in the framework of Andalusian culture with which Gilmore is intimately acquainted, the issue comes to life with a good deal of local flavor. Though cautious in drawing conclusions, the author raises provocative questions in a field of study that a new generation of female anthropologists have increasingly considered to be their own. Knowing these *People of the Plain* so well helps Gilmore to move with greater assurance in increasingly female territory.

These summaries of the studies by Spiro and Gilmore are greatly simplified. Both anthropologists use sophisticated theoretical arguments and, in the case of Gilmore, pay attention to the new wave of anthropological literature on women. However, the main thrusts of the two works should be clear. Spiro conducted a crude experiment in nature. That is, he created a before-and-after experiment that enabled him to suggest why the people of his kibbutz failed in their efforts to minimize differences between men and women. As is usual with natural experiments, there was a problem of controls (in this case, cultural influences). However, Spiro makes an arresting case that precultural factors were responsible for the failure of the revolutionary attempt by the kibbutz founders to reduce the gap between men's and women's roles. In retrospect, it should not be surprising that they failed in their attempt to do what no other people have done. Some division of labor by gender exists in all human societies. For whatever reason, child care is pretty much the province of women, though fathers and others sometimes can play important roles here. In the home, women are likely to be the fuel gatherers, fetchers of water, and clothes launderers. Outside of the home, women rarely engage in activities such as hunting, fishing, mining, metal working, and clearing land. Using machines and collective productive arrangements, the kibbutz founders tried to develop a society in which men or women could do most jobs with equal effectiveness. Though many changes have taken root in their little community, they have not been able to eliminate some division of labor and other differences between men and women. After reviewing cross-cultural studies such as Carol Ember's "A Cross-Cultural Perspective on Sex Differences," which details the areas of production where there are divisions of labor by gender, it is not surprising that this aspect of their utopian experiment failed.

Gilmore, in his exploration of the power of men and women in Andalusia, introduces us to the subject of status differences between genders and the reasons why they exist. These reasons seem to be cultural, not biological. He shows that the working-class woman pretty much rules the home. One reason for this seems to be due to the prevailing rule of residence that favors alliances between female blood relatives. As a result, the husband, outnumbered by women whose interests coincide, tends to give way. In the upper classes, however, where the rule of residence tends to favor the man, women have less power in the domestic sphere. Thus, the ability to command in the public sphere is associated with rule in the home. So, as Gilmore concludes, the issue of gender power is seen to fit into the broader issue of the power of humans over one another. One nagging question remains, however: Why, in the absence of confirming evidence for male dominance, do working-class men believe that it is they, not women, who command? Gilmore has nothing to say on this score.

The relative social standings of the sexes and the reasons for them are emotional issues that can generate some heated debate in which anthropologists, like others, often find it difficult to remain objective. It is helpful, therefore, to have studies of specific cases that do not attempt to go too far beyond the data. David Gilmore's investigation of the power of the sexes in Andalusia is an example.

Finally, it should be mentioned that, to date, no study has provided a scientific answer to the question of why, when all the indicators are added up, women have never attained a position of superiority over men. There has been a lot of speculation about this, some of it revolving around the relative physical strength of the two sexes. (For example, it has been said that "The average man can beat up the average woman.") The truth is that we just don't know why this is the case. Whatever the reasons, male dominance remains deeply entrenched; but, as is demonstrated when the world's women meet to discuss their problems, the issue is becoming more and more subject to debate.

AGE

In *When I Was Old* the French novelist and writer of detective stories, Georges Simenon, tells us that there came a time when he began to feel that he was getting old. He began to keep a journal on what was going on in his life and wrote on this subject for a couple of years until it had no more interest for him. Then the journal (which was later published) came to an end.

Simenon says that he does not know what it was that prompted him to keep the journal, but he does mention that he was approaching the age of sixty at the time. Possibly he was thinking of that number as some kind of marker, which in the Western world is a time when people begin to feel increasingly irrelevant. If so, it is one of a number of culturally defined age categories through which he would have passed during the course of his life. As people grow they assume, more or less, the expected behavioral characteristics of these age categories or grades. Maybe, as might have been the case with Simenon, people may be bothered by the implications of old age. Then, they may reject the relevance of this particular category for them personally by saying, "You are only as old as you feel"; but even so, most people are likely to recognize the significance of the category, especially when someone reminds them to act their age.

People in the West tend to think in linear and in absolute chronological terms about age. A person is thought to grow and decline over a number of years, which even in the best of circumstances rarely exceeds a hundred. People must have passed through a number of these years in order to do such things as apply for a driver's license, attend college, enter the army or work force, marry, collect Social Security from the government, vote, or run for political office. They are put in a certain age bracket in sports competition and in physical and psychological assessments. A mother tells us with pride how advanced her child is in speaking, walking, or in holding its head up.

Chronological measures of development from birth to death infuse all aspects of life in state-organized, industrial societies.

It is true that Europeans and Americans sometimes use physical or behavioral criteria as indicators of age. A boy may be said to be capable of doing "a man's work" or a girl said to have the physical attributes of "a grown woman." Such people are thought to have matured more than their chronological age would indicate. Americans sometimes put aside thinking about age in absolute chronological terms by referring to the generations. A mother is senior to her daughter, and a grandmother is senior to both of them. This location of a person in a generational sequence, which is an indication of relative age, also has behavioral implications, as, say, the obedience of a younger generation. There are cultural norms for how daughters, mothers, and grandmothers should act and be treated.

Because the peoples of the world have a variety of ways of thinking about age and because it is more or less important in organizing their behavior, anthropologists have to be wary about using their own notions, which are likely to be culturally biased. People may use chronological age, evident maturation, position in a generational sequence, or other markers in thinking about the subject, but whatever the way of looking at it, some notion of life stages in a life course seems to have prevailed in all societies.

Consider the category of young men (*ritai'wa*) among the semi-nomadic Akwe-Shavante, hunters and horticulturalists who once were established in savannah country in the Mato Grosso of Brazil. In *Akwe-Shavante Society*, David Maybury-Lewis points out that young men can be distinguished from uninitiated boys and mature men (*predu*). Entering the category of *ritai'wa* at a time that Westerners know as adolescence, and "graduating" into the category of mature men in their forties, the young men seem to embody many of the qualities that the Akwe-Shavante admire. They are supposed to be warlike, handsome, and good performers in ceremonial runs, dancing, and singing. They should be alert and wakeful (not sleepy or sluggish). These young men are exceedingly vain and spend a lot of time oiling and painting their bodies and doing their hair. As do the mature men, they have the right to sit together at their own site in the center of the village. Villagers also can see them dancing and singing as they parade around at all hours of the day and night.

The mature men are more judicious in their behavior. The site where they congregate should not be approached without a special invitation. Here, these elders consider the latest news and gossip about it. It is in the meetings of these men that much of the governing of this society is accomplished. A person who demonstrates rhetorical power is respected and may be in line to become chief.

In anthropological lingo, the categories of young men and mature men among the Akwe-Shavante are age grades, that is, a category of persons distinguished by age (something like the American adolescence and adulthood, only more formalized). There are pressures against deviating too far from the norms of these categories, and social sanctions are leveled against those who do. For example, if the Akwe-Shavante young men do not dance and sing in the night, mature men may comment for all to hear that they are too sleepy. In comparison, at an American university, a youth who does not party or drink enthusiastically may run the risk of derision by his fellows, if not his elders. It may help to think of an age grade as having the qualities of a subculture (discussed in Chapter 2).

An association of age mates that continues throughout the life of its members has been identified in a number of societies. Anthropologists refer to these enduring groups, which are usually formed in adolescence, as *age sets*. Among the Akwe-Shavante, there are eight age sets, each of which has its own name and is comprised of persons who differ in age by no more than five years. The youngest age set is formed by the congregation of boys in the bachelors' hut between the ages of seven and twelve. They move along into the category of young men after a particularly significant initiation rite sometime between the ages of twelve and seventeen. Then follow moves at five-year intervals upward on the age set ladder until they become mature men. At this time, some of them have begun to die off, and their identification with their age set also has given way toward an association with the elders of the tribe. When it is time for the next set to come on board as young men, the youngsters will take the name of what was the most senior set and possibly be assisted in getting started by some of its remaining members. And so the cycle continues.

Mention of the categories of age raises the question of the transitions or passages that people go through from one stage of the life course to another. Among the Akwe-Shavante, where stages are particularly marked, the passage of an age set into the grade of young men is associated with rituals that involve jumping up and down in water, running, dancing, and singing for extended periods. Rituals like this were first investigated extensively by Arnold Van Gennep in his famous *The Rites of Passage* and by others including Victor Turner (in *The Ritual Process* and other works). These rituals appear not only to mark a transition socially, but also to ease it for those involved. Death, of course, can be viewed as one such transition.

CASE STUDY

McCabe on Gender Differences in Later Life

People have so many notions of age and aging that one may begin to despair of finding common threads, other than the basic biological ones, that tie them all together. One persistent notion is that as people age past adulthood the social and psychological gap between the genders tends to dissolve. Justine McCabe, in "Psychological Androgyny in Later Life: A Psychocultural

Examination," has investigated this hypothesis in a southern Lebanese village that reveals marked segregation and differences in behavior of adult males and females. Generally, the first half of the life course of the Lebanese village woman is characterized as passive and compliant. She is a nurturer and spends a lot of time attending to others in the domestic sphere. Young men, on the other hand, tend to be an active, self-indulgent, and assertive lot in and outside of the home. McCabe was interested in learning whether these differences persisted into later life.

This anthropologist employed traditional anthropological methods, including participant observation and use of informants, in fourteen months of fieldwork in 1974–1975. She also used a specially adapted Thematic Apperception Test (TAT), which required a sample of twenty-five village men and women to describe and tell a story about figures making up what respondents took to be a two-generational family. The responses on the TAT and the information gained by other methods showed the expected male-female differences. Younger men usually were thought of as self-assertive, active masters of situations in and outside of the home, while young women were usually thought of as self-effacing nurturers and mediators. On the TAT the younger women in the picture were often seen as being quiet, simple, and having no opinions. In contrast, the older women were generally thought to be more assertive and dominating and the older men as more conciliatory and nurturant. McCabe points out that these changes, which have been identified in some other societies, extend beyond the home when, after middle age, the woman begins to get out more. In McCabe's words, the wife no longer "kowtows" to her husband as before.

What accounts for this shift in the roles of the two genders? One hypothesis that has been suggested is that the shift reflects biological factors that have emerged in the course of evolution to promote reproduction. During the reproductive years, the behaviors displayed by younger Lebanese and other men and women tend to ensure the survival of the domestic unit, which is needed to produce children and ensure their survival. McCabe, however, favors a cultural hypothesis. She thinks that because opportunities in the public sphere are not very great, men, by the time they reach middle age, begin to think of themselves as unsuccessful, while women are able to build on and expand the power they have been accumulating in the domestic sphere. Now, the older man increasingly retires to his wife's domain where she is very much in charge. In addition, as Gilmore found in Andalusia, the Lebanese women gain support from female kin and friends outside of the home. Men, on the other hand, have been carrying on a competitive life outside and therefore have little social support to rely on. So, the older women change in the direction of younger men in their behavior, while the older men become more like what their wives once were.

There are problems with McCabe's study, some of which the author recognizes. But the fact that all of this anthropologist's data fall in the same direction gives us greater confidence in her conclusions. In addition, investigators have found the same pattern of transition in a number of other societies, which adds weight to McCabe's findings and suggests the need for further cross-cultural investigations to test her cultural explanation against the biological one.

McCabe's extremely interesting study provides one example of how age may be seen to affect the behavior of people. It is of particular importance in drawing our attention to the fact that gender differences are not immutable, but change through the life course. This means that it no longer is possible to speak of general differences or similarities in the roles of men and women. Gender roles may differ by social class, as the summary of Gilmore's study in the previous section indicates; and now, through McCabe's investigation, we see that they may differ by age as well. This study is only one example of a welcome increase of anthropological interest in age as an ascribing factor, particularly in the later stages of the life course. The importance of such study in an industrialized society such as the United States with its expanding population of older people is obvious.

Applied Significance

It was suggested earlier that in contemporary Western society older people, who make up an increasing proportion of the total population, tend to have less power in the affairs of their world than middle-aged adults. Anthropological investigations in societies such as the agricultural Tiriki of Kenya and the Irigwe of Nigeria, where one's social power tends to *grow* throughout the life course, suggest that certain sociocultural factors are responsible, and therefore, that the condition of declining elder power in the West is not inevitable. Perhaps some political activists among the elderly in Western society, such as the Grey Panthers, are aware of their political clout. But they probably have not explored the issue of social power of the aged so deeply and extensively as have David Kertzer and K. Warner Shaie in *Age Structuring in Comparative Perspective*—a broad-ranging comparative study of the relationship between social structure and different aspects of the individual life course.

Also of applied significance for Westerners is the remarkable cross-cultural investigation of the life course by Jennie Keith, and associates (*The Aging Experience: Diversity and Commonality Across Cultures*), in which seven societies of varying degrees of complexity have been investigated. These authors use their cross-cultural data to point up a central issue in the life of the average aging Westerner for whom life has been made easier and longer by techno-scientific advances (medicines, prosthetic devices, and nutrition, for example), but who also may have to struggle to satisfy social and psychological needs. Consider, for example, an older American in a top-of-the-line nursing home with a special diet and expert medical attention. Certainly, this person's physical needs are better attended to than are those of a poor person in America or one of the older San or neighboring Herero, the simplest societies in this study. At the same time, this older American may miss the interaction with relatives and friends and feelings of consequence that are taken for granted in some societies and so experience a decline in feelings of well-being. Is some form of home care in which such interaction is more a fact of life a viable alternative? Using evidence from the various societies in their study, the authors suggest certain alternatives that might be considered. Other cross-cultural research may help to show that though aging and death are inevitable, some things that we associate with the last stages of the life course may not be as inevitable as we may think.

KINSHIP

God gave you your relatives, but thank God you can choose your friends.

This was a saying of my father, and I think he spoke for many Americans who are impatient with the bonds of kinship. In a society where achievement is the ideal, relatives can be a drag. They are supposed to offer love and security, but they also represent obligations that can interfere with the plans of career-minded individuals. Connections with relatives are an ascribing factor, which many Americans like to downplay. There are Americans who don't think like my father, or if they do, prefer to keep such thoughts to themselves. But even they would be surprised to find out how important kinship can be in some societies.

So it is with Christopher Newman, the hero of Henry James' book, *The American.* A success at home in what appears to be late nineteenth-century America (in manufacturing some kind of gadget), Newman heads off to France looking for a wife. He wants the best, and it seems as if he's found her. James makes it clear that both individuals are admirable people in their own ways and that they complement each other perfectly. Moreover, there is a mutual attraction between them. But the woman's family stands in the way. They are poor but proud aristocrats who feel that the American does not meet their standards. He is not of the "right" class. Nevertheless, being poor, they reluctantly come to an understanding with the rich, young American. He agrees to provide for his wife in a way that is agreeable to her family. He promises to love her and take care of her. All is set for the marriage, but at the last minute the family backs out. The daughter, not being able to go against her family's wishes, enters a nunnery, and the American returns home empty-handed and desolate after experiencing this triumph of kinship and status obligations over love.

To young Americans these days, James' account might sound old-fashioned, but much of the world still operates in something like the traditional

French way. Even in America today, parental wishes about marriage partners cannot be totally disregarded. Kinship and other obligations still play some role in sorting people out for marriage. Impressed by the importance of kinship in structuring many of the societies they have studied, anthropologists have gone to great lengths in treating this subject. A glance through any introductory text in anthropology will suggest just how important the study of kinship continues to be among anthropologists. Kinship may be an important organizing factor in some societies—agreed, but it may not be the same type of kinship that exists in the West. Not all people think of relatives in the same way that Americans do. As is usual in anthropological matters, one has to guard against ethnocentrism. As David Schneider points out in his pathbreaking work *American Kinship: A Cultural Account*, Americans tend to regard kin as people related by blood and marriage. Of these, the blood relationship is considered to be the most important. For Americans, it seems only "natural" (a nice way of suggesting ascription) that people who are related by blood should feel close. "Blood is thicker than water," they say. As for relatives-in-law, they are acquired and can be unacquired through divorce or separation.

Such a biogenetic view of kinship poses problems for cross-cultural analysis. What is one to do in a culture where the biological facts of paternity are not known? How does one trace the blood relationship between a father and his children in that case? Also, Americans tend to think of kin as sharing degrees of biological substance. Because of this, they feel more closely tied to primary relatives on both sides of the family than to secondary kin. But many peoples emphasize kin on one side of the family, say the father's. In that case, relatives on the mother's side, though still considered as relatives, are seen as farther removed. This means that it is possible for people who share an equal degree of biological substance to be thought of as closely or distantly related. Finally, different peoples draw the line far or near when tracing relatives, and the cutoff point may not be determined by biological distance but by social factors. In such cases, people who are equally related biologically may or may not be considered relatives. This suggests that the notion of shared biological substance is not naturally given but culturally constituted, which means that people learn how to think about kinship just as they learn other aspects of their culture.

The Basics on Kinship

Consider marriage to be a social relationship involving sexual, economic, reproductive, and other rights and duties. Though some might quibble about its universality, marriage does seem to exist in all societies. Men and women come into this relationship in a number of ways. The partners may have a lot to say about whom they marry, as in the United States, or less, as in the French upper-class family described by Henry James. A number of kinds of marriage partnerships may be worked out. One type consists of one man and one woman (monogamy); another, of one man and several women (polygyny); another, one woman and several men (polyandry); and still another, two or more spouses of both sexes (group). The last two of these are rarely encountered. The most frequently occurring marital *ideal* in the societies of humankind is polygyny. However, granted the usual sex ratio and the desire of most adults to marry, it can never be the most frequent form in a given society. The Tiv of central Nigeria provide a typical example of the way marriages are distributed in a polygynous society. Among these people, the more important men tend to have several wives, while the majority of married men have only one. Since wives are considered by the Tiv to be the ultimate form of wealth, a man who has many wives is thought to be not only wealthy, but also a big success. Male economic activities among the Tiv, therefore, tend to be aimed at acquiring a number of wives.

The sorting out process whereby people acquire mates and, later, children, everywhere is subject to social controls. One is not free to marry just anyone, as the French woman who was the object of Christopher Newman's quest in James' book well knew. There are, first of all, an array of tabued relatives that one is not supposed to marry or even fool around with. When people do have sexual relations with such relatives, they are violating a cultural rule. Unless they have been granted a special exemption (as with Hawaiian or ancient Egyptian royalty where the marriage of siblings was considered desirable), this puts them at social risk. The range of tabued relatives varies and can be extended on the father's side, the mother's, or both. It always includes a prohibition of sexual relations between members of the nuclear family, that is, the group consisting of a biological father, mother, and their offspring. The universality of this tabu has been explained in a number of ways. It has been said to be derived from either a natural (built-in) or learned aversion that prevents harmful biological inbreeding. It has also been said that it derives from a learned adaptation that promotes advantageous social relationships that can be gained by "marrying out." The fairly widespread violation of the tabu, the demonstrated existence of lust and even sexual relations between close relatives and those who have been raised together, the asymmetric extension of tabued relatives (on the father's or mother's side) in many societies, and the fact that the range of tabued relatives sometimes can change dramatically over a generation or two in a society, all suggest that the incest tabu is largely or wholly learned and, therefore, a cultural matter.

Thus, it is hard to see any biological changes in the population as being responsible for the change in the range of tabued relatives in the Burgundian agricultural village of Minot reported on by Tina Jolas, and her colleagues in *Une Campagne Voisine*. Their informants told them that early in this century it was customary to marry a cousin from within the village, and occasional marriages even between first cousins could be justified. These days, however, marriages between cousins from the village are considered incestuous and regarded with a *"reprobation profonde."*

The obverse of the incest tabu are rules about people one is *expected* to marry. In all societies there are expectations that one will find one's mate outside of certain groups (exogamy) and sometimes within others (endogamy). Speaking in these terms, the authors of the Minot study point out a trend from the beginning of the century that is certainly not unique to this culture: What was once the endogamous group—that is, the village, has become exogamous as young people have looked more and more outside it for spouses; and as there are limits to how far they venture, the authors coin the term "endogamy of locality" to describe this extended zone of opportunity.

Newlyweds must live somewhere. They may live with or near the husband's parents (patrilocality) or the wife's parents (matrilocality). Sometimes there is an option to practice either of these (bilocality). And sometimes, as in the United States, the ideal has been to establish a residence apart from any relatives in some nice suburban community (neolocality). There are a few other very rare alternatives.

The Tiv practice the most frequent option: patrilocality. It is customary for a Tiv wife to move into a compound that includes her husband's parents, his married and unmarried brothers, and his unmarried sisters. She has to get along with them all, including (because the Tiv are polygynous) any other wives her husband takes. Not getting along with her husband's parents is grounds for annulment of the marriage and can raise tricky questions about other marriages in a society where wives and payments for them pass between kinship groups. It has been suggested that the more there is at stake in a marriage, whether in the form of property or social obligations to others, the more difficult it will be for the married partners to break up. This may be why the traditional Tiv wife usually makes such an effort to get along with others in her husband's compound. She is not totally helpless, though, since she can call on her original kin group for assistance under certain circumstances. She also has the right to leave her husband if he does not, for example, prepare some land for her to farm or if he mistreats her for frivolous reasons.

Most people—even in the United States where between 40 to 50 percent of all marriages currently end in divorce—seem to want marriages to succeed. Though there are provisions for termination of marriages in all societies, this seems everywhere to be regarded as regrettable. Those who fall out of a marriage may be subject to social difficulties like legal rigamoroles and economic penalties. In rural Greece, it was once customary for a widow to be a target of abuse and social ostracism even though she was not responsible for the termination of her marriage. The societal cards seem to be stacked in favor of, if not this marriage, then the next, as well as the families that follow. The nucleus of familial arrangements is what Americans have preferred—that is, a married couple and their offspring. This nuclear family appears to be a recognized social unit in most, if not all, societies, but sometimes it is not the most important domestic unit. Consider again the household of a Tiv man of some status. It consists of that man, several wives and their offspring, not to mention parents and unmarried brothers and sisters. It is a recognizable social unit, the demands of which often take precedence over those of the different nuclear families that comprise it. Anthropologists have used a variety of labels for larger domestic groupings like this, depending on whether kin connections are through blood or marital ties. It would seem possible to call all of them extended families and keep in mind that in many societies they are the most significant domestic unit. It is also important to remember that where they exist, these extended families do not completely swallow up their composite nuclear families; sometimes the interests of the two entities will conflict.

To some Americans, the family might seem to be all of kinship worth mentioning, but in many societies it is only the beginning. Individuals can be intimately involved with relatives beyond their family who are tied together by what anthropologists call rules of descent. In the United States, where relatively weak connections extend through both mothers' and fathers' relatives, bilateral descent is said to prevail. Where one is affiliated with kin of both sexes through men only, the rule is patrilineal. If the affiliation is through women only, it is matrilineal. In a society where the latter rule prevailed, I would feel closer to my mother's than my father's sister. There are two additional possibilities, ambilineal and double descent, which are mentioned in the literature but rarely occur. The social groupings or categories larger than the family that are based on these rules of descent have been called (in order of greater inclusiveness) lineage segments, lineages, and clans (where their organization is unilineal) and kindreds (where it is bilateral).

Among the Tiv, the patrilineally organized lineage segment or lineage could be extremely important to the individual. At birth, children automatically become members of patrilineally organized lineage segments and lineages of both their father and mother. Those connected through the father are said to constitute the individual's *ityɔ* ; through the mother, *igba*. The members of a lineage or lineage segment, when speaking of their common ancestor, may say that they have "one father" or "one mother," and they have a special term for all patrilineally related individuals in a compound or related compounds. In contrast to what usually happens in patrilocal situations, a Tiv wife acquires membership in her husband's lineages. Her husband's lineage membership, given at birth and therefore ascribed, does not change. All members of a lineage have certain rights and obligations. Thus, Paul and Laura Bohannan, whose work on the Tiv of a half century or so ago (*The Tiv of Central Nigeria*) has been used as a basis for describing Tiv culture, point out that members of a man's *ityɔ* *must* do things for him. They must provide him with fields, a wife, a place to live (near patrilineally related relatives), and assistance when he is involved in certain kinds of conflict with others. His *igba*, on the other hand, may help him only if they feel so inclined. In the Bohannans' words, they do things for him "because they will or like." The fact that a man tends to be more involved with members of his *ityɔ* than *igba* seems to be consistent with the patrilineal emphasis of this culture. Americans may get some idea of the comparative importance of kinship involvement in different societies by asking themselves how many of their bilaterally related relatives must respond when they are asked for assistance. Probably very few beyond the nuclear family would do so.

To understand how important kinship can be in organizing a society, think of modern, corporate Japan. It is composed of thousands of businesses that often lay kinship-like claims on their people. Certain firms such as Mitsubishi still are expected to take care of employees, if not for life, for as long as possible. In return, these employees are supposed to show their allegiance to the firm, take on uninteresting jobs, work overtime without pay, spend some leisure hours with other employees, and not leave the firm for a more attractive job elsewhere. The Japanese who work for such a firm tend to think of themselves and their involvement with their company in a way that can scare Americans, who are more individualistic and who like to think that they are free to go whenever and wherever they want.

In Japan, a large corporation like Mitsubishi is a subsociety in itself, with many specialized roles that are organized bureaucratically with very specific rules and lines of authority. Mitsubishi commands huge resources and has great economic and political power in Japan and elsewhere. It has a vast network of working relationships in and outside of Japan. To take Mitsubishi and all of the other corporate structures out of Japanese society would reduce it to a shambles.

Now, suppose that instead of being acquired, all the roles in corporate Japan were ascribed in terms of kinship. Of course, that would not be possible in a modern, achievement-oriented, industrialized society, but suppose that Japan could—just for a moment—be transformed into a more intimate, preindustrial society like that of the Tiv. In this mental experiment, corporations would be transformed into kinship groupings larger than the family. Such a transformation would produce a fair approximation of a society such as the Tiv, where much of the social organization is accomplished by kinship. On the father's side, a Tiv belongs not only to an extended family, but also to a series of lineage segments that are included in some maximal lineage. All of the members of these groupings are supposed to be descended from common ancestors. Each of the groupings has a claim on a person in certain circumstances. For example, a man may ask a particular group of patrilineal relatives (the marriage ward group) for economic assistance in marital affairs. In return, this group may require his resources for bride payments, while his maximal lineage may require his services in war. All of these social units have systems of authority that are mainly in the hands of men. They defend members' rights while insisting on their obligations. They can own property, such as land, which is distributed to members of families for farming. These and other kinship groupings that include one's mother's patrilineal relatives are involved in every aspect of Tiv life and constitute much of the social organization of Tiv society.

Although there are many differences in the ways Japanese corporations and Tiv kin groupings are structured and function, they both may be seen as having networks of social roles, each of which is "assigned" certain more or less specific activities. The Tiv counterpart of the president of a large Japanese corporation would be someone they refer to as "great father." To know this and other Tiv kin terms is to begin to understand the nature of Tiv social organization. In the American nuclear family, there are a number of prescribed roles and associated kinship terms. There is a mother, daughter, sister, and so on. To describe someone this way in America implies that certain behavior is expected of that person. In pre-revolutionary China, it was the norm for a daughter-in-law to be an obeying, deferring, and generally abused creature while her mother-in-law played a complementary role. The kinship terms used by a people can tell us something about how they sort each other out in their minds and how they expect people to behave, but how they actually do behave has to be demonstrated.

In most societies, individual relatives are lumped together or classified into certain labeled categories. Thus, as an American, I put the relatives of my generation into the categories of brother, sister, and cousin. In my parents' generation there are father, uncle, and so on. Usually there is only one father and one mother, but there can be several aunts and uncles. The Tiv do it differently. They have terms that correspond to Americans' father (*ter*), mother (*ngɔ*), and child (*wan*), but they lump all the people whom Americans discriminate as brothers, sisters aunts, uncles, and cousins together. Regardless of generation, the Tiv differentiate these family members only by gender and, sometimes, age. A separate term is sometimes used for people on the paternal side, but again, it ignores the generation of the person. Thus, the Tiv recognize the difference between relatives who are lineally connected (through the parent-child line) and collaterals (through siblings), as Americans do. However, they handle the designation of collaterals somewhat differently. By looking at any genealogical chart, it is possible to see that there are several possibilities for separating or combining relatives into categories. These possibilities, however, are limited, and as it turns out, even more limited in practice.

The different kinds of kinship typologies or classifications that anthropologists have found so fascinating, and that generations of anthropology students have learned about, all involve splitting and lumping relatives according to criteria like kinship distance, generation, lineal and collateral relations, relative age, and so forth. Drawn from a particular person's point of view, the typologies lay out the ways in which relatives are classified in one's own and one's parents' generation (affinal relatives, that is, relatives by marriage, usually are not included). According to one typology, which is based on the way peoples consider relatives labeled siblings and cousins in the United States, Americans have an Eskimo terminological system (the Eskimo or Iñupiat are one of the peoples with this form of kinship nomenclature) in which cousins are distinguished from siblings. They also may be said to have a lineal system because they distinguish between parents and their siblings (thus, for example, between mother and aunt) as well as between the generations (mother and daughter, for example). Such distinctions can mount up in some systems of classification.

Although typologies may be essential for scientific work, it is important to remember that they are ways of bringing order to a reality that is usually messy and that is continually being changed by the human beings involved. Accordingly, the various typologies of kinship nomenclature, as well as other aspects of kinship, ought to be used with care. There are several cautions to keep in mind. First, a particular type of kinship nomenclature refers to a rule or norm in a particular society. Hardly anyone's thinking will conform exactly to it. Further, there may be a number of rules or norms depending on the situation. Thus, William Lancaster, writing of the Rwala Bedouin of the northern Arabian desert (in *The Rwala Bedouin Today*), points out that though these people see everyone to be ultimately descended from a common ancestor in patrilineal fashion, they are sufficiently flexible to discard such connections if other kinship structures turn out to be politically or economically advantageous. Similarly, Marilyn Strathern, in her study of an English village near Cambridge in the 1960s and 1970s *(Kinship at the Core)*, points out how kinship ties of a group of families who constitute the core of the village are manipulated (by emphasizing certain blood ties) to close down on connections or (through marital ties) open them up. Second, the anthropologist constructs the norm from an investigation of the thinking and behavior of the people involved. Needless to say, any construction will reflect the point of view of the investigator and the various vicissitudes of the investigation. For example, David Schneider's construction of American kinship, mentioned earlier, owes a good deal to his students' investigations in Chicago. Third, the terminology may be used infrequently by the people being studied. For example, the Bohannans say that the Tiv tend to resort to people's names rather than kin terms. And finally, there may or may not be some specific behavior or attitude, such as avoidance, joking, nurturance, punishing, or deference, that goes with the term. Keeping such cautions in mind, one still can get a remarkable "lift" toward understanding some cultures through their kinship patterns.

Connections

Kinship is a particularly interesting area for exploring the connections between different aspects of a culture. Consider American kinship terminology as a starting point. The norm is not to distinguish between paternal or maternal relatives. An aunt is an aunt regardless of whether maternal or paternal. The same applies to cousins. Gender has no bearing either as far as cousins are concerned. This suggests that Americans are not concerned with specifying relatives as maternal or paternal, and in the case of cousins, that they are uninterested in distinguishing one from another. Their apparent lack of concern with these relatives is to be expected in a society where the nuclear family stands out and other relatives are considered less important. Further, it seems that from the way they label kin Americans do not favor one side of their family over the other, which is to be expected in a system where bilateral descent prevails. Thus, different aspects of kinship fit together in this society in a way that can be readily understood.

Other systems may not be so simple, nor their connections so neat. As was pointed out in Chapter 2, different aspects of a culture may change at different rates, and cultures have tendencies to fragment as well as hang together. Still, it often is possible to discover some coherence between kinship nomenclature and other features of kinship. Even among the Tiv, who pose many problems of analysis because they rarely use kinship terms, there are special labels for collateral relatives on the father's side, which suggest the importance of the patrilineally organized *ityɔ*.

Both Tiv and Americans distinguish between lineal and collateral relatives, but most people do not. In the parental generation, many lump together father and father's brothers under one term and mother and mother's sisters under another. The peoples who use this kind of terminology do, indeed, distinguish their own biological mothers and fathers in practice; but the terminological merging suggests that, say, mothers and mothers' sisters have more in common in these societies then they do in America. Indeed, this is often the case. Where such a system prevails, some kind of unilineal descent involving clumps of relatives based on male or female ties often exists. A further corollary of this arrangement is that the children of the mother's sister and father's brother (parallel cousins in anthropological terms) are usually given the same term as siblings and are sexually tabu. At the same time, it appears to be open season on sexual dalliance with mother's brother's and father's sister's children (cross-cousins), who are given different terms. Thus, among the aboriginal Ojibwa Indians of North America, a man was supposed to avoid not only his own sister, but also all parallel cousins who were also called sister; it was, however, possible for him to joke around sexually and pursue cross-cousins.

Cross-cultural studies have shown that certain kinds of kinship terminology tend to be associated with certain rules of descent. The Eskimo form, mentioned above, for example, is associated with bilateral descent. Also, rules of descent and residence are related. Patrilineality is associated with patrilocality, matrilineal descent with matrilocality, and bilateral descent with bilocality and neolocality. The reason for this would seem to be that feelings of kinship are promoted among people who live close together. According to George P. Murdock, an American anthropologist, whose cross-cultural investigations of kinship (see, for example, his *Social Structure*) have been particularly influential, the rule of residence is the key element of any kinship system. If it changes, other aspects of kinship will tend to follow until they line up with it.

However, there does not appear to be one key determinant of the rule of residence. Important activities that require the organized effort of either males or females do seem to be associated with patrilocal or matrilocal residence. Thus, big game hunting and warfare are often found together with patrilocal residence. Neolocality and the nuclear family that goes with it are found in a variety of circumstances. One of these is a niggardly environment. The Shoshone Indians, for example, once inhabited a region of the western United States that supported only a few wild animals and edible plants. This environment could sustain groupings of these hunters and gatherers that were larger than nuclear families for a small part of the year only.

Such an explanation of neolocality and the nuclear family will not do for industrialized societies, however, where such kinship arrangements predominate. In this kind of society, even if the environment is naturally niggardly, it is possible for high technology (disease-resistant crops and more efficient machines, for example) to make it productive. Higher technology and larger productive systems, as in the case of a modern factory, make kinship more and more redundant. In a Spanish factory I became acquainted with during field research, a relative of a high government official had been given an important post simply because of his kin connections. It turned out that he was an incompetent and unable to do the job effectively. As a result, he was gradually transformed into a figurehead while more capable managers took over. Emerging factory systems can tolerate—even use—kinship connections, as did the water-powered mills of the eastern United States during the nineteenth century (reliable employees could be hired through family connections). However, as the scale of operations increases and job requirements become more complex, kinship connections can begin to interfere with industrial work and must be modified or discarded. Achievement comes to the fore.

Similar things happen in an economy as trading begins to play a more important role. In the days when they produced most of the goods they needed, inhabitants of Minot, the Burgundian village mentioned earlier, exchanged produce with neighbor-relatives in and outside of the family. The distribution of economic resources, therefore, tended to follow the lines of kinship. However, as more produce came to be sold abroad and a good deal of what was used came from outside, kinship became a less important factor in the way goods were distributed. More rapidly changing and impersonal market forces gradually took over.

In the modern, Western world, kinship and other ascribing factors play less and less of a role in sorting people out and structuring certain tasks. Larger networks of relatives and other intimates dissolve until the nuclear family stands alone. Even this unit is hard pressed to survive in the face of forces that pull its members this way and that. In America today, for example, the nuclear family no longer is the typical household unit (one-parent families are common as well). Kinship networks have difficulty handling the large-scale organizational tasks of a modern society. In their place, large, bureaucratically organized corporations or state agencies have become central facts of everyday life. Within these structures, relationships are, ideally, impersonal, rule-oriented, and highly specific. Individual work roles tend to be achieved rather than ascribed. Like the Japanese corporations mentioned earlier, large corporations may attempt to create a sort of kinship in their firms, but such a system can have only limited success in an industrial and post-industrial world.

CODA

Looking at human societies generally, gender, age, and kinship certainly are the most important ascriptive factors that people have used to organize themselves. This may be because these factors are more closely tied to universal biological facts, which are harder to escape. But as I hope I've made clear, though societies cannot wholly escape the dictates of biology in sorting people out, they do have a great deal of leeway in how they interpret and use them.

There are other ascriptive factors—for example, locality, status, and ethnic group membership—which may be even more important in some situations. Consider the black population of South Africa, which with the establishment of foreign, white domination of the region, was relegated to an inferior position that continues still. Though dramatic changes are under way in that country, people born black in South Africa still find their status in life strongly dependent on the color of their skin. Similarly, in India, people born into a certain hereditarily defined caste have found opportunities that are available to members of other castes closed to them. But there are forces at work in societies throughout much of the contemporary world that are helping to undermine these and other ascriptive factors and to make them increasingly irrelevant for organizing societies. In India, for example, certain affirmative action policies are now in place that favor lower caste applicants.

In the past, ascription was a good way to sort people out in societies that didn't change very rapidly and where narrow horizons and low technical expectations prevailed. In such societies, people's potential occupation and social connections were basically laid out for them early in life. They may not have been happy with what they were doing, with the others they were obligated to, or with the various deprivations they experienced, but any discontent was minimized by a lack of alternatives. Even if they were doing menial labor such as cleaning latrines, which was the work of one Indian caste, they carried on. Some among them may have grumbled or tried to do things differently, but unless some major upheaval was in progress, their initiatives stood little chance of success. As many informants have told anthropologists in a resigned way, "That's the way things are." Even when living a hard life, though, people in such a closed society had a sense of intimacy and certainty that people everywhere seem to value to some degree.

As the world has opened up through industrialization, commercialization, and other forces, life's possibilities have increased dramatically. It is no longer necessary for a woman to be simply a domestic laborer. Often, she will add a job, say, in a factory, to her domestic chores. And although some jobs in the factory may be closed to her, her life has been expanded. As the American anthropologist Helen Safa points out in *The Urban Poor of Puerto Rico*, even the poor who gave up a rural existence for a life in a shantytown in San Juan, Puerto Rico, could sense increased possibilities in life there and gain hope from them. They would soon learn, however, that there is a negative side to an increasingly open existence. People often become uncomfortable when they lack solid social foundations. In his book *Loss and Change*, the British sociologist Peter Marris notes that migrant people in African cities often show the same symptoms as bereaved persons. Cut off from a more secure, ascribed existence in the bush, they act like people who have just lost a loved one. They show many of the symptoms of the bereaved and look about— sometimes desperately—for something solid to hang on to. Some of them may find it in secular or religious revolutionary movements, others in reconstituted tribal enclaves in refugee camps, or kinship networks in the city, but all seem to be yearning for the kind of certainty and involvement they left behind in a more ascriptive culture.

In the enormous fluidity of contemporary life, people can be afflicted with what amounts to a permanent identity crisis. For better or worse, most get sorted out socially, but it is becoming more and more difficult to find one's place in life. Social foundations have become so soft and shifting that even when people achieve success, they still may have doubts about where they stand and who they are. Adolescents are particularly struck by such doubts as they move toward adulthood. Older workers, cast out of a firm to which they have given years of devoted service, can display a look of incomprehension accompanied by periodic bursts of rage. And elderly people, afflicted with declining faculties and feelings of irrelevance, are especially subject to disorientation. As I noted earlier in this chapter, my father wanted to be able to choose his friends and his position in society. He only gradually came to realize, I think, the full consequences of this.

SELECTED REFERENCES

BERLAND, JOSEPH, "Qalander," in *Encyclopedia of World Cultures*, ed. Paul Hockings, pp. 245–48. Boston: G. K. Hall, 1992.

BOHANNAN, LAURA, and PAUL BOHANNAN, *The Tiv of Central Nigeria*. London: International African Institute, 1953.

EMBER, CAROL, "A Cross-Cultural Perspective on Sex Differences," in *Handbook of Cross-Cultural Human Development*, ed. Robert L. Munroe and Beatrice B. Whiting, pp. 531–38. New York: Garland Press, 1981.

———, *People of the Plain*. New York: Columbia University Press, 1980.

GILMORE, DAVID, "Men and Women in Southern Spain: 'Domestic Power' Revisited." *American Anthropologist*, 92, 1990, 953–70.

JOLAS, TINA, MARIE-CLAUDE PINGAUD, YVONNE VERDIER, and FRANÇOISE ZONABEND. *Une Campagne Voisine*. Paris: Éditions de la Maison des Sciences de L'Homme, 1990.

KEITH, JENNIE, CHRISTINE FRY, ANTHONY GLASCOCK, CHARLOTTE IKELS, JEANETTE DICKERSON-PUTNAM, and PATRICIA DRAPER, *The Aging Experience: Diversity and Commonality across Cultures*. Thousand Oaks, CA, London, and New Delhi: Sage Publications, 1994.

KERTZER, DAVID, and K. WARNER SHAIE, eds., *Age Structuring in Comparative Perspective*. Hillsdale, NJ, Hove, and London: Lawrence Erlbaum, 1989.

LANCASTER, WILLIAM, *The Rwala Bedouin Today*. New York and London: Cambridge University Press, 1981.

MARRIS, PETER, *Loss and Change*. Garden City, NY: Anchor Books, 1975.

MAYBURY-LEWIS, DAVID, *Akwe-Shavante Society*. Oxford: Clarendon Press, 1967.

McCABE, JUSTINE, "Psychological Androgyny in Later Life: A Psychocultural Examination," *Ethos*, 17, 1989, 3–31.

MEAD, MARGARET, *Sex and Temperament in Three Primitive Societies*. New York: William Morrow, 1963.

MURDOCK, GEORGE P., *Social Structure*. New York: Macmillan, 1949.

MURPHY, ROBERT, and YOLANDA MURPHY, *Women of the Forest*. New York: Columbia University Press, 1974.

SAFA, HELEN, *The Urban Poor of Puerto Rico: A Study of Development and Inequality*. New York: Holt, Rinehart and Winston, 1974.

SCHNEIDER, DAVID, *American Kinship: A Cultural Account*. Englewood Cliffs, NJ: Prentice Hall, 1968.

SPIRO, MELFORD, *Gender and Culture: Kibbutz Women Revisited*. New Brunswick, NJ: Transaction Publishers, 1996.

———, *Kibbutz: Venture in Utopia*, Augmented ed. Cambridge, MA: Harvard University Press, 1975.

STRATHERN, MARILYN, *Kinship at the Core*. Cambridge: Cambridge University Press, 1981.

TURNER, VICTOR, *The Ritual Process*. Chicago: Aldine, 1969.

VAN GENNEP, ARNOLD, *The Rites of Passage*. Chicago: University of Chicago Press, 1960 (1908).

WHYTE, MARTIN K., *The Status of Women in Preindustrial Societies*. Princeton, NJ: Princeton University Press, 1978.

Government

WHO'S IN CHARGE?

The newspaper said that a state of emergency had been declared in a bit of French territory in the southwestern Pacific near Samoa called Wallis-et-Futuna, two islands in what was once a considerable colonial empire. They were governed by a French administrator, who declared the state of emergency because the normal operation of the government had been threatened by a dispute between the French and local people. It was pointed out in a communiqué that "certain Wallisiens" had threatened to remove the administrator's deputy by force; at the same time, the two natives who had been elected to the French parliament had expressed support for the existing regime. Meanwhile, some thirty state police had been sent to reinforce the seven gendarmes who normally kept order on the two islands.

Such an event is not unusual in today's world, but not too long ago, when more than 80 percent of the globe was under the control of Western, white nations, it occurred less frequently. Then, Western colonial empires were well established, and though native populations fretted and occasionally rebelled, the colonial regimes seemed to be there to stay. As some British colonists once said, "Whatever happens we have got / The Gatling gun which they have not."

After World War II, however, the great European-based empires fell apart with astonishing rapidity, sometimes under the impetus of open revolution, as in French Indochina, and sometimes under less violent conditions, as with the British in Nigeria. Some parts of empire remained, but they were not free of the questioning and resistance of native peoples. The incident in Wallis-et-Futuna was a tiny manifestation of this.

It is at times when governmental authority is questioned that its true nature is laid bare. Regarding the events in Wallis-et-Futuna, a statement by a French official is revealing. He proclaimed that, as always, the authority of the state and of local custom would be preserved. What is revealed by this statement is the existence of two domains of authority, the boundary between which had come into dispute. Discussions with local leaders had been under way to resolve the problem. Ultimately, though, the authority of the French state, backed up by force, was to prevail. To answer the question posed in the heading for this section, the French state, with its apparatus of laws and its capability of using force if necessary, was ultimately in charge here. However, this tells only a part of the story of how society is governed.

THE ANATOMY OF GOVERNANCE

Those British philosophers who, in the seventeenth century, believed that people once sought to move out of a state of nature by banding together into groups also had ideas about how those groups should be governed. For Thomas Hobbes, the groups would be subject to the control of a king who could not be deposed, while John Locke favored a government that could be changed by the will of the people. These philosophers were thinking in terms of Western political systems, which represent only some of the various ways in which human beings may govern their societies. Anthropologists, on the other hand, are concerned with all of the systems of governance humans have ever created.

Governance requires not only governors, that is, people who have more or less power to shape the actions of a society, but also people who are governable. Human beings usually respond to the threat or use of force. The French were counting on this in Wallis-et-Futuna. But a society in which everything is handled by force would be like a prison; it would not resemble the usual society of human beings. So much effort and so many resources would be used in controlling people and the settings in which they act that other necessary areas of life would have to be neglected. No established human society has used force or the threat of force as the only means of social control. People have a variety of interests other than the avoidance of pain and death that can be manipulated by those in power. Do I, an American, want to be a success? Why not, then, follow the example of someone who has succeeded and who attributes personal achievement to following the rules?

Am I, a poor Burmese Buddhist, impatient with my condition in life? Why not do the socially acceptable things, such as giving the last of my weekly earnings to help build a pagoda, that are supposed to guarantee a better existence in the next life? The reasons for following social prescriptions or norms are at least as various as are human motivations.

In humans there are anarchic or revolutionary tendencies that put people in opposition to any social arrangement, but they also have an evolutionarily based desire to associate with, care for, and get along with others. If properly socialized, they will have an active disposition to adhere to the cultural norms of some society and follow its notions of right and wrong. This disposition, whatever its specific motivational underpinning, constitutes the basis of morality. As A. Irving Hallowell, whose work has been referred to earlier, points out, human societies are moral orders composed of individuals who are capable of assessing themselves in terms of some social standard and feeling good or bad about their assessments. They are not made up simply of mutually adjusting individuals, as is, say, an ant society, but of self-reflective persons who evaluate themselves and their actions. The trick, then, in governing a society is to socialize its members so that they evaluate themselves more or less in terms of the same or compatible standards of right and wrong. Each individual's moral sense is thus collectivized, and a basis for social control is established.

People want to feel good about themselves, and every society provides its members with rewards for adopting an appropriate social posture and sense of self. Rewards may range from a simple lack of abuse, through the positive regard of others, to more tangible things of value. Sometimes, it may not take a lot to get a person to go along. In Laurence Wylie's book, *Village in the Vaucluse* (France), a boy says that he does what is expected of him so that *les autres* (the others) will let him alone. This suggests that his attitude of self-regard and actions are already linked to the opinion of others, albeit in a somewhat negative way.

Most people in a stable society try to do the right thing—at least a part of the time. In so doing, they feel good about themselves. But there is also a negative side of self-regard that motivates people. When it is activated by behavior—or the thought of behavior—that violates some norm, a person may feel shame or guilt, which can be painful in the extreme. One way of avoiding these painful feelings is to change one's thinking and behavior in a more socially acceptable direction. Does one lust after one's mother? Think of her, rather, as pure and self-sacrificing. Does one hate one's neighbor? Better to think that we are put upon this earth to love one another. Does a carousing college student wake up one morning with a terrible hangover, or worse? Maybe it would be better to hit the books in the library. All people do wrong at times by their own and their society's standards, but most of them have the capacity to alleviate the painful feelings that result by acting in a socially appropriate way. All societies make use of people's capacity to feel guilt and shame, as well as the fears from which those feelings are derived, in order to control them.

The concepts of guilt and shame have been developed to refer to negative feelings people have after assessing themselves in terms of others' expectations. For example, I may feel worthless today because I failed a test in engineering, a subject my father thinks is important. Or I may feel a vague disquiet on the day following a particularly luxurious sexual dream in the night. The concepts of guilt and shame differ in one significant way: They involve differing degrees of internalization of others' expectations. Guilt-ruled people are capable of experiencing negative feelings about themselves in a vacuum. Thus, I have thoughts of forbidden pleasure and immediately feel a twinge of conscience. That is the internalized "other" part of me that can be seen as doing the twinging. Shame-ridden people, on the other hand, need others to be present to confirm their failings to them. Without others' presence, the feeling of shame will not be activated. Guilt and shame have been defined here as pure types of internalized social control. The majority of people probably are capable of entertaining both feelings in different degrees. Some anthropologists have suggested that people in a particular society tend toward the shame type of personality while people in another lean toward guilt. Thus, Ruth Benedict in *The Chrysanthemum and the Sword*, a study of Japanese national character written during World War II, argued that though they were capable of experiencing guilt, the Japanese tended to be a shame-oriented people and that shame was essential for the functioning of their society. Recent, more careful investigations, such as those of Takie Lebra reported in Chapter 3, have shown that both shame and guilt play a significant role in internalized control.

Sometimes it may be difficult to know whether shame or guilt is at work in the controlling process, but there are occasions when it is quite obvious. For example, Laurence Wylie was conversing with a teacher in the little village of Roussillon in southern France about a teaching problem. As an example, the teacher pointed to one of the children and, in her presence, began to list her faults. Other children, who hadn't measured up in some way, were forced by the teacher to carry little signs indicating the nature of their failings. In both cases, the aim obviously was to use shame to get the children to mend their ways. As for guilt, the legendary Jewish mother is supposed to be able to turn it on in her offspring with hardly any effort. And typical Japanese do not need to be reminded of their failings in filial obligations. Their latent guilt feelings are readily activated at any time.

People's moral sense depends on a sensitivity to others' views. In every society, there are some individuals (the psychopaths) who have very little, if any, of this type of sensitivity. They make social control difficult. There are others who may have a moral sense that is shared by members of some subgroup but that is incompatible with others' notions of right and wrong. Thus, terrorists may be acting on the basis of a morality that is not shared with the people they attack. Because of this, no amount of exhortation, shaming, or guilt-selling by these people will make them relent. The others, to whom they respond in moral terms, speak with a different voice. This recalls a conversation I had with an informant in Spain. We were talking about the custom of bribing local officials, and I raised the question of whether it was moral for an American expatriate to do this. He said, "What is moral? I'll tell you what it is. It's what everybody expects you to do." He meant, of course, what the locals expected you to do. For the Americans, however, the matter was not so simple—there being at least two reference groups with which they could identify. But whatever one's identification in this cross-cultural situation, it was a means of submitting to social control.

In some societies, the moral sense of people and the mechanisms that activate it may be able to handle a good deal of the task of social control. In a particular Society of Friends (Quakers), for example, periods of talk and meditation may be enough to arrive at some kind of moral consensus. There is a coming together about what is the right thing to do under the circumstances. But, as we who live in the contemporary world know all too well, a moral consensus is not so easy to arrive at. Contending factions may arise around particular issues, and there will be a good deal of pulling and hauling before a consensus is reached. Sometimes it never is reached, as was the case in one Quaker group with which I was associated. The best that can be hoped for at times is a kind of superficial getting along without deep moral backing. Whatever the basis, decisions about collective action have to be reached if a society is to survive. The processes of developing and carrying out a collective will for such action are essential aspects of governance in which governors and governed play their parts.

Who are these people? Certainly, one cannot accept without question some chart of political organization that includes kings and queens, presidents, prime ministers, ultimate leaders, functionaries, and the like on face value to identify the governors. There are too many examples where formal (*de jure*) political organization is contradicted by real (*de facto*) arrangements, as when a big company actually dictates governing policy. Certainly, one cannot assume that power is concentrated in the hands of one person (a queen, perhaps) or in a small group of people constituting an oligarchy. There are too many reports by anthropologists of societies in which leadership is spread around. Thus, among the Mbuti Pygmies, a group of hunters and gatherers of the central African forest, there is no single, permanent leader. One person may take the initiative one day and another the next. The truth is that sometimes it may be difficult to distinguish governors and governed. Even in the most autocratic of societies the governed possess some power to acquiesce or not. This may help us to remember that (to paraphrase an American comic book character, Pogo) governance is a matter of us all, that is, all those who are involved in working out a certain sociopolitical arrangement. That "working out" involves a continuous interaction among a variety of individuals and factions, all of whom have an interest in the nature and direction of the arrangement.

GOVERNING ARRANGEMENTS

The San

Among the aboriginal San, hunters and gatherers of southern Africa, a variety of social mechanisms exist to prevent power or importance from falling into the hands of one or a few individuals. Some people do stand out from others in socially valued ways, but they rarely have the opportunity to cash in on these attributes. Thus, in *The !Kung San*, Richard Lee reports that a successful hunter will hear a number of belittling remarks about a prize animal he has killed. Lee himself received many disparaging remarks about the ox he had provided for a feast. By these and other leveling tactics, the San act to prevent any significant monopolies of power or importance from developing. Many people, therefore, participate in the the process of governance.

Since the San are not saints and since no one among them has much power over others, it might be thought that their bands (numbering, on the average, around twenty) would constantly be teetering on the brink of anarchy. These people do pursue individual interests at the expense of others. There are some serious disputes. Lee thinks that they do have a high homicide rate. But there are social mechanisms that prevent these small communities from falling apart. Sometimes, one of the parties in a dispute will leave and join another band. Other times, public discussion and opinion work to resolve differences. But above all, it is the collective orientation of these people, which develops early in the socialization process, that holds the bands together.

The Tiv

The horticultural Tiv, who are mentioned from time to time in this book, reveal greater differences in social status than the San. They are organized into opposing lineages and lineage segments, which, when conceived spatially and administratively, are called *tar*. A minimal *tar* consists of a number of adjacent compounds and farms and may number from a hundred to a thousand people. Members of nearby *tar* are usually more closely related genealogically (in this case, patrilineally) than those who are farther away. People who live nearby will ally themselves more readily on issues affecting their members. How broad or narrow an alliance is depends on the issue involved. Thus, several adjacent *tar*, which may be opposed on a number of other issues and even fight from time to time, will band together to seek retribution if a member of one of them has been killed by someone from a distant *tar*.

As reported by Laura and Paul Bohannan in the 1950s (in *The Tiv of Central Nigeria*), the Tiv have leaders, but no political offices such as a chief or prime minister. These leaders, whose base of operations is a *tar*, can have considerable influence and may take initiatives in a variety of circumstances, but they cannot give orders. They act as arbitrators in disputes and represent their kin groups in dealing with others. Those with great influence have to be skilled in discussion because public opinion plays such a large role in this society. They have to be wise in the ways of the people around them. They are likely to be older, wealthier, and more lavish in their hospitality. But most important of all, as far as the Tiv are concerned, they are possessors of valuable drums and titles, and they are thought to have coveted magical powers *(swem)* that are associated with their *tar*.

Individual Tiv share in the prestige of their leaders, and they seek their help for protection from others, but such is the egalitarian streak in these people, that those who rise too far above their fellows have to watch their step. People of higher social rank are envied, feared, and hated, and they must be constantly on guard against those who would bring them down (by witchcraft, for example). In such a situation, it is difficult for any individual or group to gain great power or prestige. It is not surprising, therefore, that the British were frustrated when they assumed administrative control over the Tiv at the beginning of the twentieth century. There was simply no centralized political institution to latch on to.

Fiji

The British had less difficulty establishing a colonial regime in the Fiji islands in the southwestern Pacific, where a system of hereditary chieftainships was in place. In "The Role of a Fijian Chief," Clellan Ford describes how this system works. Power is so concentrated in the chief that no decision of importance in his district could be taken without his approval. He is responsible for all visitors (including anthropologists), for directing collective activities such as fishing, gardening, and house building, and he supervises ceremonies such as funerals. Disputes between people are brought before him and resolved. If there is a special community project that needs to be done, he can command the labor to do it. Finally, he collects and redistributes a significant amount of the community's surplus production.

A Fijian chief is expected to be even-handed and generous. He should be tactful and carry himself with dignity. Although he assumes no special privileges at feasts, there is no question that the chief is in charge. An informant tells the anthropologist that, without the chief, all would be lost. Clearly, in Fijian society, power is centralized and differences in social rank are well established. Early Western visitors found similar systems of governance in many of the Pacific islands.

Buganda

A Fijian chief has the kind of power and social importance that no San would dream of acquiring. But his high status pales by comparison with that of the Bugandan king (*Kabaka*) described by the British anthropologist, Audrey Richards, in "Authority Patterns in Traditional Buganda." In the early nineteenth century, Buganda (located in a part of what is now the nation of Uganda) was an east African society at the height of its power. Blessed with abundant natural resources, its people subsisted on a combination of horticulture (plantain, bananas), fishing, hunting, and animal tending (sheep, goats, cattle, poultry and buffalo), and trade. This society was ruled through an elaborate system of public offices arranged in several kinship, territorially based status hierarchies. At the apex of these was the *Kabaka,* whose power was enormous. Holders of public offices were dependent on him and struggled for his favor. An effective *Kabaka* would use these struggles as one means of maintaining social equilibrium.

Bugandan society was stratified into two main classes: lords or chiefs and commoners. Some commoners could rise to high status, as in the case of the prime minister or a special aide to the king, but all were subordinates owing immediate allegiance to a lord. Those living on a particular lord's estate provided him with labor, produce, military service, and (should their lord desire them) women to serve as his wife or concubine. Always, the commoners were supposed to demonstrate publicly their respect for him. They are said to have crept about in his vicinity, to do immediately whatever was asked of them, to flatter him, and to accept his decisions in arbitration without question. The same pattern of dominance and submission pervaded the entire society. Richards points out, for example, that it prevailed in Bugandan households where the father was a kind of king.

At the top of this society, the *Kabaka* commanded more deference than any of his subordinates. Great lords fell flat before him and rushed to do his bidding. They were expected to show their loyalty by being present at court for a part of every year. A lord who was absent might fall into disfavor and even be punished—something to be avoided in a society where the king could kill at will. He had complete rights over his subjects and could mobilize them for grand projects, some of which might do little more than feed his ego. Whatever reservations people had about all of this, they seem to have taken pride in the splendor of their king's court, his accomplishments in war, and his ability to keep the peace. Richards points out that they combined attitudes of terrified submission with great tenderness toward him.

The different systems of governance summarized here will seem more or less familiar to the reader. For example, one may find the Buganda system with its *Kabaka* not unlike despotisms one reads about in the paper. Most

Americans, however, will feel a distinct lack of sympathy for such a form of governance. It is a far cry from the ideal of participatory democracy. Much has been written in favor of different kinds of governing systems, and proponents have gone so far as to claim that a particular form is more "natural" than another. Thus, the founding fathers of the United States claimed that all men were created equal and argued for a system of political control that would complement this aspect of human nature. Their views were codified in the essential laws of the land that make up the Constitution of the United States.

Any survey of the political systems of humankind makes it difficult to claim that any one is more in tune with human nature than any other. Those who argue that there is a natural system of social control modeled after something in the mind of God, in a flock of chickens, in a contemporary group of hunters and gatherers, or whatever, as supporters of particular forms of government have done, must face the fact that many systems of governance have existed and that humans have expressed satisfaction with quite different political arrangements. In this regard, it is interesting to turn to Geert Hofstede's *Culture's Consequences*, which reports on the job-related attitudes of employees in a large multinational firm. One attitude he refers to is the "power distance" between employees and their boss. Respondents were given a range of choices that varied from an extremely democratic relationship, in which employees had great input, to an extremely authoritarian system, in which they had no influence. A wide variety of preferences were revealed, with responses varying significantly by country (that is, by culture). Employees from Denmark, for example, were among the more democratic respondents, while those from the Philippines were among the more authoritarian.

TRENDS AND CONNECTIONS

The examples given in the preceding section cover much of the gamut of human systems of governance. The range could be filled out and extended to include complex industrial societies, but the four societies we have examined would seem to provide a basis for a preliminary analysis of human political arrangements. A number of aspects of such arrangements have been of interest to anthropologists. For example, they have been concerned with techniques used to secure compliance with collective rules—techniques that can range from the use of brute force to gentle persuasion. Force is resorted to in all four of the societies just discussed. The San, for example, kill one another from time to time, and Tiv *tars* may fight. But in established societies force is never the predominant method for gaining compliance. A variety of human dispositions besides fear and anger may be tapped to get people to comply with the rules of a society.

Anthropologists have also been interested in the ways in which people organize themselves politically, that is, in the kinds of social organization people create to govern. One might speak here about the delegation of power or the allocation of the various tasks of governance, as in the various branches of U.S. government and their subdivisions; but more basic issues concern the distinction between governors and governed and the nature of the relationship between them. In some societies like the San, such a distinction hardly exists. People play both roles from time to time, depending on the situation. In Fijian society, however, the chief is clearly a governor, while very few others have anything to do with governing. Governors exist because they have taken or been granted the power necessary to create, maintain, and enforce collective activities. They may depend a lot on input from below, in which case there is (to use Hofstede's term) low power distance between governors and governed; or they may range to the extremely autocratic who tend to ignore input from the governed, in which case there is high power distance between the two.

In the four cases just summarized, there are general trends (from first to last) towards an increasing separation or distinction between governors and governed and an increasing power distance between them. In terms of the social contract metaphor, one might say that there is a greater tendency for peoples to "contract out" to one or more of their number the task of running their societies and give them the power to do so. Anthropologists, who are always looking for the ways in which different aspects of a culture are tied together, have noted that a number of other characteristics of culture are associated with this trend. First, the size of the group being governed (whether measured in terms of territory or numbers of people) tends to increase. The typical San band, where governors and governed are hardly distinguishable, is a small, strictly local unit, while the Buganda kingdom, with its autocratic *Kabaka*, is large and embraces a number of communities. There is, therefore, a tendency toward higher, more inclusive levels of social integration. Second, there is a general increase in the level of technology. The Bugandans have a more complex technology than the San or the Tiv. Third, from first to last, the societies become more productive. Hunters and gatherers like the San tend to produce less than the horticultural Tiv. Fourth, the capacity to mobilize resources, human and otherwise, increases. More power in the systems is potentially available to the governors. The scale of public activities, such as warfare or buildings, tends to increase as a result. Fifth, there is an increasing social differentiation or specialization (as between governors and governed, and between governors themselves), which is to say that societies tend to become more complex. Finally, the societies become more hierarchical, in that there are increasingly marked differences in social status. This trend is associated also with the emergence of status groupings or categories—classes or castes—and thus an increasing stratification of society. Differences in social status have been measured in terms of three criteria: power, prestige, and control of economic resources. The Buganda *Kabaka* and his lords constitute a ruling class or aristocracy that dominates a great mass of commoners. This hierarchical system seems to have been generally accepted; it had become a fact of life. Among the Tiv, on the other hand, where status differences are not as pronounced, there is an ambivalence about them. The leveling tactics that are used against people who seem to have risen too far are a manifestation of this.

The trends just described are general tendencies only. There are societies where nonpolitical aspects of a culture are out of synch, so to speak, with the political. For example, the different components of social status may be out of alignment. In Yankee City (a pseudonymn), an old New England town by the sea, the people with the highest prestige (termed upper-upper class by investigators) were usually not the wealthiest nor the most powerful. The anthropological literature contains many other examples of societies in which differences in prestige are not entirely consistent with differences in wealth or power. Thus, among the Yanomamö, a fierce group of South American horticulturalists, each village headman tends to be wealthier and have greater prestige than his fellows; but because he is expected to be more generous, he may end up temporarily impoverished. Besides this, he has very little power to get people to do what he wants. He can set an example or harangue them, but if they do not want to go along on a particular project, there is little he can do about it. If one takes a broad view, however, there does appear to be some tendency in the societies of humankind for the different aspects of social status to line up with each other.

If contemporary societies can be taken as rough models for ancient modes of existence, the general sociopolitical trends just laid out would seem to describe in a general way what happened in the course of human history. Thus, the San system represents a very early form of human governance, the Tiv system a somewhat later form, and so on up to the relatively complex political arrangement in which power is concentrated in the hands of a comparative few, as in the Bugandan kingdom. Using a well-known typology that identifies discrete stages of this trend, it may be said that in human history the earliest type of sociopolitical arrangement was the band, a small, fairly egalitarian group of hunters and gatherers; the next, the tribe; then the chieftainship; and finally, the state, which is the largest, most complex, and most powerful sociopolitical form of all. So pervasive is the state form of political organization in the contemporary world that it would seem wise for anyone considering aspects of governance anywhere—even in the simplest of societies—to begin with the expectation that the hand of some state will sooner or later be revealed in the actions being investigated.

CONNECTIONS

Why did the state form of political organization come into being? Why did some humans give up their smaller-scale, more egalitarian modes of existence for larger, more hierarchical social arrangements in which power was increasingly concentrated in the hands of political specialists? Such questions have preoccupied anthropologists and others over the years, and a number of explanations have been offered. One famous hypothesis accounts for the origin of the state, the most centralized governmental system of all, in the social coordination needed to carry out early irrigation projects. This hypothesis, while applicable to some cases, needs considerable revision to make it cross-culturally viable. Irrigation projects are one type of large, complex public task that cannot be handled by a small-scale, strictly local system of governance such as exists among the San. If such large-scale tasks are to be accomplished (resolving class conflict, dealing with population pressures, and waging war have also been suggested), more centralized, leadership, perhaps associated with a codified system of laws, must emerge. The trend toward a more powerful, centralized public authority and codified laws may be explained in terms of the need to accomplish larger or more complex public tasks. People may or may not have responded to this need by developing a more centralized system of governance, of course, but some did and tended to prevail.

The nature of the complex tasks handled by more powerful, centralized governments varies enormously. For example, consider societies with large populations. Their larger scale would render the type of governance practiced by the San, or by members of a New England town meeting, obsolete. Further, consider that a society has to deal with powerful outside forces. Some of its people may begin to engage in large-scale trading. Or there may be powerful enemies that have to be dealt with. In such a situation, a people may choose or accept strong leaders who have the power to supervise and coordinate these activities. And what about health care? Can a nation such as the United States take adequate care of *all* of its people without great involvement by the federal government? In all such cases, there has to be some trade-off between the social requirements of a larger, more complex mode of existence and the interests of individuals that were shaped by smaller and simpler regimes. If grand social tasks are to be accomplished, peoples must, willingly or unwillingly, hand over power to governors or administrators. Their adaptive fate may hinge on whether they do so or not.

Who are these leaders to be? They are those who come to monopolize the things that give one social power. A list of these qualities would be endless. They can range from a certain facial expression to the use of a weapon, but in each instance, someone possesses something that gives them the power to make decisions for others. The search for key factors that underlie a people's rise to power continues. An important factor, surely, is the ability to control the production and distribution of resources. In an agricultural society, people with more land tend to become more powerful. A horticultural chief who acts as the focal point for the distribution of goods will acquire some power as a result, or a key middleman in a trading network between societies will gain prestige and power.

As with other adaptive social arrangements, new systems of governance, once started, engage new motivations and achieve a momentum of their own. People then begin to acquire a stake in the new system. It is important to keep in mind, though, that not everyone has the same stake in a particular social arrangement. The tendency for individuals' behavior in a group to vary around cultural norms is an indication of this. There is something of the revolutionary or anarchist in all of us, but those who have risen to higher status are usually the least interested in bringing their social system down. The elite of a state have great power, prestige, and wealth, which is to say they have the best their society has to offer. Even the Yanomamo headman who gives away a good deal of his wealth and who has very little power still has greater prestige than his fellows. Governors may complain about the heavy burdens of governing, but it is instructive to see where they will stand in relation to their fellows in regard to proposed changes in the status quo, such as the imposition of term limits on political offices.

CASE STUDY

Fredrik Barth on the Basseri
of the Khamseh Confederacy

In order to bring the whole discussion of governance down to earth, consider the Basseri, a group of nomadic, pastoral Muslims in southern Iran. In *Nomads of South Persia,* Fredrik Barth, a Norwegian anthropologist who, after training in Norway, the United States, and England, has made important contributions in both basic and applied anthropology, describes and analyzes the culture of this group of approximately sixteen thousand people. That aspect of his report that focuses on the Basseri's system of governance will be considered here. The time frame is the late 1950s and represents one instance of his (then-) broader interest in the peoples of Iraq, Pakistan, and Iran (later expanded to include the Sudan, Indonesia, New Guinea, and China).

Barth tells us that the tent-dwelling Basseri migrate up and down a strip of land approximately three hundred miles long and twenty to fifty miles wide in the Fars province of southern Iran. They subsist largely by herding sheep and goats that eat their way along a "tribal road" *(il-rah)* through a series of seasonally maturing pastures. The road passes over mountains, through valleys, and across rivers. Sometimes, the Basseri camp in desolate regions, other times close to towns and villages. From Barth's account, one learns that the schedule and route of migration are set in a general way by the Basseri chief *(khan)*. Migration tends to take on a traditional pattern, but from time to time the chief will institute changes.

During the course of their annual migration, the Basseri encounter various Arab and Quashqai nomads whose routes of migration cross or run parallel to theirs. They also meet sedentary agricultural villagers and people from towns, the largest of which is Shiraz. Sometimes they encounter other Basseri who have drifted away into a sedentary life or who have formed other nomadic groups. Thus, they have considerable contact with other people, both sedentary and nomadic. In addition, they deal occasionally with representatives of the Iranian government.

The minimal Basseri social unit is the tent *(khune)* in which there usually dwells a nuclear family (a few of the wealthier families are polygynous). These households cluster together into camps that vary in size (depending on the season of the year) from a few to forty or more tents. Each household owns movable property consisting of household items, riding and carrying animals (horses, donkeys, camels), and most important, a flock of sheep and/or goats that typically numbers about a hundred. This flock is the principal economic resource of the household, providing meat, hides, wool, clarified butter, and milk for use by the family and for sale outside. According to Barth, the typical Basseri household with its flock is on the move from one place to another for about 120 days of the year.

The people who make camp together have various kinship ties with each other and migrate together as a unit. They tend to settle disputes and correct social deviation through public opinion. Each camp has a headman who may or may not have been appointed by the *khan*. Whether appointed or not, a headman does not acquire any power from the *khan*. If, for example, a dispute cannot be resolved through public opinion in a camp, it usually is not taken to the headman, but to the chief who deals with the matter directly. Headmen do tend to be wealthier and have greater prestige than their fellows, but they have little power to direct or coerce the people in their camp. Barth offers an intriguing analysis of the headman's role in working through what may be the most important thing a camp must do to maintain itself, that is, decide unanimously whether to migrate or not, by what specific route, and where to set up camp again.

As mentioned before, the *general* route and schedule of migration are set by the chief. His word is passed down through the heads of patrilineal descent groupings called *oulads*. Each *oulad*, which is comprised of a number of camps, is assigned certain pasture lands and a general migratory route and schedule. Within this framework that is set and passed down by the chief, each camp works out its own decisions about moving. The headman promotes his ideas through his kin, who then communicate them throughout the camp. It is clear from Barth's account that the headman has his own opinions, but he has to be careful about asserting them. He cannot give orders nor step in to close out the meandering discussion, which Barth found exasperating because he wanted to prepare himself to move or not. But even the headman, himself, may not actually know whose ideas have won the day until he looks out of his tent in the morning and notes the direction and nature of movement of the early risers.

In contrast to camp headmen, who are little more than discussion leaders, and *oulad* headmen, who are little more than channels of communication, the Basseri *khan* or chief has a virtual monopoly on the right to command. His high status allows him enormous power as well as great prestige and wealth. He is expected to be endlessly hospitable and publicly generous. He should carry himself in a large and imperial manner. Much of his wealth is inherited, but he also has the power to impose taxes on his subjects from time to time. He and his immediate relatives constitute a real ruling class that mingles with the elite of towns and villages.

According to Barth, the Basseri chief exercises his authority in three main areas: tribal migration, dealings with outside authorities, and the resolution of disputes. The manner in which he settles disputes between subjects is an indication of the enormous power he wields. There is little formality on such occasions, but intimations of the *khan's* power are everywhere evident. For example, he may take up a dispute while engaged in other matters, such as eating a meal or chatting with visitors. His decision, which might take the form of a comment on the side, may or may not follow precedent and custom. However it may be rendered, the *khan's* decision, according to Barth, must be obeyed. There are very few areas in which the chief is unwilling to act. One of them involves disputes over inheritance, which are often handed over to judges in towns along the Basseri *il-rah*.

Barth takes pains to emphasize the enormous power of the Basseri *khan* over his subjects. One is a little uneasy, however, about accepting all of this anthropologist's assertions on face value. He provides very little concrete evidence. Particular examples of follow-through on the *khan's* decisions are missing, as are examples suggesting how much a creature he is of outside political forces. The overall picture Fredrik Barth presents, though, suggests that this system of governance tends toward the extreme type of centralized authority discussed earlier in this chapter.

A particularly intriguing part of Barth's analysis involves an attempt to explain why the Basseri system of governance is the way it is. In developing his explanation, he makes comparisons with other nomadic tribes in the same area who live in somewhat different natural circumstances. For example, tribes to the east inhabit a bleaker environment than the Basseri. As a result, the density of their populations is lower and the movement of camps more erratic. There is no regularized migration such as exists among the Basseri. Since large-scale coordination cannot work under these circumstances, no centralized authority has emerged. The Basseri, in contrast, have a need for such coordination and, according to Barth, there is an incentive for the appearance of a strong, autocratic leader. To the west of the Basseri is the Quashqai tribe, which inhabits an even richer environment. Barth points out that because it is possible for an individual and his family to flourish under these conditions, the wealthier among the Quashqai are not so tempted as their Basseri counterparts to drift away into an attractive sedentary life. As a result, they remain as power centers in the Quashqai political system. This leads to a much more complex hierarchical arrangement than among the Basseri, who have a single ruling class with greater power and a comparatively weaker mass of subordinates who provide hardly any challenge to the chief and his relatives. Among the Quashqai, on the other hand, there are always potential challengers, and force must be resorted to more frequently by the chief.

Barth also uses certain aspects of the social setting of Basseri culture to account for the emergence of their strong, centralized system of authority. There are sometimes powerful outsiders who must be dealt with along their migratory path. Suppose that an individual Basseri has problems with a farmer over damage done by his flock. The next day, that individual and his family may be on their way and incapable of handling the dispute effectively. But a powerful chief who has a house in Shiraz and who moves intimately among the sedentary elite can act for them in this matter. Such an authority is also able to supervise the development of long-term trading relationships. Barth sees large-scale trading with a variety of peoples as one reason for the rise of the *khan* and the Khamseh confederacy, in which the Basseri and other tribes once came together in a loose coalition dominated by a single kinship group.

In dealing with a society where wealth appears to be an essential element of leadership, Fredrik Barth gives remarkably little play to economic factors in the Basseri system of governance; he also tells us relatively little about the larger political order, centralized in Teheran, which undoubtedly shapes Basseri political life. Nevertheless, his analysis does illustrate the importance of paying attention to the natural and social setting of a culture. These people pass through a region that has pastures rich enough to sustain a considerable pastoral population. Some centralized leadership is necessary to coordinate such a group. The region also contains a variety of other peoples, some of them rather powerful. A centralized leadership is necessary to carry on relations with them. The creation and acceptance of a strong, centralized system of governance in the person of the *khan* and his family is seen by Barth to be the Basseri's adaptive response to such necessities.

There are no guarantees that this or any other social arrangement devised by human beings will survive, however. Drought could dry up the pastures on which the system depends. Trade routes could change and other economic factors could intervene. Neighboring, imperialistic chiefs could gain the allegiance of some of the Basseri. And the powerful Iranian government could change its ways of handling these people. Indeed, Barth reports that at one point the Iranian army, which had been charged with dealing with the Basseri, instituted a new policy of administration through local headmen. Needless to say, such a policy would threaten the existence of the *khan* and the autocratic, centralized system of government he represents.

This brief summary does not do full justice to Fredrik Barth's sophisticated ethnographic report on the Basseri. Readers who are interested in the whole way of life of this interesting group of pastoral nomads will want to read his book and perhaps other works on nomadic peoples, including those on the Qalander of Pakistan who were mentioned in Chapter Four. However, enough information has been given here to lay out the essentials of the Basseri system of governance and make an attempt to explain it. The explanation offered by Barth, which makes use of other aspects of their culture, as well as its setting, illustrates the hypothesis that more centralized, powerful systems of governance are associated with the accomplishment of larger and more complex public tasks. Evidence to support this explanation has been derived from comparisons between the Basseri society and other nomadic societies in the same region. There is also a good deal of information addressing the problem of the steadily increasing settling down of nomadic peoples in the Middle East and elsewhere. In Saudi Arabia, for example, approximately 40 percent of the population was nomadic in the 1950s as compared with less than 5 percent today. Barth's study does much to illuminate this historic trend.

WHAT ABOUT US?
GOVERNANCE IN INDUSTRIAL SOCIETIES

So far, little comment has been made about the forms of governance in those societies that loom large in the world today—that is, in industrial societies where the nation-state reigns supreme. This is partly due to the fact that there is not a great deal of information about these systems of political organization in the anthropological literature. Until recently, anthropologists have shown little concern for them. There are a number of reasons this neglect is unfortunate, one of which is that these governments are often linked to the fate of the peoples that anthropologists have been accustomed to study. What happens in the U.S. Congress, for example, can have consequences for the Mashantucket Pequots of Connecticut, whose casino-based interests are ultimately under the control of the U.S. Senate. But the lack of anthropological work in this area is no reason not to pursue this important issue. Studies by sociologists, political scientists, and other social scientists can be put to good anthropological use.

In the town where I live, for example, an elected First Selectman used to handle most of the governing operations. Now, there is a town manager, a mayor, a town council, and an array of specialists who take care of these operations. This more complex way of doing things is the way things are accomplished in industrial societies Their systems of governance may not be more concentrated than some of those that have existed under preindustrial conditions, but clearly, forms of governance such as exist among the San or Tiv will not do for them. Nor will a centralized form such as that in Fiji suffice, where a chief has responsibility for nearly everything. The work of governance is too much for one or a few persons to deal with. So specialists who handle the complex tasks of monitoring the situation, securing compliance, and carrying out public decisions appear and proliferate. Bureaucratic forms of administration take over more and more areas of social life. In China today, citizens have to contend everywhere with representatives of the state bureaucracy. In the United States, both public and private sectors are bureaucratically organized. True, bureaucracies have existed in nonindustrial societies (ancient Rome and China are only two examples), but it is doubtful that they ever attained the significance they hold in modern industrial society.

In *The Power Elite*, sociologist C. Wright Mills develops an image of the American system of governance that can be loosely applied to industrial nations generally. This image consists of a series of pyramid-like bureaucracies, the top people in each of which share common interests. In the United States, Mills says, the interests of government leaders, big business, and the military mesh with one another. This view of concentrated power in the hands of a comparatively small group of elite may sound familiar to readers who have demonstrated against the "military-industrial complex" of the United States or to Chinese entrepreneurs who are frustrated by omnipresent state-run bureaucracies. Though the degree of concentration of power obviously varies from one industrial society to another, as does the amount of control leaders have over bureaucrats and others, the essentials of Mills' image would seem to be generally applicable to all. The bureaucratic organizations in these countries, and the people who manage to control them, can shape the world in profound ways. The president of General Motors, a large industrial conglomerate, is able, by signing his name, to end employment for thousands of people in any of GM's plants around the world; and the president of the United States, by picking up a telephone and speaking in a certain way, has the power to start a nuclear war that could end all of our lives.

It is important, however, to distinguish potential power from actual power. Industrial chiefs, unlike the Basseri *khan* whose every decision is supposed to be obeyed, must contend with people who have conflicting agendas and with bureaucracies that acquire a momentum of their own. Under certain circumstances, these chiefs can be reduced to something like a Yanomamö headman who, even if he has a clear idea of what he wants to do, does not know whether people will follow him or not. Industrial chiefs, like all leaders, have problems with convincing those they govern of the legitimacy of their rule.

In all societies, the exercise of power or authority is legitimated in one way or another. Whatever the basis of the "contract" between governors and governed, there are reasons or justifications for governors' exercise of authority. These legitimations may be seen to reflect the morality of a people and their system of written or unwritten law. But what happens when a people become skeptical of any values used to justify the exercise of power? This is often the case in industrialized societies, where the point of view of one sector of society can be contradicted by so many others. It is this increasing rate of disagreement that undermines the legitimations of industrial rulers. Kings who have claimed that they rule by divine right may find that others, who do not share their view of the supernatural and its relation to the natural order of human affairs, disagree with this justification. On a smaller scale, the domination of a Chinese mother-in-law over her son's wife, once justified in agreed-upon moral terms, begins to give way in the face of new views derived from female employment outside of the home. The older generation in a French village finds that the young do not so readily accept the notion that the elders "know best." This decline in the plausibility of the legitimations of those in power is associated with a decline in the power distance between them and subordinates who now feel entitled to a greater say in the governing process. It is not a return to the near-egalitarian conditions of a small-scale society like the aboriginal San of not too long ago, which would be impossible in an industrial society given the greater scale and complexity of public tasks. But it is obviously at some remove from the autocratic systems of governance in Buganda and among the Basseri, discussed earlier.

Many authors have pointed out this egalitarian trend. In *Democracy in America*, Alexis de Tocqueville, a French observer of the early American republic, suggests that this young nation was at the forefront of a growing egalitarianism among societies of the Western world. Significant status differences are evident in the United States, but they are not accepted as inevitable or right, as they are in truly hierarchical societies. Writing in *Homo Hierarchicus*, Louis Dumont, a French anthropologist, notes that (more industrialized) Westerners, who have become accustomed to relationships of greater equality, have trouble understanding a hierarchical society such as India where, even today, vestiges of a hereditarily based caste system remain.

The implications of this are important for overseas Americans, who must deal with host nationals of less industrialized countries where people in authority pay less attention to the views of subordinates. In such countries, American expatriate homemakers often try to cultivate a relationship with maids they could not afford at home. Doing business in these countries, American managers have sought input from host subordinates. That these Americans often fail in these endeavors is to be expected in societies where those in authority are expected to assert themselves, not consult.

Concrete evidence for the equality-inducing effects of industrialism is provided in the cross-cultural study by Geert Hofstede, which was mentioned earlier. Hofstede, it will be recalled, asked employees of a large multinational corporation how much they expected to be consulted by their bosses. He found that, generally, the higher the level of industrialization of their countries the more employees expected to be consulted, which is to say that the power distance between bosses and subordinates tends to decline with industrialization. Though this study touches on the socialist world only light-ly, the evidence suggests that though the basis of power may differ, the trend is evident there as well.

In order to survive, therefore, industrial nation-states must develop complex, centralized systems of governance, but their leaders, like governors everywhere, have to contend with various limitations on their power. Among these are the difficulties of legitimating any governing arrangement among an often distant and various people. Intra-societal differences that raise questions about the legitimacy of their rule may be leftovers from a preindustrial condition, as in the competing nationalisms in the Balkans, or generated by the increasing differentiation and extension of industrial society itself. Also, leaders of industrial states must contend with a greater desire of the governed to have some say in the governing process as well as the well-known intractability of proliferating bureaucratic organizations that are supposed to help governors decide and administer. Anthropologists, for whom the political *resistance* by peoples in the developing world is of special interest, so far seem not to have been drawn to these matters in the developed world where the industrial or post-industrial state reigns supreme.

While there are factors that undermine their governing, industrial chiefs—even those in the more democratic societies—still have formidable ways of asserting themselves, causing some authors like George Orwell to warn of an advancing totalitarianism in our world. First, industrial chiefs have inside information and connections (aided, perhaps, by political sound-ings or networks of spies). Second, by generating and controlling the flow of information, they can tap a variety of motivations and promote consensus for their policies. For example, the propaganda organs of the former Soviet state worked diligently (if, finally, unsuccessfully) to accomplish this. The depth of the consensus industrial chiefs manage to obtain can never be as great as in a small-scale, tradition-bound society, but it can be impressive nevertheless. Third, if they manage to control the various bureaucratic structures, indus-trial leaders may be able to get a large array of social activities running in their favor. In France, for example, it is sometimes said (only half facetiously) that those who control the *fonctionnaires* (governmental employees) control the nation. The bureaucratic machines run continuously, and their operations can have a great influence on human behavior. Fourth, as we are reminded on an almost daily basis, industrial leaders can always tap into the fertile ground of nationhood, which may coincide with the boundaries of the soci-ety they govern. By stirring up sentiments of ethnocentrism and possibly racism, as the Nazis did in Germany, they can evoke an image of a collective condition that is presented as being natural and right—not what it really is, namely, a political construction by human beings that emerges out of a cer-tain set of social circumstances and continues or ends depending on how those circumstances develop. Fifth, developing cynicisms among the gov-erned about their governors can be placated by various societal safety valves that can include such activities as sports and consumerism. Finally, by controlling powerful police and military forces, industrial chiefs can coerce people into doing what they want them to do. This, according to the newspaper report referred to earlier, is what the French had to resort to in their little colony of Wallis-et-Futuna.

SELECTED REFERENCES

BARTH, FREDRIK, *Nomads of South Persia*. Oslo: Oslo University Press, 1961.

———, "Political Leadership among Swat Pathans," *London School of Economics Monographs on Social Anthropology*, 19, 1959.

BENEDICT, RUTH, *The Chrysanthemum and the Sword*. Boston: Houghton Mifflin Co., 1946.

BOHANNAN, LAURA, and PAUL BOHANNAN, *The Tiv of Central Nigeria*. London: International African Institute, 1953.

COLES, ROBERT, *The Moral Intelligence of Children*. New York: Random House, 1997.

DE TOCQUEVILLE, ALEXIS, *Democracy in America*. New York: Anchor Books, 1969.

DE WAAL, FRANS, *Good Natures: The Origins of Right and Wrong in Humans and Other Animals*. Cambridge, MA: Harvard University Press, 1996.

DUMONT, LOUIS, *Homo Hierarchicus*. Chicago: University of Chicago Press, 1970.

FOGELSON, RAYMOND, and RICHARD ADAMS, eds., *The Anthropology of Power*. New York: Academic Press, 1977.

FORD, CLELLAN, "The Role of the Fijian Chief," *American Sociological Review*, 3, 1938, 542–50.

FOUCAULT, MICHEL, *Power/Knowledge! Selected Interviews and Other Writings*, ed. Colin Gordon. New York: Pantheon Books, 1980.

GIDDENS, ANTHONY, *The Nation State and Violence*. Cambridge: Polity Press, 1985.

GLEDHILL, JOHN, *Power and Its Disguises*. London and Boulder, CO: Pluto Press, 1994.

HOFSTEDE, GEERT, *Culture's Consequences*. Beverly Hills, CA: Sage Publications, 1980.

LEE, RICHARD, *The !Kung San*. Cambridge: Cambridge University Press, 1979.

MILLS, C. WRIGHT, *The Power Elite*. New York: Oxford University Press, 1956.

RICHARDS, AUDREY, "Authority Patterns in Traditional Buganda," in *The King's Men: Leadership and Status in Buganda on the Eve of Independence*, ed. L. A. Fallers, pp. 256–93. Oxford: Oxford University Press, 1964.

SIMIC, ANDREI, "The First and Last Yugoslav: Some Thoughts on the Dissolution of a State," *Anthropology of East Europe Review: War among the Yugoslavs*, 11 (Special Issue), 1993, 16–22.

WOLF, ERIC, "Distinguished Lecture: Facing Power-Old Insights, New Questions," *American Anthropologist*, 92, 1990, 586–96.

WYLIE, LAURENCE, *Village in the Vaucluse*. New York: Harper Colophon Books, 1964.

Languages

TO DISCOVER LANGUAGE

People going abroad often hear from experts on the subject that the key to adaptation will be their ability to learn and use the host (native) language. These experts will tell you that if you do not know the language you will not be able to get what you want nor understand what your hosts are thinking. Sometimes, Americans will learn the language on their own with some assistance from "the locals" and a couple of books, as I did when I first went to Cuba to undertake fieldwork. But more often, they will take a course beforehand. There is controversy about the best way to learn a language, but we do know that children are apt to learn it more quickly and retain it better than adults and that, at any age, as with other things, the more you use it the better it will go.

In one course I know of, language learning involves not only speaking and writing, but gesturing as well. The teacher's idea is that a good deal of meaning is communicated by physical signs such as (with speakers of French) pursing the lips or shrugging the shoulders. Using gestures, early Western explorers were able to communicate with natives. There is evidence that certain facial expressions tied to emotions are understood in many cultures, and certain signs such as putting the hands to the mouth (to indicate wanting to drink) seem to be widely understood. But gestures, bodily movements, and postures that play a part in communication vary widely between cultures. For example, if a person gazes directly and constantly at another during a conversation it may be interpreted as threatening or insulting in Japan, but polite or appreciative in the United States. A raised thumb, indicating something positive in America, may be taken as an insult elsewhere. The use of nonverbal signs is universal, but the frequency and nature of their use varies. In no culture, however, do nonverbal signs rival speech-based forms as a means of communication. Among humans, spoken language, with or without its written counterpart, is the principal means by which communication is accomplished. Like other social animals, humans need to communicate in order to survive, and since at least the time of the earliest *Homo sapiens* they have relied on spoken language to do so. It is only this form of language, which is unique to modern humans, that will be considered in this chapter.

Let us suppose that the person heading overseas takes the advice of the language expert and begins to learn the appropriate language. Such learning will involve acquiring a vocabulary of words and their meanings, a task that is aided immeasurably by having a dictionary on hand. It is not enough to know just the words and their meanings, however. You must also learn how the words go together and how they change in form according to their uses— the grammar. In English, for example, one says "I go," not "I goes." In French, the corresponding expressions are *"Je vais,"* not *"Je va."* (For some languages the parallels are much less obvious.) Generally, students find the grammatical part the most boring and difficult part of learning a language, but for linguists the grammar of a language is quite interesting. Finally, one should learn how the formal properties of a language are used in specific contexts to produce meaning. Whether a person is teasing or not, for example, depends less on what is being said than on how it is said and in which situation.

As Americans gain experience with different languages, they begin to comprehend that some are easier to learn than others. For them, Spanish is a comparatively simple language to learn while Chinese is difficult (and even harder to write). It has been customary for anthropologists to take on some of the most difficult language learning tasks. Not only have they had to learn languages of cultures that are very different from their own, but these languages often have had no written counterpart. So unless they are willing to use a translator or rely on someone else who has already worked out the language in phonetic notations, they must do it on their own. An American anthropologist, Jules Henry, once told me about his beginning interviews with Pilaga Indian informants in southern Brazil. At that time, he was still trying to gain a minimal competence in that language and was writing things down very slowly in phonetic transcriptions. Because of this, his informants sometimes got bored and went away.

So, as you begin to learn a language, you realize the enormity of this human creation. Until now, you probably have taken your native language pretty much for granted. Like other aspects of your culture, it was something that you didn't think about very much. But now, as you learn a new way of communicating, it all becomes more problematical. If you are of a reflective nature, you may begin to raise questions and make comparisons between your own language and the new one. The nature of these languages and other languages may become interesting to you. Now you can begin to profit from the work of scholars who have made it their business to understand different languages, groups of related languages, or all of the languages of humankind, written or unwritten. From the anthropological point of view, the consideration of all languages is of great interest, but anthropologists also want to know about the nature of specific human languages, how they are different and how similar, how they relate to other cultural elements, and why they are the way they are. In short, anthropologists raise the same kinds of questions about language as about other aspects of culture.

WHAT IS LANGUAGE?

To point out that language is an aspect of culture should bring back all of the things about culture that were discussed in Chapter One. First of all, language is learned, and though the importance of precultural programming is increasingly being insisted on by language experts, one could never come to speak, say, the Tiv language, without learning it. Second, a language, like a culture, is associated with a group of people. Linguists use the term language community when speaking of such a group. Third, the language practiced by the people in the group varies, as does any other culture trait, around norms. Not everyone speaks it in the same way. To give only a few examples, people in northern Castile (Spain) tend to speak differently than those in Andalusia in the south; people of higher social rank in Samoa use more emotion-laden expressions than those below them; and women in a number of cultures (including the United States) are said to engage in more "sympathetic" conversation than men. Fourth, one should expect a language to be linked to a culture and its setting in various ways. Consider only the specific terms that have to be learned in any vocation. Computerese goes with computers, not with hunting and gathering. And finally, a language has a history. An investigation will show, for example, that the language of the dominant group in the United States has changed over the course of three centuries, but the change has not been so great as to make it impossible for a typical Texan of today to communicate with (were they still living) an ordinary citizen of colonial Boston.

Different aspects of a culture may be seen as oriented toward different collective tasks. The task of language is communication. Without communication people could not adapt to each other and their society would fall apart. All of the projects that require some kind of collective effort would founder because the individuals involved could not let each other know very much about their intentions nor adjust them. Something of the problem involved is experienced by people in an overseas training group who are given a task to complete without an agreed-upon language to work with. Or one can think of an immigrant who has been in an accident and has been transported to an emergency room of a hospital where the personnel speak a different language. Doctors usually depend on their patients to tell them something about what ails them, but in this case, that aid to diagnosis would be lacking. Other examples of communication failures could be added in endless succession, all of which would attest to the importance of adequate communication in carrying on human social life.

A little probing, perhaps with the aid of a linguist, will reveal that there is more to language than people are generally aware of. At the minimum—the atomic level, so to speak—are meaningless sound bits that may or may not correspond with minimal written units such as the letters of the Roman alphabet as used in the English language. These bits, which can be distinguished from each other—as, for example, a single vowel can be distinguished from a consonant—are phonemes. They can be described in terms of the features of sound production, for example, whether the lips are open or closed or how the tongue is used. French speakers make more varied use of the front of the mouth in speaking than do Americans. The total repertoire of sound-bits available to humans for speaking is vastly superior to that of any other animal, but it is limited. Each language of humankind is drawn from this total repertoire of possible sounds, with the smallest number of sounds in a language being about fifteen and the largest about sixty. In English, the number of written letters is twenty-six, while the number of phonemes (because some written letters represent a combination of phonemes) is greater.

Regarding phonemes, it is important to remember that they are meaningless, just as most letters are meaningless, and that there are certain acceptable ways of putting them together to create meaningful units. Thus, in English, three phonemes make up the word "bat" or, in reverse, "tab," but in my dictionary there are no "tb" sequences. In the tonal language that the Tiv use, there are certain sequences of pitch and not others. Thus, every language, even as it has a certain repertoire of phonemes, has rules for how those phonemes go together. Though a language may have comparatively few phonemes, and though the possibilities for their combination are limited, the number of ways in which sounds are combined to generate meaningful sound units is very great. This means that language is very efficient as a way of communicating because it can produce a lot of meaning with only a limited array of sounds.

The minimal meaningful units of a language are called morphemes, which may be whole words or not. The word *fermier* in French is similar to "farmer" in English in that it combines a first morpheme (*ferm*), which signifies the act of farming, with a second, *ier*, the agent who does it. An "s" added at the end creates a third morpheme, the plural. Thus, the combination of meaningful units produces a further meaning: *fermiers*, in this case. Beyond words, there are phrases and sentences (the realm of syntax) that have meaning in themselves and that are stated according to certain rules governing the combination of words. A sentence that says, "Dell the in farmer the" does not communicate meaning in English, although someone who knows the old round might give you the benefit of the doubt and rearrange the words into a meaningful sequence.

Any language contains not only basic elements, but also an organization of those elements. The way in which the elements change in form according to usage and the way in which they relate to each other is called a grammar, which, if we are lucky, someone has already analysed and written down before us. But before that, it evolved over the years. The difficulties adults have in acquiring a new language illustrate the immensity of this creation, which, like a great work of art, becomes more fascinating as we enter more deeply into it. Finally, there is the manner in which linguistic forms go together with certain settings to produce meaning. Students may not speak to their buddies in the same way as they speak to their professors, and they have different ways of communicating in different situations.

Language, then, is a special form of communication that requires extremely complex operations by the people who use it. On the "sending" end, a person in a specific situation has some meaning that he or she wants to get across. This meaning has to be coded in linguistic terms, that is, in terms of the elements and grammar of a language. The coded message, containing strings of grammatically arranged, meaningless sound-bits (phonemes), is sent by activating the proper articulatory muscles. On the "receiving" end, the coded message is perceived and decoded on the basis of a "codebook" that (hopefully) is shared with the person sending the message. All of this takes place very rapidly, under the control of something like a linguistic computer in the brain, which appears to be specialized for its linguistic tasks.

DIFFERENCES AND SIMILARITIES

In order to chart the variability of human languages, or any other kind of variability, it is necessary to have some catchall framework that will apply to all cases. In this sense, language can be compared to another cultural phenomenon, marriage. So, taking marriage to be a certain kind of socially recognized relationship between men and women, it is possible to chart its variation in terms of the number of men and women involved. In the case of language, it is fairly easy to note the variability within a language community. It is not terribly difficult to note differences for a couple of related languages such as French and Spanish or the various Bantu languages of Africa.

It becomes progressively more difficult to make comparisons, however, as the differences between languages increase. Besides embracing all of their differences, any comparative framework ought to have a minimum of ethnocentric bias, that is, it should not favor the nature of one language over others. Because there are unwritten languages, a scheme based on something like written English will not do. Any system that uses words as a minimal basis of analysis will fail to do full justice to the subject matter. A too-particular form of grammatical analysis, such as the Western form that goes back to the Greeks and Romans, would also generate problems. It would turn out to be rather inadequate when applied to, say, Chinese. But if the essentials of all languages are kept in mind, it is possible to develop schemes that enable us to chart the differences and similarities of the thousands of versions of this uniquely human form of communication.

For example, Joseph Greenberg, a linguist and anthropologist, in his fascinating little book, *A New Invitation to Linguistics,* uses such a scheme to show how speakers of English, Russian, Turkish, Classical Arabic, Hausa (from West Africa), Thai, and Quechua (from western South America) would handle a sentence that he renders in English as "The boy drank the water." He charts the variation in the form of the noun subject (in English, "boy"), verb ("drank"), and noun object ("water") in terms of nine traditional grammatical categories, such as case (whether the noun varies in form as subject or object, as in "I" versus "me" in English), gender (variation of nouns as in the masculine, feminine, and neuter forms in German), and number (variation in form for singular and plural).

After an extensive analysis of the seven languages from around the world, Greenberg reports that there is only one category in which the languages are all alike. This category refers to whether the verb form indicates completion or not (in English, "drank" versus "was drinking"). But Greenberg also points out that these and other languages do have a number of other properties in common. First, all languages have a fundamental vocabulary that includes a word or words such as "boy," "drink," and "water," and that such words are intertranslatable. Linquists have found out that there is a common fund of things that people in all cultures seem to want to communicate, and, as has been pointed out elsewhere, the words that are used more frequently tend to be shorter. Second, all languages have words and sentences, as well as morphemes and phonemes. Third, all languages distinguish nouns and verbs in some way and specify nouns as subjects or objects.

Moreover, as Greenberg indicates, the categories for far-ranging linguistic analysis that have been developed seem to embrace most of the significant variations in human languages. Take, for example, the category of word order. It is known that if a sentence contains subject (S), verb (V), and object (O), as does "The boy drank the water," there are limits to the ways in which they can be arranged. The S-V-O, V-S-O, and S-O-V orders are most frequently used, while V-O-S is rare, and O-V-S and O-S-V never occur in simple sentences. So, there appear to be not only language universals, but also constraints on linguistic variability; and as the list of these continues to grow, one begins to wonder about them. The question, "Why all these languages?" then begins to give way to "Why language?"

EXPLANATIONS

The explanation for the differences in human languages given by anthropologists has tended to be the same as for other cultural differences: They represent different learned adaptations to different life circumstances. To take a simple example, people in northern and southern regions of the world must learn a word for snow, while those in equatorial regions have little or no need for such a word. The way in which differences come about becomes apparent in tracing the histories of related languages. Emerging from a common stem, they gradually diverge from each other in a way reminiscent of the formation of new species. Thus, the Romance languages of today are further radiations of what originally were merely dialects or regional varieties of basic Latin. No one has ever claimed that these radiations are due to biological changes in the peoples carrying these languages, however. The usual view is, rather, that they came about as the peoples involved learned new ways of expressing themselves in circumstances of increasing isolation from each other or contact with neighboring languages. So what were once simply dialects gradually diverged until they became different languages. A good example of this can be found in the controversy over Black English or Ebonics in the American inner-city where a black underclass seems to be developing. Whatever the origin of the differences of this language from standard English, there are grounds for believing that they are currently increasing, a fact that suggests that various social barriers are at work.

It is more difficult to argue, however, that the commonalities of languages are learned. Which of our common life circumstances generate through learning the universalities and constraints mentioned above? There may be universal influences such as those that come with "mothering" that everywhere shape the developing individual's linguistic capacity very early in life. A more likely source, though, would seem to be certain pan-human biological dispositions toward linguistic or language-related cognitive capabilities. Whether built-in or acquired, it is important to know the exact nature of these factors. Are they language-specific, or do they involve broader cognitive capabilities? There has been a good deal of scientific work concerning such issues.

A number of authors have pointed out the ability of infants to discriminate sound patterns containing linguistic structures from others (for example, noise, music). Peter Eimas, in "The Perception of Speech in Early Infancy," reports that a series of ingenious experiments with infants who suck differently in response to certain sound stimuli suggest that children everywhere are born with perceptual mechanisms tuned to the properties of speech. The implication of all of this work is that human infants are set up early in life to zero in on whatever language happens to be used by their care-takers. If this capacity is, indeed, built into the organism before birth, it then constitutes an evolutionary specialization that has emerged in the same manner as other traits that provide an adaptive advantage for humans. The development of the large brain increased hominids' cultural capacity; and the development of a linguistic capability, by increasing the ability of these creatures to communicate, has added to that capacity. As a result, each gen-eration has been able to communicate more and more of what they have learned, not only to each other, but to succeeding generations as well.

The physical basis of humans' evolving linguistic capacity is rather shadowy, but the emergence of upright posture undoubtedly was an impor-tant early development. It was followed by the emergence of a J-shaped vocal tract that had a vastly increased sound-producing capacity. Apes, who have been used as a loose kind of model for the earliest hominids, have a vocal tract that resembles a slightly curved tube. In it, sounds involving the tongue can only be produced in a one-dimensional way, that is, by moving the tongue up or down. But humans have, among other things, the back of the tongue to work with and they can make sounds by moving that part back and forth. Evidence for a corresponding cerebral development is not so clear. For most humans, language is processed in the left hemisphere of the brain. Some anthropologists say that they can detect an increased lateralization in favor of this hemisphere from endocasts made of the inside of the skulls of early humans, such as *Homo erectus*. Experiments with monkeys and apes also sug-gest it. Scientists are always straining for more evidence about early human developments. It would be best to have some written observations on early humans, but unfortunately, writing goes back only a few thousand years, which is not very long as far as human evolution is concerned. Undoubtedly, more evidence about the evolution of human linguistic capacity will be forth-coming, but crucial details probably will continue to escape us.

However and whenever the human capacity for language evolved, it is apparent that it became a specialization that probably does more to set humans apart from other animals than any other trait they possess. Experiments with apes initially suggested that these animals had a signifi-cant capacity for language. They could not speak, of course, but contrary to what some believed ("Apes don't speak because they have nothing to say"), they seemed to be able to communicate a remarkable amount of meaning. Thus, one chimpanzee, who was trained to use the American Sign Language for the Deaf, acquired a vocabulary of several hundred words, which it used in communication with its trainer and even other chimpanzees. The apes clearly have some linguistic capacity and the brain development that goes with it, but later research has raised serious questions about how much. A particularly thorny issue concerns the apes' capacity for grammatical constructions, which is a crucial aspect of human linguistic ability. It appears that apes are fairly limited in this regard.

Another line of research pointing to pan-human linguistic capacities has been followed by scientists who have probed for the underlying grammatical structures of human languages. The work of the linguist, Noam Chomsky, and other "structuralists" involves getting at the "deep structure" of a language, which, through certain transforming processes, generates a number of "surface" grammatical structures. Investigations like this point to the existence of some basic grammatical principles that are common to all languages. These principles or preferences could be determined by the structure of the human brain, though very early pan-human socializing influences have also been suggested.

The way a child acquires a language is often cited in support of the notion of such universal principles. On the speaking side, there are at first (within the first several months) a period of crying-fretting that increases, then declines and levels off as it becomes more intentional and communicative. There is also a babbling sequence, the equivalent of which even exists in deaf infants of deaf parents who use the American Sign Language for the Deaf as a first language. Later, children appear to leap into linguistic competence. The current evidence suggests that the same general communicative sequences exist among all peoples, not just Westerners with whom most research has been carried out. Of course, humans have to learn the elements of some specific communicative style, including language, but they seem to be able to become full-fledged communicators with only limited teaching or example. As was pointed out about socialization in Chapter Three, linguistic neophytes come on as active, rather than passive, learners. They do not acquire linguistic competence bit by bit, as adults who have surpassed the critical period for language acquisition (up to about age fifteen) must do, but often do so in large chunks. People who insist that all aspects of a language have to be learned and that the human organism is an empty vessel at birth that has to be filled up with learned acquisitions are in for a hard time when confronted with such facts.

Ochs and Schieffelin on Language Acquisition In Different Cultures

There is still plenty about a language that has to be learned, however. Not only the meaningless and meaningful units and the way they go together, but also the ways in which these essentials are used and in what contexts they must be learned. In English, the word "great" can mean different things depending on the tone and the situation in which it is employed; and different speakers talk differently when addressing infants rather than adults. Native speakers normally learn all of this as part of their socialization.

In order to get a handle on the actual process of language development, it would seem best to observe closely the acquisition of language in young children. Such observation, if done in several cultures, can help decide whether developmental sequences are innate or culturally or situationally dictated. Elinor Ochs and Bambi Schieffelin do this in their cross-cultural study, "Language Acquisition and Socialization," the main points of which will be summarized here. The authors start with the assumption that there are certain biological dispositions that shape the process of language acquisition anywhere, but the exact way in which a language is acquired and used reflects the influence of cultural expectations that are transmitted to the child in the socialization process. To demonstrate this, they analyze language-related socialization patterns in three cultures: the Euro-American middle class; the Kaluli of Papua, New Guinea; and the Samoans of the Southwest Pacific.

Ochs and Schieffelin take an ethnographic point of view, that is, they look at the socialization process as an anthropologist looks at any aspect of a culture. They focus on what actually goes on between infants and their caretakers from birth until around three years of age. In two of the cultures, Kaluli and western (American) Samoa, one of the authors observed these transactions firsthand. As far as the Euro-American middle class was concerned, they sought out descriptions in the psychological and linguistic literature and use them as ethnographic reports. In their article, they construct typical developmental stories for each culture, show how they fit into a whole way of life, and make comparisons in terms of a scheme that emerges from their data.

The (Western) middle-class socialization pattern may sound familiar. The process usually involves two people, a mother and child, who share a great deal of eye contact. From the time of birth, the mother tends to regard her baby as a communicative partner. The mother has expectations that the child will begin to communicate through cries and other signals, and later, through language. In linguistic transactions between these partners, the child often takes the initiative with some utterance or other, and the mother responds with a question ("What do you want Mommy to do?"). She then expands on the question ("Open it up?"). Finally, she interprets the response ("Oh, what a nice smile"). During this process, the mother simplifies adult language into what has been called baby talk, which is one aspect of her general accommodation to the child. As the infant develops linguistic capabilities, adjustments are made, but the general pattern continues. The infant is exposed to a regime in which gestures and vocalizations may not be immediately understood. The child learns to deal with this ambiguity through a process of give-and-take that produces progressively more accurate meanings, which the infant can agree with or not. Finally, the infant comes to understand that communication and understanding involve a two-person transaction in which language plays an important role.

The Kaluli, according to Ochs and Schieffelin, do not believe that new-born infants are capable of understanding and do not regard them as communicative partners. A typical Kaluli mother is responsive to her infant's needs, but in the first few months she rarely addresses the infant directly. Instead, she often faces the child away from her so that it can see and be seen by others who address it. Then, the mother, speaking through the child, responds in a high-pitched nasal voice while moving the child up and down like a puppet. Except for the special tone, the language she uses is adult-like. Later, at six-to-twelve months of age, the child is given a few orders, but is still not regarded as a communicative partner. The infant may then be vocalizing and gesturing or even be saying a word or two in the Kaluli language. But until it says the words for "mother" and "breast," it is thought to be incapable of language. From this time until about three years of age, the infant is put through a routine that involves the mother and other participants. The child often becomes a third party in what amounts to a conversation between the mother and another child. It is told to say things to that person in adult language ("Whose is it?" "Is it yours?"). If the child makes a mistake, the process is repeated until it gets it right. Throughout this process, it is considered the child's responsibility to accommodate to the adult world, which frequently involves three or more people in communicative transactions. Since the Kaluli believe that one cannot know what another thinks, they do not explore for meanings as do Western middle-class adults. Rather, they specify a lot in order to make things perfectly clear. The child is socialized in a way that is compatible with such linguistic practices.

As in Kaluli, infants in Western (American) Samoa enter a social world that often involves three or more parties who may be carrying on several conversations at once. In addition, because the Samoans have an acute awareness of social rank and the behavior and discourse that goes with it, children are expected to learn to speak in a manner appropriate for their low rank in the family. This begins with a child being asked to repeat something a caregiver has said to a third party and involves the expectation that the child has paid attention to the situation and will report accurately on what has been going on. Earlier, because caregivers do not attempt to fathom what is on children's minds nor help them express it, infants have begun to learn to take full responsibility for their communications; Ochs and Schieffelin report that infants are more likely to be talked about than to, and when caregivers do talk to them, it is not as conversational partners for whom the task of language acquisition is made easier by the use of a simplified mode of discourse, such as in middle-class baby talk. So, a heavier share of the burden for attaining linguistic competence tends to fall on the Samoan child.

It is apparent from this cross-cultural investigation that children in different cultures acquire language in different ways and with different kinds of input. They may be drilled into it in a highly specific way; they may acquire it through verbal explorations with others; they may learn from listening to the conversations of others; or they may realize that some sound they have produced amounts to something significant. Their caretakers may accommodate or not accommodate to them. There are a variety of courses of language socialization, but whatever the course, most children manage to acquire a linguistic competence that is more or less appropriate for their culture. Ochs and Schieffelin argue that this could not be accomplished without certain biological dispositions for language that produce an active language learner with certain basic acquisitional tendencies; but neither could it come about without input from some sociocultural context that begins to operate on them even before language emerges. There must be some kind of appropriate input from outside.

To sum up what we have learned from the ethnographic study of language acquisition in three cultures by Ochs and Schieffelin, it would seem that children everywhere not only acquire a language, but also an understanding of the way to use it. They are taught their language in certain ways that would seem to reflect other aspects of their culture. For example, from the way in which they are socialized, they ought to learn what people are like as communicators, the social conditions in which certain expressions should be used, how expressions are to be communicated, and to whom. Ochs and Schieffelin suggest that the child not only acquires a code for language, but a sociocultural code that goes with it. And they and others might want to go even further by raising questions about the personal and social consequences of different modes of language learning, which is, after all, an important aspect of the socialization process. For example, consider as one research question which mode of language acquisition of the three discussed would tend (other things being equal) to generate people with the greatest individual initiative?

THE USES OF LANGUAGE

Talk is cheap.

Actions speak louder than words.

These expressions, often associated with Americans, testify to the belief that, compared with concrete actions, language is of lesser importance. These people tend to think that actions, like money across the table or help given in time of need, mean more than words. Perhaps the expressions are a throwback to an earlier era, when the exchange and processing of information had not yet moved to the center of the American stage. Even so, language has always been an important aspect of American culture, as well as other cultures. One way of measuring its importance is by examining its uses.

Earlier, the significance of language for communication was discussed. Without language, very few human social projects could get off the ground. Think, for example, of trying to coordinate a big-game hunt at night without language or of carrying out a complex heart operation in a modern hospital. Those engaged in these projects have to know, at the minimum, the symbols for animals, organs, implements, and people as well as for what is going on. By using language to refer to things in the world humans have the capability of manipulating that world to their advantage.

Language refers not only to things "out there," but also to things in the mind. Things can be more or less specifically designated and thought about. Thus, the word *agua* in Spanish includes a variety of specific waters (*caliente, frio,* etc.), "cousin" in English includes a number of specific relatives (first, second, etc.), and "incest" covers a range of specific sexual relationships between relatives. Using linguistic symbols, people can classify things and relate them to each other, as in the suggested causal relationship "alcohol loosens inhibitions." Although humans are not alone in their ability to think such things, language obviously enhances their ability to do so.

It has been suggested that the way different people think about things is dependent on the nature of their languages. Edward Sapir, an anthropologist and poet, and Benjamin Lee Whorf, an insurance man from Connecticut, thought that such important concepts as time, space, matter, and color would vary according to the nature of a language. They developed this idea on the basis of observations they made of a number of different peoples, including the Hopi of the American Southwest, Americans, and Europeans. As an example, they note the dominant American tendency to think of a phase of time, such as summer, as a noun subject or object with various qualities (for example, a "hot summer"); while among the Hopi the same concept is not "objectified," but refers to when conditions are hot, for example. So, in our case it can be manipulated and divided up; in the other case, it cannot. A good deal of additional research has followed, all of which has run into the difficulty of stating this exciting hypothesis in a more precise, cross-culturally testable form. Considering the amount of interest in the hypothesis, it is surprising that researchers have come up with so little confirming evidence. Nevertheless, it still may be that there are categories of thought that vary with language. And, of course, one should not rule out the notion that the relationship between language and thought is a two-way, not a one-way, street, which is how some scholars prefer to shape the Sapir-Whorf hypothesis.

References to the world outside or in the mind are not the only uses for language. It also can serve as a sign or index of the context in which communication takes place. Are we serious or only teasing? Is the subject sacred or mundane? Are we men or women? Are we of different social ranks or the same? Is this person speaking as a tourist or a native? Is what is being said speculative or not? Sometimes linguistic utterances refer to social position or the nature of social relationships, thus helping to structure a society. For example, the use of language to mark the degree of formality (and, therefore, social distance) of a relationship is something that students of German learn very early. Like many other languages, German has a formal and informal way of indicating "you" (*sie* and *du* respectively), and one learns that in the beginning of a social relationship it is better to use the formal form.

A good deal of anthropological effort has gone into the exploration of the use of language in social positioning. William Labov, in one of the many studies by him and his associates, found that the natives of Martha's Vineyard, an island off the coast of Massachusetts, distinguish themselves from summer residents and other visitors by, among other things, the way in which they use their tongues to pronounce certain phonemes. Elinor Ochs, in *Culture and Language Development*, shows how social class is indicated in Samoa by the use of personal pronouns. The Samoan language has emotion-laden pronouns, including some that seem designed to get the listener to feel sorry for the speaker. She notes that high-status persons are much less likely to use this affect form than those of lower status, which is consistent with the Samoan expectation that higher-status persons act in a more restrained and detached manner. There also appear to be differences between male and female speech patterns in many cultures. For example, Deborah Tannen has suggested, in *You Just Don't Understand,* that among her American women subjects conversation tends to be a means of establishing connections between equals, while among her male subjects it is a means of preserving independence and negotiating a position in some kind of hierarchical pecking order. Thus, men want to find out quickly where they stand and push themselves forward (and upward), while the womens' talk tends more to convey understanding or sympathy. Though this difference has been suggested for a number of other cultures, it also has been found to be highly dependent on the situation in which the conversation occurs; and, of course, as we learned in Chapter Four, one has to remember that different peoples construct their ideas of gender or sex differences in different ways. This means that we are far from being able to declare any universal differences in language usage between the sexes for all of humankind.

Finally, to close out what is only a suggestive listing of the ways in which language can, through sometimes complex processes, contribute to social positioning, let me refer to studies of how a single linguistic form can point to different dimensions of social structure, namely gender and social status. Investigations of Black English (Ebonics) in the United States have shown that the use of double negatives (a form also found in a number of other languages) such as in "I ain't goin' [to] do no dancin'" tends to increase as one goes down the status ladder and to be significantly higher among males than females at all status levels. Whatever the source of these differences, it is obvious that they must be taken into account in, say, constructing a school curriculum for an American inner-city.

It should be clear from all of this that language plays a role in the functioning of all aspects of sociocultural life including the passing on of the way of life that a people has created for itself through socialization. A person does not just act in an objective social situation, but in a meaningful context that language has helped to structure. Without language, the Tiv people, who are mentioned from time to time in this book, would have been hard put to sort out their relatives and the nature of their obligations to them. Tribal elders could not hear, discuss, or pronounce judgment on a case involving a dispute between neighbors. Buying and selling in the marketplace could scarcely begin. Bride purchase, which involves discussion between men of different kinship groups and with their wards, could hardly have existed. There would be no gossip about the latest elopement. People could not tell their children about the witches that fly at night. Songs could not be sung, and nights would have been long for a lack of storytelling. There might have been some dancing, but it would have been harder to teach. Some rituals could have been practiced, but without accompanying language and belief. Finally, what part of the Tiv material world—their drums, dwellings, agricultural implements, weapons, cooking utensils, and all the rest—could they have been able to fashion without the aid of language.

Language has many uses in human life, and it vastly enriches our existence. Think, finally, of a group of chimpanzees living in the forest. The chimpanzees can think, though not as well as humans. They can learn and they have a form of social organization as well as systems of authority. Collective rituals have been noted among them. On the whole, though, whatever culture they have is only rudimentary. They do not pass on much of what they learn from generation to generation. Why is this? An important reason would seem to be their lack of language, which is something that humans alone possess.

SELECTED REFERENCES

BERLIN, BRENT, and PAUL KAY, *Basic Color Terms: Their Universality and Evolution.* Berkeley: University of California Press, 1969.

BROWN, CECIL, *Language and Living Things: Uniformities in Folk Classification and Naming.* New Brunswick, NJ: Rutgers University Press, 1984.

CHOMSKY, NOAM, *Reflections on Language.* New York: Pantheon Books, 1975.

COLLETT, PETER, "Meetings and Misunderstandings," in *Cultures in Contact*, ed. Stephen Bochner, pp. 81–97. Elmsford, NY: Pergamon Press, 1982.

EIMAS, PETER, "The Perception of Speech in Early Infancy," *Scientific American*, 252 (1) (1985), 46-52.

FREED, ALICE, and ALICE GREENWOOD, "Women, Men, and Type of Talk: What Makes a Difference?" *Language in Society*, 25, 1996, 1–26.

GREENBERG, JOSEPH, *A New Invitation to Linguistics*. Garden City, NY: Anchor Books, 1977.

HAUSER, MARC, *The Evolution of Communication*. Cambridge, MA: MIT Press, 1996.

JACKENDOFF, RAY, *Patterns of the Mind*. New York: Basic Books, 1994.

LABOV, WILLIAM, *Sociolinguistic Patterns*. Philadelphia: University of Pennsylvania Press, 1973.

OCHS, ELINOR, *Culture and Language Development: Language Socialization in a Samoan Village*. Cambridge: Cambridge University Press, 1988.

OCHS, ELINOR, and BAMBI SCHIEFFELIN, "Language Acquisition and Socialization: Three Developmental Stories and Their Implications," in *Culture Theory: Essays on Mind, Self and Emotion*, ed. Richard Shweder and Robert Levine, pp. 276–320. New York: Cambridge University Press, 1984.

PINKER, STEPHEN, *The Language Instinct*. New York: William Morrow, 1994.

TANNEN, DEBORAH, *You Just Don't Understand: Men and Women in Conversations*. New York: William Morrow, 1990.

WHORF, BENJAMIN LEE, "The Relation of Habitual Thought to Language," in *Language, Culture and Personality: Essays in Memory of Edward Sapir*, ed. Leslie Spier, A. Irving Hallowell, and Stanley S. Newman, pp. 75–93. Menasha, WI: Sapir Memorial Publication Fund, 1941.

Idea Worlds

WHAT ARE THEY THINKING

All humans live not only in an objective world—the world *out there*—but also in a subjective world of ideas; and even as our actions are related to the world out there they reflect our *inner*, subjective world as well. We dream, plan, fantasize, speculate, calculate, and formulate all through our lives. Other animals have thoughts, too. Studies of chimpanzees, for example, have revealed some conceptual abilities. But no creature has a mental life that comes close to that of humans. So important is this aspect of human life that it must be routinely considered in any discussion of humanity. Because anthropology is the science that has humanity as its principal concern, the study of human idea worlds has always been a part of its work. Indeed, for those anthropologists whose notion of culture is confined to mental representations, one may say that they are pretty much stuck on this aspect of human action.

Through the use of participant observation and informants, anthropologists try to enter into the thought worlds of the people they study. It is essential to understand people on their own terms and to reconstruct what W. I. Thomas referred to as their "definition of the situation" or what A. I. Hallowell called their "behavioral environment." If you have ever tried to make sense of a stranger's apparently incomprehensible actions you will understand how difficult this can be.

The anthropologist is not totally at a loss, however, in trying to comprehend idea worlds. An informant can discuss what he or she is thinking or meaning; and if the investigator is especially astute, it may be possible to dig up something that the informant is not consciously aware of. Also, people objectify their subjective worlds in language, art, philosophy, scientific treatises, folklore, myth, and religion. These shared or extrinsic symbols, which Hallowell thought to be uniquely human, can be a major entrée into the idea worlds of a people.

Consider the extrinsic symbol *vaillance*, which Bernadette Bucher (in *Descendants de Chouans*) suggests is a "primordial value" or "code of conduct" of an agriculturally oriented people who live in an area along the west coast of France (the Vendée) between Bordeaux and Brittany. These people tend to think of it as expressing a highly desirable personal quality that, according to Bucher, implies a melange of courage, adaptability, tenacity, and capability. An understanding of this value would give an anthropologist a good start in comprehending their actions. How might the anthropologist handle this interpretive operation? First, one distills from observed behavior and comments of informants the essential meaning(s). Next comes the holistic task of relating this value to other values, as Bucher does with the "dominant values" être de service ('be helpful'), *ne pas être fier* ("don't be haughty"), and *ne pas être à part* ("don't be aloof"). Bucher shows how all of these aspects of what might be called a personal disposition toward others fit together. Finally, there may be a comparison of these values with those of other peoples. In Bucher's case, this mainly involves noting differences between the code of conduct under study and that of "honor and shame" of certain Mediterannean societies, such as in the Lebanese village studied by Justine McCabe (see Chapter Four) in which, when push comes to shove, community cohesion tends to give way to individual and family preoccupations. Something of the excitement of such operations, whether narrowly or broadly conceived, is conveyed in *The Interpretation of Cultures* by the American anthropologist Clifford Geertz. But, as was mentioned in Chapter Two, interpretive audacity sometimes may carry anthropologists beyond the realm of ethnographic fact, and they may have to make a conscious effort to keep our feet on the ground, so to speak.

THE CASE OF RELIGION

A religion provides a particularly interesting example of a world of ideas and its associated actions. Its practitioners are involved in using and generating ideas concerning the nature of the world and the place of humans within it. These ideas are expressed in oral or written beliefs and ritualistic behavior. For example, in the strictest of early Protestant sects God was seen to be a powerful father figure who had a plan for the world and its creatures. This plan, the exact nature of which was not revealed to humans, included the salvation of some humans in an afterlife. One's actions in this life could not affect salvation (which was up to God); they were, ideally, only a way of honoring God. Collective rituals in a place that Westerners have come to call a church were to celebrate God and his works, not to help humans in this or the next world.

Although many Westerners may find this type of religion not their particular cup of tea, most will have little difficulty recognizing it as a religion. This may be because God is involved. The early Protestants' idea of God referred to a supraempirical being who possessed qualities going beyond the world of the senses. All Jews and Christians have an idea of some such being, as do Muslims, Hindus, and Buddhists. So Westerners should have no trouble calling such people religious. They probably would not want to put the polytheists of the world beyond the pale either. They would count them as religious too, although some might raise questions about the "correctness "of their religions. The idea of supraempirical powers as an essential element in religious ideas is an attractive one and has drawn many to a definition of religion as something that is concerned primarily with the *supernatural*.

There are problems with this Western-oriented definition, as with any definition; but it has good cross-cultural utility, which is essential for the comparisons that anthropologists like to make. If we are going to compare a mainline American religion such as Catholicism with a sect such as the Hare Krishnas, or either of these with the religion of the Balinese or the ancient Aztecs, we will find common core ideas in all of them relating to a supernatural realm, which will permit us to make comparisons. If we employ this view of religion relentlessly, we will have to include not only gods, but also angels, witches, fairies, demons, souls, giant talking birds, and animate rocks as elements of religion. We may feel a little uncomfortable about putting all of these together in the same category, but that feeling of uncomfortableness may come from our own ideas about the *reality* of these things. Our particular god, angels, and souls may be real, we might think, but other supernaturals are fantasy, or even superstition.

Such concerns with the realness or rightness of ideas cannot preoccupy anthropologists in their work. All believers have some kind of evidence to support the realness or rightness of their views. There is, however, no *scientific* evidence for or against the existence of supernaturals, so anthropologists have to put whatever faith they have about them in brackets, so to speak, while doing anthropological work. To take only a couple of examples, Michael Gilsenen (with Sufi Muslims in a Cairo café) and Peter Stromberg (with Protestants from the Immanuel Church in Stockholm) do this when they try to make sense of what their informants believe to be experiences of what might be called divine grace. For the anthropologist it is enough to know that people *really* believe in the existence of supernatural powers and act in terms of their ideas of them. A group of such people, whatever the quality of the supernatural realm they believe in, can be said, then, to have a religion.

To sum up, for anthropological purposes a religion may be thought of as organized around some group's ideas of the supernatural. Accompanying these ideas is a set of beliefs and behaviors (ritualistic and other) that reflect the ideas. The really religious are supernaturally guided, that is, by their ideas of supernaturals. The scientist cannot make any judgment about whether these ideas refer ultimately to something real, and so, *as a scientist*, the anthropologist is not concerned with wagers such as that considered by the French philosopher Pascal concerning the existence of God. Resolving the question about the reality of supernaturals may be important to others and possibly even to the scientists themselves *outside* of their work, but as far as science is concerned, it is a waste of time.

WHY RELIGION?

Paul Radin says in *Primitive Religion* that religion comes from life and is directed to life. By this he was suggesting that religion can be explained in terms of (empirical) life circumstances. Many such explanations have been offered. Intellectualists have found the cause of religion in the human mind, as, for example, in the need to explain extraordinary events. Emotionalists have argued that feelings such as awe, excitement, fear, and anxiety give rise to religious ideas. The sociologically oriented have emphasized social conditions or needs such as legitimation or integration. It will not be particularly useful to go over grand explanations like these in detail since each has been found wanting in one way or another. A principal criticism concerns the scanty and conflicting evidence on which they are based.

Often, the grand theorists of religion have sought its cause in some archetypical condition of human life, especially primitive life. Sigmund Freud, for example (in *Totem and Taboo*), thought that religion arose from a guilt complex derived from conflict between father and sons in the "primal horde." Direct evidence for such a horde does not exist; nor is there direct evidence for most of the life circumstances of the earliest humans such as *Homo habilis* or *Homo erectus.* Some material evidence suggesting the existence of religion among prehistoric hunters and gatherers (artwork, burials, and possible ceremonial arrangements) has been found, but it is not extensive and its religious significance is open to question.

When grand theorists refer to primitive religion they often make use of indirect evidence from contemporary primitives whose cultures are supposed to be similar to those of the ancients. Emile Durkheim, for example (in *The Elementary Forms of the Religious Life*), thought that he had found evidence of the earliest religion in the totemism of the Australian aborigines. He considered their societies to be primitive because they were small and undifferentiated. But totemism, a kinship-oriented religion involving plants or animals with supernatural qualities, is not always found in such societies, and there is no direct evidence to indicate that it existed among the earliest humans.

Today, anthropologists have largely given up the search for the ultimate origin of this or that sociocultural trait. It is just too speculative. But some things can be said about the origin of religion. Almost certainly it arose (perhaps as early as a hundred thousand years ago) among some people whose brains had evolved enough to permit a robust mental life that included ideas of supernatural powers, that is, of unseen things. If the sense of reality of these things was great enough, humans could have established relationships with them and acted in terms of these relationships. But what kinds of circumstances would have brought about the creation of supernatural beings in primitive minds? The question seems a little wrong-headed when one looks at people in our society who are not committed to the scientific frame of mind. For them, a subjective world that includes supraempirical beings may be nothing extraordinary, and the question "Why supernaturals?" might be profitably turned around to "Why not?"

Some of us have supernaturals on our minds more than others, however. Even as some peoples appear to be more religiously involved than others, the degree of religiosity seems to vary from person to person. Paul Radin notes that only a small percentage of people in any society are truly religious. People like Bernadette Soubirous of Lourdes, the modern Indian mystic, Sri Ramakrishna, Jesus of Nazareth, or Handsome Lake, the Iroquois prophet, all appear to have had an extraordinary capacity for supernatural involvement. They are examples of "religiously musical" people (to use Max Weber's felicitous expression) who practically live in a supernatural world. We know about them because they have acquired significant followings. No doubt there are others, equally gifted, who have not acquired followings and who are not known to us. Whether successful or not, these "formulators" (to use Radin's term) would seem to possess special qualities. It has been suggested that they have specific personality attributes such as intense psychic conflict, and they have been branded as "neurotic epileptoid" or "paranoid schizophrenic." Some have argued that their religiosity comes from ingesting certain substances such as mescaline or ayahuasca. Certain "altered" states of consciousness have been related to bodily deprivations such as a lack of sleep or food. Possibly some of these people might be religious frauds. If so, their alleged religious involvement would be found in qualities associated with con-artistry.

There is little solid scientific evidence about factors associated with religiosity, but at least one study has produced encouraging results. In "Aspects of Cognition of Zincatecan Shamans," Richard Shweder, comparing Zincatecan (Mexican) shamans (that is, people who divine and solve problems with supernatural assistance) with non-shamans reports a difference in mind-sets. When responding to unstructured stimuli, the shamans are quicker to impose their own order. They show greater mental productivity and more "inner-directedness." In other words, they are the kind of people who tend to impose their richer subjective world on the objective world *out there*. This conclusion, which is consistent with some earlier speculations, has to be treated with caution as a cross-cultural generalization, but it does suggest lines of fruitful research. The reasons for variation in religiosity between individuals and societies are only beginning to be discovered.

Variation in the *quality* or *kind* of religion is a question that has always been of interest to anthropologists. Some early grand theorists saw religion varying through time in some evolutionary way. Culture evolved from some primitive state, and religion, as a part of culture, was seen to evolve as well. Some saw humanity gradually falling away from a "pure" primitive monotheism. Others saw religious evolution as a relentless march *toward* monotheism. These and other grand evolutionary designs have little basis in fact and are rarely encountered in the anthropological literature these days. Instead, one finds anthropologists searching cross-culturally for the sources of religious variability. Although there continue to be many impressionistic observations, some scientific evidence has begun to emerge in the form of statistical studies that demonstrate associations between kinds of religion and personality or social factors. For example, in *The Birth of the Gods*, Guy Swanson, taking his cue from Durkheim (one might also have suggested Karl Marx), has found that religion tends to act either positively or negatively to support the moral codes of socially stratified societies. It appears to provide supernatural sanctions that keep the socially deprived "in their place" and to justify a situation of social dominance and subordination. In the same cross-cultural study, Swanson also reports that beliefs in monotheism, polytheism, active ancestral spirits, reincarnation, witchcraft, and immanence of the soul (believed to be a part of the body and not transcendent) are also associated with specific kinds of social arrangements.

On the psychological side, a number of cross-cultural studies have found a significant statistical association between belief in benevolent or malevolent supernaturals (good guys or bad guys) and what amounts to acceptance or rejection by parents in childhood. When the father of Anthony Eden, a British foreign secretary, looked out the window on a typical dreary day and shouted, "Oh God, how like you," he might have been saying something not only about his god, but also about his own personality that had developed under harsh socializing circumstances.

This is only a little of the evidence that has linked religion's quality with secular, this-worldly factors. It is not exhaustive, but is only designed to give some idea about how anthropologists try to explain religious variability. They are nowhere close to explaining fully that variability; nor is it likely that religion will ever be explained away in terms of secular facts of life. But recent anthropological work does suggest that religion, whatever its ultimate origins, is clearly constrained by such facts.

THE NATURE OF A RELIGION

Whatever the factors that bring it into existence and maintain it, a religion, sooner or later, acquires a life of its own. It becomes, in Clifford Geertz' terms, a cultural system that has to be understood and described. The way anthropologists look at a religion derives from the particular definition they employ as well as certain invariant properties that most anthropologists use. Following the line taken in this chapter, any religion can be seen to revolve around certain ideas in the minds of its believers. These ideas, which refer to supernatural powers, are the focal point of an array of ideas that may be called a belief system. For example, at the core of any Islamic belief system would be the twin assertions that "there is no God but Allah" and that "Muhammad is His Apostle." Any anthropological description of a religion will include a discussion of its belief system and how it is organized. For example, structuralists like Claude Levi-Strauss have attempted to decipher this organization in terms of supposed universal properties of the human mind (for example, a tendency to think in binary terms). In addition, the rituals of the religion and related behaviors such as the various rites of the Ndembu of northwestern Zambia, so sensitively analyzed by Victor Turner in *The Ritual Process,* have received anthropological attention. Some anthropologists assign primacy to ritual and others to belief, but most of them recognize both of these aspects of religion and the fact that they are intimately interrelated.

Because a religion is seen to be anchored in life circumstances, the anthropologist usually discusses the social and environmental setting in which a religion exists and by which it is constrained. There is also a concern with the characteristics of its believers and the way in which they organize or arrange themselves. Are they poor or well off? Are they part of a large, complex organization such as the Catholic Church or a small face-to-face group with some charismatic leader like Jesus of Nazareth? The usual anthropological description of a religion is not, therefore, some dry-as-bones discussion of doctrine and ritual, but of something that is being practiced by specific human beings who have organized themselves in a certain way at a specific time and place. Religion thus becomes a *human* social fact, and it is the anthropologist's task to understand this and to describe it with the utmost fidelity and sensitivity. Not all anthropologists are equal to this task. No matter how well trained, some of them are less religiously "musical" than others.

Finally, we should keep in mind that anthropologists are, by nature, comparers. By using invariant properties in their descriptions, they help others to make comparisons and to make general statements about what kinds of beliefs, rituals, contexts, and believers tend to go together.

CASE STUDIES

In order to bring this discussion of the nature of a religion down to earth, it will be helpful to refer to some specific religions. Two anthropological accounts will be summarized here. The first one, by Seth and Ruth Leacock, is reported on in their book *Spirits of the Deep*. It deals with the Batuque, an Afro-Brazilian religious cult in Belém, Brazil. The other, by Melford Spiro, is offered in *Buddhism and Society*. It treats one of the great religious traditions as it is practiced today, especially in a Burmese village setting. Although the theoretical approaches of these studies are different, they have both been carried out from the anthropological perspective that has just been discussed and that pervades this book. Based on intensive fieldwork and impeccable scholarship, these studies permit us to see contemporary, non-Western religions in action. The summaries that follow can only hint at the richness and sensitivity of the original reports.

The Leacocks on the Batuque of Belém, Brazil

Seth and Ruth Leacock, who developed an intimate acquaintance with their subjects during two field trips covering a period of nine months, tell us that the Batuque is one of a large number of Afro-American religions, such as Cuban Santeria or Puerto Rican Espiritismo, that stress spirit possession. Their description of the historical context of the Belém Batuque includes a treatment of the importation and subsequent integration of African slaves into Brazil, a discussion of the region around the mouth of the Amazon (where Belém is located), and a search for the Batuque's African, Christian, and American religious roots. Their Batuque, like all Batuques, has taken on the coloration of a particular locale, which in this case is the Brazilian, urban, lower class. The Leacocks emphasize the poverty of the neighborhoods from which the Batuque draws its members. These people are nominally Catholics, but they do not usually attend church. Elements of Catholicism are mixed into the Batuque religion, however.

　　Batuque members believe in *encantados*, or spirits, who are thought to be capable of taking possession of the bodies of individual humans. When this happens, people take on the character of the spirit, whatever it is. If the spirit is an important one, the person in trance acts in a very serious, even pompous, manner; if the spirit is a known carouser, the person may act giddy and even drink beer or rum. Excepting the important fact of the ability to possess people, the *encantados* are not unlike Catholic saints in that they have supernatural qualities that can be tapped by people who develop a personal relationship with them. They require things of these people and will punish them if offended, but they also give supernatural assistance in, for example, maintaining family harmony, curing illnesses, or providing information. For Batuque believers, the *encantados* are thought to have a more specific, day-to-day interest in a person's life than the Catholic saints or God.

The Leacocks emphasize that the rituals of the Batuque are more loosely structured than those of more conservative cults like Xangô or Candomblé. The central ritual takes place in a *terreiro* or cult center, which is headed by a *mãe de santo* (mother) or *pai de santo* (father). The public ceremonies (which are directed by the *mãe* or *pai de santo*) involve, first, a prayer to Catholic saints, then a series of drum-accompanied songs and dances that "call on" and honor various *encantados* who are thought to reside above or under the earth. These spirits are believed to make their appearance as members of the company become possessed by them and take on their characteristics. In many ways a spectacle, the ceremony attracts large crowds who press against the railing of the *terreiro*. The spectacle is enhanced by the ornate clothing of the participants, the burning of gunpowder in bare hands, and the drumming, dancing, and singing that goes on long into the night. Another important activity involves consultations concerning personal problems, which are given by mediums during the public ceremony or at other times at their homes.

In Belém there are a number of mostly independent *terreiros*, each headed by a *mãe* or *pai de santo* who have a somewhat competitive relationship with each other. They do not have a great deal of power over their members, who generally tend to be poor, over thirty, female, and native to the city. Some of the members of a *terreiro* are mediums, who are capable of being possessed, and some are not. Among the mediums, there is a rank order leading up to the *mãe* or *pai de santo*. The Leacocks emphasize that trance-possession is learned, but that not everybody can learn it; and for those who do, some learn to "control" it better than others.

Spiro on Buddhism in Yeighi, Burma

The focal point of Spiro's investigation is a small agricultural village located not far from Mandalay in the heart of Burma (now Myanmar). The principal crop of the village of Yeighi is rice. Additional information was acquired in other agricultural villages, in Mandalay and some other cities, in other Buddhist countries such as Thailand, and through historic documents. Spiro generalizes widely from his Yeighi data because he found little variation in the essentials of the religion in space and time, but the people of Yeighi and their religion constitute the focus of his investigation.

The religion in question is Theravada Buddhism, which Spiro contrasts with the Mahayana Buddhism of northern and eastern Asia. Different aspects of Buddhist belief have been emphasized in different times and places. The history of Buddhism in Burma and recent historic developments that have affected it are considered. Spiro is careful to specify the sources of his data on current practices. In Yeighi, they come from questionnaires administered to almost every household, interviews with a "blue-ribbon panel" of fifteen religiously involved laymen and with monks in the local monasteries, and participant observation in and outside of the community.

In contrast to the Batuque, which does not stress this subject, Theravada Buddhism, like Christianity, is very much concerned with the matter of personal salvation, that is, the fate of the individual after death. In the Buddhist conception, such salvation is seen in a context of reincarnation, which involves a series of deaths and rebirths into different earthly existences until the individual ceases to exist. By following the teaching (*Dhamma*) of the Buddha, one of a number of supremely enlightened individuals who are thought to have released themselves from the "wheel of earthly existences," that is, reincarnation (each involving a life and death), a person is believed to be able to alter his or her fate and ultimately attain deliverance.

According to the Nibbanic version of Buddhism, the individual can attain deliverance through the practice of morality, charity, and meditation, which if carried out with the correct intention, can lead to a condition of mind oblivious to worldly desires. In Kammatic Buddhism, a more popular form of the religion, the aid is more proximate, that is, to improve one's worldly existence in subsequent births through the accumulation of merit in this life. Thus, a woman can hope that by accumulating merit she can be reborn as a man in this male-dominated culture. She might therefore make contributions to the construction of a pagoda. Both of these religious traditions emphasize that personal salvation is to be attained by the *unaided* effort of the devotee, the Buddha acting only as a model and message-giver. The other forms of Theravada Buddhism tend to be more this-worldly in their orientation and prone to beliefs in supernatural powers, which include gods (*devas*) and spirits (*nats*)—powers that an individual can relate to directly for this-worldly ends.

Just as the Buddhist belief system is more complex than the Batuque, so is its ritual. Spiro goes over the rich array of Theravada Buddhist ritual practices. He deals with such rituals as the Confession of Faith, the various rites connected with events in the Buddha's life, and the extremely important (in terms of gaining merit) initiation of a boy. He also speaks of cycles of rituals: the calendrical cycle (daily, weekly, monthly, annual), the life cycle (initiation, death), and crises of natural or supernatural origin. Rituals are performed in private and in public. They focus on the Buddha, his teaching, and the Buddhist monastic order (*Sangha*).

Monks teach and perform rituals that can help laymen, but more importantly, they conduct practices that will affect their own *karma*, a supernatural force for good or bad that is linked to one's present and past actions. A monk, in pursuing what appears to be a mostly selfish course, is conceived to be expressing the highest aspirations of his society, and it is by supporting and revering him that laymen can affect their own *karma* in a positive way. Monks at ordination take a vow of poverty, chastity, and homelessness, and they attempt to follow the monastic Rule, which stresses sexual abstinence, reverence for life, care about claiming the achievement of supernatural powers, and acceptance only of those things that are freely given. Violation of these and many other elements of the Rule require confession and either expulsion or an expiation ceremony.

Unlike the Batuque, which consists of largely independent cults, Theravada Buddhism has an elaborate organization that extends beyond the village. One can think of it, perhaps, as something like a loosely organized Catholic Church. At its heart is the monastery, which has a structure not unlike Western monasteries. The head of the monastery is under the loose jurisdiction of the district and national organizations of a branch, which, in turn, is linked with other branches in the Burmese order. Lay devotees (both men and women) cluster around monasteries, whose members are all male. Spiro notes that women demonstrate the most ceremonial devotion. He also points out the qualities of the male initiates into the monastery. They are mostly boys of rural origin who have received a religious education in a monastery rather than a secular education. They have come under the influence of a monastic teacher and are on the way to becoming what Spiro refers to as "world rejectors." The author speculates that they have strong dependency and narcissistic needs and that they are emotionally timid. The Burmese recognize that, with or without the aid of monastery life, only a few become *arahants*—people who are supposed to be delivered from the fetters of worldly existence and placed on the immediate path to *nirvana*, that ultimate state in which the individual ceases to exist.

The summaries just given are inevitably inadequate. They attempt to distill only the descriptive parts of two anthropological studies of religion (the authors' attempts at explanation and integration are barely touched on). Readers will have to read the books themselves in order to experience the religions in detail. But the summaries do give some idea of the kind of picture that anthropologists "take" of a religion and of the possibilities of comparing these pictures. The religions are practiced in different parts of the world and in different settings. One is a "great" codified religion of considerable complexity. The other is comparatively simple. They offer vastly different views of the world and how people should act in it. In Theravada Buddhism, the aim of most believers is to do better in one's next earthly existence. The ultimate goal, however, is to be done with all earthly existences altogether. Batuque members hope that their beliefs and practices will ameliorate a poverty-ridden existence in this life. What happens after that is not dwelt upon. Catholicism may serve as a kind of backup where serious matters of the afterlife are concerned. As in the case of belief, the ritual system of the Batuque is much less complex than that of Theravada Buddhism.

The authors of these two studies are acutely sensitive to, and properly respectful of the religions they have studied. They deal with these religions on their own terms, lacing their descriptions with quotations and observations that lend them a compelling personal immediacy not usually found in accounts by other scholars. They do not make any judgments about the "correctness" of the religions. That issue is beyond the scientific pale. Above all, they deal with religion as something that is lived: an aspect of human life practiced by flesh-and-blood people who arrange themselves in a certain way in a specific historic setting. Through a consideration of its believers, religion is made to come alive.

What now is to be done with descriptions such as these? A natural step is to compare the religions with each other in a fashion intimated earlier. Next, one might want to make comparisons with one's own religion. The inevitable result of this would be to erode culture-bound conceptions of religion. We come to see our religion (if we have one) as being more like this or that other religion and as located somewhere in a range of variability exhibited by all the religions of humankind. A further, more analytic procedure might be to search for the causes of differences and similarities between religions, in a manner discussed earlier in this chapter, and of their consequences.

THE CONSEQUENCES OF RELIGION

A religion is shaped and maintained by the conditions of life in some group or society. This is something that has come to be taken for granted in anthropology. However, religion can acquire the power to act back on those conditions through the actions of its believers. In Iran today, it is easy to see the power that a religion can have in shaping a society. Modern Iranian religious zealots, waiting for the return of the redeeming twelfth Imam, believe that their Shiite version of Islam has the power to transform them, their society, and the world. Even the United States, which has been considered by such Iranians to represent the interests of Satan, can be transformed. Whether we believe these people or not, we can recognize that they are offering us a particular view of religion's this-worldly consequences. And indeed, the social transformations that took place in Iran after the revolution against the Shah lend credence to their view.

What, then, does religion do for the individual and for society? Anthropologists have had their own views on this subject. Through their use of the concept of function, they have attempted to show that religion makes certain contributions to individual and social life. Thus, they have argued that the idea of an afterlife may make it easier for people to face death; the concept of the divine right of kings could contribute to a king's authority; a God-given value system, if shared by a community, could foster community solidarity; certain religiously based food taboos could promote adaptation to the environment; and malevolent supernaturals could serve as a safety valve for this-worldly hostilities.

A particularly interesting, if tricky, illustration of religion's alleged functions is found in studies that explore the relationship between religion and physical well-being. In a famous article on the concept of "Voodoo Death," Walter B. Cannon, a physiologist, has proposed the exact psychosomatic mechanisms whereby magically inspired fear could cause a person to die. His views (which have been disputed) are not the same as those of Haitian believers, but he agrees with them that death, in fact, is the result of the application of certain religious practices. On the brighter side, the role of religion in restoring or maintaining bodily health and emotional well-being has been claimed by believers, who postulate the operation of supernatural forces, and scientists, who think in terms of psychological processes. Thus Peter Stromberg's Swedish informants see themselves as better off because of God's will, while Stromberg himself sees them using religion's symbols to resolve personal conflict.

We know now that too many of religion's consequences have simply been assumed rather than demonstrated. Anthropologists should now realize that a religion may work in a variety of scientifically demonstrable ways for, or against the adaptation of individuals and societies. The manner in which it works and the people whose adaptation is affected have to be carefully specified. An example of this more sophisticated type of functional analysis is found in Spiro's discussion of the worldly consequences of Theravada Buddhist beliefs and practices. Spiro considers both psychological and social functions. Among the social consequences, according to Spiro, are two of an economic nature: (1) Buddhism's effect on the distribution of wealth in Burmese society, and (2) its effect on Burmese economic development.

In Yeighi and the rest of Burma, Spiro encountered a socially stratified society—some people are wealthy and a lot of people are poor. In our society, this state of affairs is something that is (at least publicly) lamented. Not so in Burma, where Buddhism provides a moral justification for social inequality. People believing in the Buddhist notion of karma would attribute their present economic situation to past actions in other lives. Spiro finds that this view is especially prevalent among the poor, and he speculates (in the manner of Swanson, who was mentioned earlier) that this leads them to accept a condition of economic deprivation. Because the poor tend to accept their situation and do not try to change it, and because the attitude that leads to this acceptance stems from its key beliefs, Buddhism, through its concept of *karma*, is seen by Spiro to function to conserve or maintain the system of social stratification in this society.

The Kammatic Buddhist variant, it will be recalled, stresses the concept of merit, which can be accumulated through such actions as religious giving. In Yeighi, Spiro says, approximately one-quarter of the income of a household is spent in religious giving, and the estimate is even higher for other villages in the area. The money is spent on such religious items as initiation ceremonies (a loose equivalent of the Jewish Bar Mitzvah), provisions for monks, pilgrimages, and construction and repair of pagodas. Because of this, a smaller proportion of the Burmese income is plowed back into productive economic operations such as agriculture or industry than in, say, present-day China. This means that whatever efforts the Burmese government makes in the direction of economic development will be hampered by the Buddhist belief in the possibility of accumulating merit in this life for a better existence next time around. Spiro, contrasting this with the Protestant Ethic in early industrial Europe and America (which emphasized economic productivity as a sign or means of salvation), concludes that Buddhism is, therefore, *dysfunctional* for Burmese economic development. Through its concept of merit (as well as *karma*), Buddhism is seen, rather, as functioning to maintain a less productive economic system.

Spiro also speculates on the uses of Buddhism for the maintenance of political power, but in the light of the brutally repressive actions of Myanmar's military rulers against Buddhist monks and their sympathizers, as well as other protestors, one has less confidence in his analysis. If these rulers deny Buddhist claims for political participation, how is it possible to see Buddhism as supporting political legitimacy? This shows how careful the anthropologists must be in developing functional explanations.

Functional analysis, which seeks explanations for actions in terms of their consequences, has been the subject of a good deal of recent criticism by anthropologists and others. This is in part due to certain assumptions of early functionalists who often seemed to be oblivious to the forces of social change, conflict, and fragmentation. The concept of dysfunction had to be coined to take into account the obvious fact that everything did not always work out for the best. But it is clearly evident that a religion does have consequences for the people who believe in and practice it, as well as for others. Functional analysis, if properly deployed and adequately demonstrated, can show how these consequences are brought about.

It may be possible now to recapitulate what has gone before in this chapter. Religion, here, has been taken as one example of human idea worlds in action. It has been conceived as a social institution that is based on certain ideas or beliefs in supernatural powers. Anthropologists have been concerned with describing the religions of humankind, and their studies have made us aware of the enormous variety of these religions. Besides describing, comparing, and ordering religions, anthropologists have also been concerned with finding their causes and consequences. In their studies, they have, knowingly or unknowingly, followed Paul Radin's dictum that religion comes from life and is directed to life, which is to say that it is part of some culture that guides people's actions.

WHAT TO BELIEVE?

As scientists, anthropologists cannot be advocates of a particular belief; nor can they provide the grounds for assessing the truthfulness or correctness of a belief. On the contrary, simply by describing the many religions of the world and their believers, an anthropologist may raise doubts about particular beliefs (Which one is the right one?). In a course in anthropology a student may find a heretofore unexamined world-view put into question. Faith can be shaken by encounters with other ways of thinking. The taken-for-granted quality of daily life in a stable society is something in which we have faith. When a famous religious formulator like Josephy Wovoka, a Paiute Indian of Nevada, developed a new formula for life that responded to the distress of his people following white domination, that formula was tried on, adjusted, and reiterated until it became a faith not only among the Paiutes, but also among neighboring Indian tribes (the Ghost Dance, one kind of "revitalization movement," discussed also in Chapter Nine). It was to continue as a faith until other views, derived from other conditions, acquired currency.

The conditions that are necessary to sustain faith are suggested almost daily by converts to certain American religious sects. Their relatives and friends, seeing strange things happening to the neophyte that have included suicide pacts, may begin to think that some kind of "brainwashing" is responsible, that is, that they are being manipulated by some "guru." As Anthony Wallace has pointed out in *Religion: An Anthropological View,* the acquisition and maintenance of belief in such situations is dependent on separation from nonbelievers who carry information that is irrelevant or contradictory to the faith in question. Within the new "cocoon," an initiate, who goes through an intensive learning experience, begins not only to see the world in a different way, but also to take the new way for granted. The intensity of initiates' new religious convictions will depend on their personal needs and the nature of the life they lead in their new religion.

Always there is the possibility of a lapse of faith, especially if outsiders (including possible counter-brainwashers) are able to impose their views on the devotee. This kind of thing, of course, could hardly occur in the archetypical primitive society where a routinized existence is not jeopardized by many contacts with others holding different beliefs. In the contemporary world, however, such an existence is not the norm. Social mobility and social differentiation encourage the development and confrontation of multiple points of view. Even in modern totalitarian societies such as Cuba, this condition exists, and the Cuban government has problems with those who may not put the ongoing revolution foremost in their minds. The possibility of acquiring and holding onto a deep set of religious convictions is much more difficult in such a society. People who feel upset when they encounter others—real people—who believe differently than they do, are experiencing something that comes naturally in a modern society: the fruits of a way of life in which there is more freedom, but in which faith—especially religious faith—is more difficult to acquire and maintain.

REFERENCE

BUCHER, BERNADETTE, *Descendants de Chouans: Histoire et Culture Populaire dans la Vendée Contemporaine*. Paris: Éditions de la Maison des Sciences de l'Homme, 1996.

CANNON, WALTER B., "Voodoo Death," *American Anthropologist*, 19, 1942, 169–81.

DURKHEIM, EMILE, *The Elementary Forms of the Religious Life*. Glencoe, IL: Free Press, 1947 (1915).

FREUD, SIGMUND, *Totem and Taboo*. New York: Vintage Books, 1952.

GEERTZ, CLIFFORD, *The Interpretation of Cultures*. New York: Basic Books, 1973.

———, "Religion as a Cultural System," in *Anthropological Approaches to the Study of Religion*, ed. M. Banton, pp. 1–46. New York: Praeger, 1966.

GILSENSEN, MICHAEL, *Saint and Safi in Modern Egypt: An Essay in the Sociology of Religion*. Oxford: The Clarendon Press, 1973.

HALLOWELL, A. IRVING, *Culture and Experience*. Philadelphia: University of Pennsylvania Press, 1955.

LEACOCK, SETH, and RUTH LEACOCK, *Spirits of the Deep*. Garden City, NY: Doubleday Natural History Press, 1972.

LEVI-STRAUSS, CLAUDE, *Totemism*. Boston: Beacon Press, 1963.

RADIN, PAUL, *Primitive Religion*. New York: Dover Publications, 1957.

SHWEDER, RICHARD, "Aspects of Cognition of Zincatecan Shamans: Experimental Results," in *Reader in Comparative Religion*, ed. W. Lessa and E. Vogt, pp. 402–12. New York: Harper and Row, 1972.

SPIRO, MELFORD, *Buddhism and Society*, 2nd ed. Berkeley: University of California Press, 1982.

STROMBERG, PETER, *Symbols of Community: The Cultural System of a Swedish Church*. Tucson: University of Arizona Press, 1986.

SWANSON, GUY, *The Birth of the Gods*. Ann Arbor: University of Michigan Press, 1960.

TURNER, VICTOR, *The Ritual Process*. Chicago: Aldine, 1969.

WALLACE, ANTHONY F.C., *Religion: An Anthropological View*. New York: Random House, 1966.

WEBER, MAX, *The Protestant Ethic and the Spirit of Capitalism*. New York: Scribner's, 1930.

Economies

OIKONOMOS

It has been said that the word *economics* is derived from the name of a steward of a noble household in ancient Athens. This man, a slave named Oikonomos, was responsible for provisioning the household. He decided what crops would be grown, what animals to raise, and what commodities to purchase. He made sure that equipment and labor were available to do all of this and he organized the work teams to do the various tasks. He was in charge of distributing what was bought and produced to household members. In discussions with the household head, it was decided how much to save and how much to sell. Every day he made adjustments to take advantage of current conditions. Those were his duties.

In effect, the steward (with or without consultation) was doing pretty much what an economy is supposed to do, that is, provide the things needed to satisfy whatever wants people have acquired. Because the satisfaction of one want may involve the frustration of another, and because the means to satisfy a given want are various, a number of choices have to be made. Economics attends to (among other things) the choices that people make in the course of providing for their wants.

IS THIS AN ECONOMY?

Anthropologists interested in economic life encounter the same kind of problem they face in studying any other aspect of culture. They begin with some notion of the subject, which is most likely derived from their own culture. Then, they find that some elements of that notion are not cross-culturally applicable. There follows a period of adjustment during which they work out a preliminary definition that will permit them to identify their subject in a variety of cultures. The science of economics grew up in the capitalist, market-oriented, money-using cultures of Europe and America. To what extent do such views on economies and how they operate apply to other cultures? Anthropologists interested in this aspect of culture are not in complete agreement. They have different approaches to the subject, and they are always revising their thinking in the light of new information. But it does seem possible to venture at least a rough, preliminary definition of the field of economic action that will be cross-culturally applicable.

Consider that an economy involves all those activities that relate to the satisfaction of a people's wants. Probably best thought of as a social process, it includes the production of exchangeable things (commodities), the transfer of the rights to these from one person to another (a change in ownership, for example), and their consumption or use. These activities constitute only a part of any culture, but they can be singled out for investigation. A person may be said to be acting economically (as opposed to, say, religiously) when playing any part in this economic process. Most economists would insist that economic actions involve "economizing," which means that people are trying to maximize their benefits and minimize the costs to themselves in a given situation. In other words, as an economist-colleague said to me, "they are trying to do the best they can with what they've got." The ways in which different peoples do this in working out the production, transfer, and utilization of commodities of various kinds are the subject of anthropological investigations of this aspect of culture.

To test the usefulness of this preliminary definition and show some of the problems of applying it cross-culturally, take two cases from very different cultures, each involving something that is potentially exchangeable.

The first case involves a typical small producer of premium wines on the Côte d'Or of Burgundy, France, a comparatively small, but well-known wine-producing area. Burgundians often idealize this figure even though the bulk of their wine production is handled by merchants (*negociants*) in town. This *vigneron*, who has become a familiar figure to me as a result of a number of field trips to the region, lives with his family in one of those villages and towns along the "Golden Slope" that have names that wine lovers may dream about. He inherited some of its immensely valuable land from his father, acquired a little more from relatives, and leases some more. Now he grows and attends to the famous and notoriously capricious *pinot noir* grapes, the equally famous *chardonnay,* and some *aligoté* in a number of parcels of land in several different locations that produce grapes ranging from the ordinary up to the highest and most expensive (*Grand Cru*) category. In all, he owns and leases perhaps twenty acres. Attention to soil, the vines, and the grapes is a year-round task, but there are surges of activity, especially at harvest time, when additional hands may be necessary. The grape-growing and winemaking work involves all of the members of his family and possibly a hired hand or two. Still more people (students, for example) are brought in for the harvest in September. A number of machines are used, such as a tractor and wine press, but on the whole, this tends to be a labor-intensive operation.

Throughout the year, this *vigneron* makes decisions, any one of which can have important consequences for him and his family. When and how to spray against insects and fungi? What to do about the possibility of hail, which can damage a crop irreparably? How many additional workers should he hire and when? Who among his neighbors should he cooperate with and how? Which vines to uproot and replant? When and how to prune, to thin, and weed? How and when to harvest his crop? Whether or not to buy a new machine that might help him to make better wine? And in the end he must decide what price to charge for the crop and the wine that comes out of it. Social and natural constraints guide him in making many of these decisions, of course, but ultimately all of these choices are his and he and his family must live with them.

Suppose that this is a year when the harvest is especially good, as, say, in 1995 or 1996. What is to be done with it? Should he sell his grapes to one of the *negociant* houses in town (which process most of the wine from the Côte d'Or and elsewhere in Burgundy and sometimes have substantial vineyard holdings), make them into wine, or choose some combination of these? Under certain circumstances, say, in a not-so-good year, selling the grapes or the young wine may be the best alternative. But 1995 and 1996 were very good vintages. The best alternative (granted adequate resources) would seem to be to keep most of the crop to himself, make his own wine, bottle it, and sell it to an ever-widening circle of clients who have been alerted to the goodness of these vintages by the media and word of mouth. This long and complicated process requires decisions all along the line that can affect the price he can command for his wine. In the cellar, fermentation, racking, aging in barrels, clarification, and filtering, all raise questions that each winemaker answers in his own way. By the time the wine is bottled many months after harvest, a series of problems, any one of which can affect the salebility of the wine, have had to be negotiated.

Meanwhile, there are the buyers near and far, the representatives of what has become a worldwide market, who establish the level of demand for his product. Good and not-so-good wines from this highly respected producing area seem to be always in demand, but if the *vigneron's* reputation is especially sound and the vintage outstanding, the pressure from buyers can be very great. The *vigneron* sells his wine to them at a price that he has worked out after considering a number of factors. What are the others charging? What was last year's price? What price did this year's nascent Burgundies command at the traditional auction for charity? And if, as in some years, there is reduced demand, how long should he wait before lowering the price, keeping the wine back for better times, or selling it to a *negociant* or some other buyer?

But this is an extraordinary vintage. The demand is so high that price is not the major concern. The principal problem may be to decide who will get what and how much. Loyal clients expect preferential treatment. They want more than their share of the best of the vintage. So not everyone is completely satisfied at the time of the sale when the rights to the wine pass from producer to distributors and then on to consumers who, themselves, must make a number of economic decisions about when to serve it, how much, in what circumstances, and so on.

The second case involves the San of southern Africa, who, before they settled down, practiced mainly a wandering, hunting and gathering way of life (some could be involved as laborers for agricultural peoples living nearby). Among the things they gathered were mongongo nuts, which they valued second only to hunted meat as a food. Mongongo trees are found in wild groves scattered over the territory in which the San then lived. In contrast to the situation on the Côte d'Or, where land is exclusively held by individuals or corporations, and where territorial disputes can be serious matters, mongongo groves were owned only in a loose way by people in a particular band. Everyone in a San band had the unquestioned right to gather nuts from their groves, but people from neighboring bands could usually gather there also if they asked permission. The anthropologist Richard Lee, whose book on one of the San groups (*The !Kung San*) is the principal source for this brief account, does not report any significant conflict over mongongo trees and their fruit.

Unlike the grapevines of the Côte d'Or, which require a great deal of human intervention, mongongo trees grow wild, and it is only in harvesting their fruit (and possibly while getting firewood or water) that humans have anything to do with them. The harvest commences in April when the nuts begin to fall to the ground and continues throughout the year until the nuts are used up or next year's fall occurs. Both men and women gather, but it should be kept in mind that men are mostly hunters and that unlike some other hunter-gatherers, children do comparatively little gathering. Sometimes, the gatherers eat part of their harvest on the spot before carrying the rest back to camp for eating and processing. The harvesters may fill several carrying bags or nets for their own and others' needs. Shortly after the mongongos fall, both the soft outside and the hard inside of the fruit are used; later, as the soft part deteriorates, only the hard nuts inside are of interest.

In their mongongo and other gathering activities, the San operate in terms of an order of food preferences, and in a given location they appear to eat their way down this scale, that is, they first gather the most valuable mongongos, then other less and less valuable plant foods. They also can be said to eat their way out of a given location, which is to say that they tend to gather from the closest trees first, the more distant later, and finally, when the distance becomes too great, they move camp and start the process over again. In all of this, the men, who are primarily hunters, stand ready to drop their gathering activities at the first sign of more valuable animal food. From this and other evidence provided by Lee, it is apparent that the San make a number of calculations or choices in their food-getting quests.

In a San camp, the mongongos are shared, processed (cooked, cracked), and eaten. A woman keeps a two- or three-day supply of nuts by the fire for her household. Visitors may be given some of these to eat on the spot. Quantities of nuts, processed or unprocessed, also are passed back and forth between relatives and neighbors on the basis of need and obligation. This sharing appears to follow well-defined, but generally unspoken rules. Few calculations appear to be involved in a particular exchange, which can sometimes involve a long delayed return. In some cases, the exchange may turn out to be balanced, as when two women pass approximately equivalent quantities of nuts back and forth over a period of time. In others, it may be unbalanced, as when children gather for their household without any expectation of an equivalent return, or old people take without having given.

Do the activities just described in the two examples constitute economic behavior? One involves what might be called a basic necessity (mongongo nuts), the other, a less essential item (wine). Some economists feel that only basic necessities like food, clothing, shelter, and tools should be the subject of economic analysis. Others favor including more and more things that include not only material goods, but also symbols (for example, magical spells, trademarks), as well as services, and anything else that people use to satisfy their wants. Again it should be recalled that a definition depends on the problem set and the theoretical approach used. Readers who are drawn into the field of economic anthropology will want to keep various definitional possibilities in mind, but in an exploratory chapter like this, it would seem best to adopt a more inclusive definition. From that point of view, which includes all the things produced for people's use, something like an economic process is identifiable in the San example as well as the one from Burgundy.

However, some cherished Western notions about economies still have to be excluded because they do not apply cross-culturally. If we were to consider them essential, comparative studies of economies would not progress very far. Consider, first, the idea of property. On the Côte d'Or, the conception of rights to things tends to confirm our taken-for-granted notion of private property. The *vigneron* is the proprietor or semi-proprietor of land, for example. But where mongongo groves and their fruit are concerned, the San can hardly be said to hold such a view. Second, while the Burgundians practice a familiar form of market exchange that involves an abstract, impersonal pricing mechanism, San exchanges, though they do involve shifting valuations of things, can hardly be described as price-dictated buying and selling. Their exchanges of mongongos and other foods are more like the practice of gift-giving between relatives in the United States. Uncle Joe gets a tie and will give something of approximately equivalent value in return. Cousin Florence receives something for her house and returns a gift that is in the same price range. Generally, no one quibbles and no one is left out. Unlike the Burgundians in their grape and wine dealings, the San seem to do little calculation about how much should be offered and returned. Valuations may have been worked out over time in familiar economic terms, but they have become customary and are not governed by whims or crass profit seeking. Finally, while the Burgundians use money in most of their economic activities, the San, in their aboriginal state, have very little to do with money. They do not calculate value in such terms and are not preoccupied with "making" it.

Some other taken-for-granted capitalist notions of economies may also have to be set aside if state-controlled economic systems (command economies), such as the ones that still exist at this writing in North Korea, China, and Cuba, are to be included within the scope of anthropological investigation. But enough has been considered here to show what has to be done conceptually in order to get started on comparative studies. Because some apparently ethnocentric notions about economies have failed an initial test of cross-cultural applicability, it seems wise to leave them out of a preliminary definition. What remains is to be found in both of the cases just presented. Among the San, and on the Côte d'Or, something with exchange or commodity value (wine and mongongos in this case) is created by human actions, that is, it is produced. Then, the rights to these commodities are transferred near or far in acts of exchange that involve "payment" for them. Through the system of transfer in a society, commodities are divided up and passed around. Finally, they are consumed or used (drunk or eaten here). That both peoples "economize" in some way is evident, but the kind of economizing that goes on may violate some Western notions of the term.

In the anthropological literature on economies, there is usually an unstated assumption that an economy is some kind of more or less integrated whole. What is produced, for example, is seen to be related to consumers' or users' wants; or the way in which commodities are divided up among people is related to how production is organized. It should almost go without saying that anthropologists tend to see an economy as a part of a broader culture and its setting. When investigating any aspect of the economic process, therefore, they usually have in the back of their minds some idea about the way in which it is related to that broader context. With all of this in mind, what do the different aspects of the economic process look like?

THE ECONOMIC PROCESS

Production

Human wants may not be infinite but they certainly exceed a person's capacity to satisfy them fully. Because of this, every society must make decisions about which of those wants will be satisfied, to what extent, and how. In working out their solutions to these problems, people will be constrained by their natural and human resources (what they've got). They cannot, for example, expect to kill a tiger with their bare hands, grow crops in the arctic, or produce modern technological miracles without specialized education. Working with what they've got, then, a people will develop more or less effective solutions to their provisioning problems. Whether conscious or not of the basic economic questions posed by the economist, a people must address them if they intend to provision themselves.

First, *what is to be produced*? With their labor humans produce a tremendous variety of things. A particular society may concentrate on certain things rather than others. Something like this was drummed into me in school by teachers who spoke of specific cities or places that were characteristically associated with the production of furniture, cereals, textiles, and so on. Anthropologists often have followed a similar path by classifying societies in terms of the ways they make a living. For example, a particular people is said to practice hunting (or fishing) and gathering, as with the San; horticulture like the Tiv; animal husbandry like the Basseri; construction like the high-steel-working Mohawk Indians, who have done a good deal of the steel work on American skyscrapers; manufacturing, as in the Ruhr area of Germany; mining, as in Wales; trading, as with the sixteenth-century Venetians; or service, as in the case of the twentieth-century insurance city of Hartford, Connecticut. Although any people will engage in a variety of productive activities, and though each usually has a considerable mix of products, it has been standard anthropological practice to refer to one kind of productive activity as their mode of subsistence. Among the earliest humans, the mode of subsistence was hunting and gathering. Now, this has all but disappeared among the peoples of the world, and manufacturing and service activities are preoccupying more and more of humankind.

Second, *how much is to be produced*? The significance of this question would not be lost on the peoples of the Sahel region of western Africa who have experienced famine, nor on economic planners who are trying to raise a country's Gross Domestic Product (GDP). For them, the answer to the question undoubtedly would be "more." On the other hand, the answer of some American farmers or Saudi Arabian oil producers, both of whom are sometimes threatened by surplus production, might well be "less." In both of these cases, the problem is to adjust production to wants or the prices that reflect the interaction of wants and goods available.

Finally, *how are things to be produced*? The necessary elements of any productive system are the natural resources, ideas, human labor, and materials (tools, machines, etc.) that are used in the production process—the so-called factors of production—and the social arrangement of people involved in it. What will be the social unit of, say, agricultural production? Will it be a family, as among the *vignerons* of the Côte d'Or, or a large, industrialized operation, as in the multinational IBM? Will it involve little division of labor or much? How will the labor be mobilized and applied to the task and with what material support? Will it be a labor-intensive operation with little material assistance or a capital-intensive operation with much assistance? And who will control the production process—kinship groups, religious organizations, the state, or private firms? Any people's productive system may be thought of as having addressed these kinds of questions in its own way.

To elaborate a bit, the *vignerons* of the Côte d'Or still tend to favor the household as the unit of production. There is a growing, but still modest, mechanization of activities. Some division of labor by age and sex is evident (for example, women and children do not usually drive tractors). Extra workers are hired in anticipation of surges of productive activity, and other specialists (for example, bottlers, brandy makers, and helicopter and airplane pilots who spray vines and "seed" clouds) may be brought in on occasion. In deciding how to carry out his grape-growing and wine-making operations, the *vigneron* may have to share some jealously guarded personal control with others, such as bankers (who lend money), government bureaucrats (who tax and regulate), and associations of fellow vignerons, merchants, and others who concern themselves with various aspects of the wine business.

Going beyond the mode of subsistence, anthropologists have classified productive operations in a number of additional ways. Sometimes the level of technology has been taken to be of critical importance, as with the tool and weapon "industries" of early human societies. Sometimes the tendency to rely on human labor (labor-intensive), as opposed to nonhuman factors such as machines or animals (capital-intensive), is singled out. The division of labor by sex, age, and other criteria has been a common method for differentiating economic systems and societies. Occasionally, the unit of production (whether household or factory, for example) comes to the fore. And finally, ownership and control of the means of production (for example, whether private or public) has been taken to be a distinguishing feature. Whatever the scheme used, it is a construct that derives not only from the qualities of the cultures being investigated, but also from the interest and point of view of the analyst. For example, an anthropologist interested in the consequences for economic development of following a capitalist or a socialist road, would probably concentrate on one aspect of the social relations involved, that is, ownership of the means of production (private in the case of capitalism and public with socialism), which is an important distinguishing feature of these two forms of economy.

Transfer

Anyone who has just bought a new car in the United States will appreciate the importance of this aspect of the economic process. They have figured out what kind of car they want and how much they are willing to pay for it. Then, they may have engaged in a sort of ritualistic haggling over this commodity with a series of more or less agreeable salespeople, during which the parties involved have tried to work out a price that is best for them (The maker of my car has tried to eliminate all such haggling, but it still goes on to some extent if one has a car to trade in.) Whether there is haggling or not, one party in the transfer operation hopes to buy cheap and the other to sell dear. What the selling price will eventually be depends on a number of factors, which may be worked out in the actual transaction or beforehand. The selling price, therefore, is a sign that indicates the value of the car and all the economic operations behind it. This is the market form of economic transfer in action. In real life, other factors may come into play, but in their ideal or typical form, exchange values are responsive to economic forces only.

To an individual raised in a culture where economic individualism and the market mechanism of exchange are taken for granted, it may be intriguing to find in the anthropological literature so many accounts of transfer transactions that do not conform to this norm. Some of the transactions seem to be irrational. One example is the *kula* exchange of the Trobriand and neighboring islanders of the southwestern Pacific, in which valuables (necklaces and armshells) that were never really used or permanently possessed passed between trading partners on the basis of strictly balanced reciprocity. Equally baffling were the potlatches of the Indians of the northwest coast of America in which huge quantities of goods that had been acquired were given away and even destroyed. Whatever was involved in these transactions, it was not like the buying and selling of automobiles in modern America.

A number of kinds of nonmarket transactions have been identified. All involve a transfer value that is fixed by decree, as in price fixing by the state, as in a socialist country like North Korea, or by social convention, as with the rate of giving and return of commodities among the San. In such transactions, the parties are usually freed from economic decision making because others have done it for them. The transactions range from centric, that is, focused on some person or group—to noncentric—as in one-on-one exchanges. In the ideal-typical hunting and gathering society, where exchanges are non-centric, a noncalculating, balanced reciprocity is supposed to prevail. The truth, however, is that there are numerous unbalanced transfers in such societies, as between parents and children and more and less mature adults. Moreover, as market economies penetrate the world of hunters and gatherers, their transfers—balanced and unbalanced—come to involve more calculations by the parties involved.

As the distance between producers and consumers increases, the transfer process tends to become more complex and the detachment of the parties from the basic facts of economic life tends to increase, as with present-day commodity exchanges where "mythologies" about the commodities involved (corn, for example) and their circulation are often generated. Among the San, most transactions take place between close acquaintances and involve a hands-on acquaintance with what is being transferred. On the Côte d'Or, the *vigneron* and some of his clients deal with each other on the basis of familiarity and may taste the wine together, but many *vignerons* have a substantial foreign clientele and are deeply involved in international trade where the gap between producer and consumer is filled with a series of intermediaries: brokers, merchants, exporters, transporters, and importers, each having their own notion of the excellence of the wine they are dealing with. Under such conditions, the complexities of the transfer process can be rather daunting to an investigator.

What kind of distribution or allocation results from certain kinds of transfers? In a fairly egalitarian society such as that of the aboriginal San, people's "incomes" will not differ greatly. On the other hand, in many contemporary societies, differences of income and wealth can be very great. In the United States in 1983, for example, the top 20 percent of the population received 59 percent of the income, while in El Salvador in 1974, the same top category of people received 66 percent of the income. Some people are concerned about such income inequities and are actively trying to do something about them, as for example, stockholders who try to stop what appear to be runaway salary increases of top management. A socialist activist, concerned about the maldistribution of income in the world today, may still get some inspiration from the slogan "From each according to his ability to each according to his needs." Whatever the practicality of this ideal, it addresses the question of the distribution of income, which is routinely considered by economists.

CONSUMPTION OR USE

At the end of the economic process, the various things produced by a people are applied to their wants. What kind of schemes do a people work out to satisfy these wants? When shoppers go to the supermarket with their shopping lists and only so much money, they have to make choices in terms of their priorities. They may decide to spend more on high-priority items or they may put off buying some things until later. All of these are well-known economic strategies. Sometimes goods or services may be used directly, as when the San eat mongongo nuts they have just gathered, when a handyman fixes some household appliance, or when a Tiv sacrifices an animal that was just received in exchange for something. Sometimes things are saved for later consumption or use, as when food is stored or when an excess worker is kept on the payroll for a later job. Sometimes goods are saved for later use in the production or transfer process, as with money that is reinvested in companies represented on the New York Stock Exchange, or to start up a new business. And sometimes ideas in the form of patents for a new machine are held back for later development.

On the social level, households are usually important consumption units. Each works out some arrangement for scheduling and apportioning its income. Since not everyone in the household is thought to have the same needs, the portions going to one or another member will vary. The very young and very old, for example, receive less food, and men tend to get more than women. But a particular scheme may not be properly adjusted to the needs of some household members. A consulting Western nutritionist, finding that children are undernourished and that adults are receiving more than is necessary for carrying on their daily activities, might want to make a recommendation to change the pattern of distribution. However, such a recommendation would have to contend with cultural practices in which some people (those responsible for distributing food) have more of a stake. There will be more or less acceptable courses of action to take under such circumstances, and an anthropologist might be able to suggest the most acceptable alternative.

What people want, and what others think they need, may be two different things. Do Americans *need* all of the hamburgers they eat that help to make them fatter and fatter and the big and powerful cars they drive that use up so much gasoline and pollute the atmosphere? Do the Trobrianders *need* all of the yams that they store for all to see until they finally rot? Do the Burmese *need* all of the pagodas that they have helped to erect in order to do better in the next life? A number of lists of peoples' survival needs have been offered by anthropologists and others, but human life everywhere involves cultural elaborations on such needs, whatever they are. Even in the most extreme circumstances, people don't just survive. Basic needs are everywhere socialized into culturally constituted wants, and it is with such wants that any analysis of consumption or use must begin. Here, anthropologists' ethnographic involvement in a culture stands them in good stead. Through such involvement, they hope to come to accept a people's wants and the ways in which they are willing to change them as given, not something to be judged good or bad by outside standards.

WHY ECONOMIES?

For purposes of study, analysts divide up economies into parts. However, it is important to remember that, as with cultures, the parts of an economy ought to be thought of as possibly related. Thus it would be reasonable to expect that the norms governing consumption in America are related in some way to the ways in which goods and services are produced and transferred. The nature of the relationships between the parts, and with the rest of a culture and its setting, must, of course, be determined by investigation. By establishing the nature of one of the interconnections bearing on an economy or any aspect of it, one would be able to begin to explain it.

Why are there economies? The answer should come immediately to one who has had only a little anthropology. Economies exist because peoples have wants that they try to satisfy. They do this through a social process involving the production, transfer, and consumption or use of things. Viewed in this way, economies are not unique to human beings. Other animals produce, transfer, and consume. In some cases, they also appear to be doing some calculating in the process (chimpanzees have been observed offering sexual favors in exchange for food, for example). Human economies, though, are overwhelmingly cultural in nature. Whether or not they are the most important aspect of a culture, as some believe, remains an open question. But an anthropologist would be seriously remiss not to give serious attention to this aspect of culture.

What are the factors responsible for the differences and similarities of the economies of different peoples? In what ways are the economies of the United States and China, for example, alike and unlike? As is the case with other aspects of culture, questions about the reasons for the cross-cultural variability of economies have proved to be scientifically fruitful. From the way economic actions have been treated in this chapter, it may seem that people are free to choose any economic arrangement they want. Putting economic questions in terms of choices or calculations is to some extent an artifact of the way economists think. From their perspective, there are never enough means to satisfy human wants, so choices (and sacrifices) must be made. But such choices are always limited or constrained by basic human needs and by the requirements of a culture, its setting, and its history. It is to such factors that anthropologists have tended to turn in attempting to explain why economies are the way they are.

One such explanation is to be found in Bernard Magubane's historical analysis (in *The Making of a Racist State*) of white supremicist South Africa. He argues that, after Europeans conquered the area in the late nineteenth century, foreign capital was employed to open up and maintain gold and diamond mining operations, which came to be crucial elements in the South African economy. The conquered black population provided a source of cheap labor in the mining operations. In the early stages of colonialism, these and other South African black workers went along with what the Europeans expected of them; but gradually they began to assert themselves against these expectations. Though employers did raise wages, improve working conditions, and grant some limited rights, they found it difficult to keep up with the wants and other aspirations of their workers. This was so because the employers were interested in making a profit, which depended to a considerable extent on cheap labor. Eventually, according to Magubane, the conflict between owners and workers, that is, in the social relations of production,— came to pervade all of South African society. Thus, Magubane explains the developing conflict in the South African economy, and in South Africa generally, in terms of a historical process that began more than a century ago. Needless to say, this analysis still has relevance today even after the advent of a government that stands for the equality of all races.

In referring to the ways in which South Africa came to be dominated from the outside through the process of colonialism or imperialism, Magubane also shows how the social setting of a culture can be used to explain its economy. Natural settings have also been used to account for the character of economic systems, especially when they have only simple technologies. Americans with their use of machine technology have managed to make themselves more independent of their natural environment; but hunters and gatherers, who do not have an elaborate machine technology to help them, are much more dependent on natural conditions. Their economies, therefore, are more likely to reflect those conditions. One indication of this is the tendency among hunters and gatherers for the size of animal and human groupings to be associated. Where animals exist in large herds, as did the bison of the Great Plains of the United States in the nineteenth century, larger groups of hunters ensure greater success; but because animals that exist singly or in small groups cannot be followed profitably by larger groups of hunters, as was the case among Canadian Indian forest dwellers in winter, smaller human groupings were the adaptive response. A similar principle appears to apply to gathering activities as well. The Shoshone Indians of the western United States tended to concentrate in larger groupings when and where piñon nuts were available. During the remainder of the year, they scattered into smaller bands, sometimes consisting only of single families.

Other aspects of culture (economic and noneconomic) may be used to explain why certain economic practices prevail. For example, the oft-noted association between complexity of technology and division of labor has been explained in terms of the technical requirements involved. As technology becomes more complex, increasing numbers of specialists are needed to handle a productive operation. Thus, the Côte d'Or *vigneron* of today, confronted by increasingly complex technical operations in all areas, comes to realize that he can't do it all and resorts to laboratory specialists to analyze his wine, meteorologists to predict weather, soil analysts to check the quality of his soil, plant specialists to predict problems in vine development, helicopter pilots to spray, and accountants to go over his records.

Some think that advancing technology will reduce labor time. As machines become more powerful and efficient, people will have to labor less. For example, by using a tractor and attachments, *vignerons* can now do vineyard work in a fraction of the time it once took with a horse or by hand.

However, this commonsense notion receives a rude jolt from our knowledge of the aboriginal San, among whom the working day, according to Lee, was six hours on the average. The advance of machines in Europe and America, though it has sometimes been associated with a reduced workload in and outside of the home, has nowhere produced so much leisure time.

In the discussion of economic transfer earlier in this chapter, the issue of the distance between exchange partners was raised. Does the nature of exchange vary with the (geographic or social) distance between the partners involved? Marshall Sahlins (in "On the Sociology of Primitive Exchange") has arranged transfer transactions between parties on a continuum extending from a "solidary" extreme, in which people do not expect to gain at each others' expense, to an "unsociable" extreme, where each party seeks to maximize their own gain at the expense of the others. He goes on to show that the character of a transaction tends to be associated with kinship distance, social rank, and a number of other factors. Considering kinship distance, he argues that people who think of themselves as closely related are less likely to take advantage of each other in an economic transaction (toward the solidary extreme). Parents and children who love each other unconditionally would most likely operate in the same way. At the other extreme is a French butcher I knew who, having been informed by his wife at the cash drawer that he had overcharged a customer he barely knew, comments, *"Tant pis pour elle"* ("Too bad for her").

Frederick Pryor (in *The Origins of the Economy*) pursues this same line of thought in his analysis of the conditions that lead to the emergence of market transactions and the use of money (practices that approach Sahlins' "unsociable" extreme). Pryor argues that such economic practices tend to come about as economic systems (and societies) become more complex. An agricultural people, with their generally more complex technology and division of labor, therefore, would be more likely to engage in market transactions involving money than would a hunting and gathering people. Using a cross-cultural sample confined to preindustrial societies from around the world, Pryor shows that this is indeed so, and he goes on to demonstrate that market exchanges in goods, credit, land, and labor emerge at different levels of economic complexity. His impressive study, which also considers other factors, is particularly important because it puts to rest much of the theoretical speculation about this aspect of economic life. Still further questions await this kind of treatment, such as the notion that people involved in more complex economic systems, because they lack direct or personal experience with the commodities, people, and operations involved in them, have a greater tendency to develop what might be called a "mythology" of commodities. A Wall Street trader, for example, may begin to take rumors as facts, or a wine merchant may formulate a wildly enthusiastic advertisement on the basis of a taste-test of one barrel by a friend visiting Burgundy.

CASE STUDIES

An Analysis of Production:
Scott Cook on the Brickmakers of Santa Lucia del Camino

As part of his interest in small-scale, nonfactory forms of industry, Scott Cook, an economic anthropologist specializing in Latin America and other developing countries, turns his attention in *Peasant Capitalist Industry: Piecework and Enterprise in a Southern Mexican Brickyard* to the brickyards of a small community, Santa Lucia del Camino, on the fringes of the city of Oaxaca in southern Mexico. Once primarily agricultural, the people of this community now lean toward brickmaking and other nonagricultural pursuits that are increasingly dependent on an urban market. At the time of Cook's study in the mid-1980s, approximately one-half of the households in Santa Lucia had one or more members working in the brick industry.

Cook begins his analysis by laying out the setting and history of the brick industry in the Oaxaca valley. He describes a landscape pitted with clay pits that produce the raw material for bricks. The proximity of Oaxaca, with its demand for bricks and other commodities produced in the hinterland, is emphasized. The outreach of a centralized government, which regulates, taxes, and plans the nature of Mexican development, and of large-scale private enterprise, such as the construction industry in Oaxaca and elsewhere in Mexico and beyond, are seen to have a strong influence on the brickmakers and their work. In addition, the local brick industry, which had experienced a surge of development since the late 1930s (when people began to build with brick instead of adobe), is described. Cook locates this small-scale Mexican industry in a global context of capitalist industrialization.

Brick producing in Santa Lucia is carried out in small enterprises headed by a man (a *patron* or *dueño*) who owns or rents a brickyard. Usually, he has not come into brick production by inheritance, but from some other line of work such as agriculture. He employs members of his family, hired workers (*mileros*), or both. Hired workers are paid mostly on a piecework basis, that is, according to the number of bricks they produce. Most of these workers originate from outside of the community. In his analysis of this productive system, Cook concentrates on the hired, pieceworking *mileros*, their employers, and the social relations between them (that is, on the social relations of production).

The brickmaking process, which begins with the digging of clay soil and ends with the delivery of finished, kiln-fired bricks, is described in detail. For example, the actual making of bricks, the most demanding and time-consuming phase of the production process, is done by individuals who mold clay into bricks for sun-drying and, eventually, kiln-firing. The description of this and other phases of the production process is enhanced by comments from worker informants and detailed observational studies similar to those carried out by American efficiency experts.

The calculations of the principal actors in this economic system, which produces several hundred thousand bricks per month, receive extended treatment by Cook. The typical *patron* buys or rents a piece of land and turns it into a brickyard. The heavy start-up costs for land, buildings, equipment, and possibly a truck are paid for with capital acquired from patrilineally related relatives and on his own. There are operating costs (for example, fuel for the kiln, gasoline for the truck) and costs associated with the replacement of equipment (shovels, buckets, molds, etc.). But the greatest cost in this labor-intensive operation is for labor, much of which is done by *mileros* who are in short supply. Employers, their families, and the families of *mileros* are also active in brickmaking operations. The employer tends to deal with those who work for him in a paternalistic way. He is viewed by the workers as a father figure and his actions are usually consistent with such a role.

Mileros are paid by the piece (in this case, by the brick) instead of by the hour or day. By this system, the members of a worker's family can contribute to his output without, themselves, being compensated. Thus a *milero's* wage may reflect not only the worker's own labor, but also the labor of the worker's family. What that wage will be depends on the demand for bricks, the employer's short- and long-range costs, and the number of workers in the area. Cook shows how the piecework rate is adjusted by employers to meet current conditions, compares it with a rate based on time, and describes the sometimes intricate give-and-take between *patrons* and *mileros* in regard to wages. In this exchange, which follows the market form, both employers and workers try to do the best they can within the framework of an emerging capitalist system of production. Although each has their own interests, both the *patrons* and the *mileros* are committed to this system and to a paternalistic form of relationship. The kind of conflict that is found in larger enterprises in the city, where unions strike and people may talk of revolution, does not exist here.

Cook takes issue with those who see this small-scale, labor-intensive form of production as an inefficient and regressive way of satisfying the wants of a developing society. He argues that the capitalist-dominated setting has a variety of market niches, not all of which must function according to the principle of economy of scale (lowering unit cost by increasing the size of an operation). There is a place for artisinal or petty-commodity production such as that practiced by the Mexican brickmakers and the *vignerons* of the Côte d'Or. According to Cook, economic planners with their grand designs based on the principle of economy of scale would do well not to lose track of the value of small-scale productive operations in what is a complex economic setting. They also should not lose sight of the human beings who make any economic system work. Cook, though he is fully aware of the issues that preoccupy Western economic planners and of the science of economic behavior that guides them, brings real human beings into the picture. These people are dealt with sympathetically and respectfully, and the job they are doing is taken seriously. That they come across mostly as economic creatures, without the other human dimensions traditionally treated in an ethnography, can be excused in light of the depths he has plumbed in order to explore one important aspect of their culture.

This brief summary hardly does justice to Scott Cook's sensitive and sophisticated treatment of the brickmaking operations in Santa Lucia del Camino, but it provides something to build on. With an understanding of this particular culture and some of the reasons why it is as it is, an anthropologist might heed the call to compare. Cook attempts to do some of this by pointing to other kinds of small-scale production in the developing world. Perhaps readers of this chapter have already begun to make some comparisons of their own—with some small, family-based enterprise that they know of, or with the *vignerons* of the Côte d'Or discussed earlier. The *vigneron* may also be considered a kind of peasant capitalist, but with a "luxury" product and a different clientele of consumers or users. What are the various similarities and differences that exist between the *vigneron's* system of production and that of the brickmakers, and how might one explain them? The search for answers to such questions would seem to follow naturally from an interest generated by Cook's work and the work of other economic anthropologists who have concerned themselves with comparing economic systems.

Allen Johnson on Time Use among the Machchiguenga

As Cook's study shows, assessment of the amount of time people use in their daily activities can be an important tool of economic analysis. In American society, where people may say that "time is money," an efficient use of time and other resources is thought to be essential for the success of a business enterprise. In his study, "In Search of the Affluent Society," Allen Johnson, an anthropologist with extensive experience in Latin America, deals with the subject of time use among the Machchiguenga, an Indian people who live in small villages scattered around the Amazonian rain forest of Peru. They are hunters, fishers, and gatherers, and they also practice horticulture in gardens they have cleared in the forest. Every five to ten years, as these gardens give up their fertility, the people move to another part of the forest, where they cut and burn out a new section for planting their crops. Johnson points out that the Machchiguenga do not have much in the way of material goods, but they have many other qualities that people in industrialized societies might value. They are honest, peaceable, warm, of good humor, and relatively content with their existence. In short, like the San, these "primitives" have created a culture about which there is much to admire.

Allen Johnson and his wife studied these people during several field trips for eighteen months in all. One thing of special interest to them is how the Machchiguenga use their time. In order to analyze this, Johnson divides up the day into production time, which includes all forms of work; consumption time, which refers to the time spent in using goods and services; and free time, which includes such things as sleeping, resting, playing, conversing, and visiting. His records thus document the amount of time these people spend in each activity. An extremely interesting fact emerges from this investigation: The Machchiguenga spend more time in activities classified as "free" than in producing or consuming. On the average, they spend more than fourteen hours per day in this type of activity.

Next, referring to data gathered in France, Johnson compares Machchiguenga time use with that of a sample of urban, middle-class French adults. He breaks these down by gender and by whether a person works inside or outside of the home. This is particularly important because productive activities in the home, often accomplished by women, are sometimes ignored in analyzing systems of production. Johnson's comparison of the two peoples produces some intriguing results. He reports that French men and women spend more time in producing and consuming than do the Machchiguenga, with the difference being particularly marked in the area of consumption. In both cultures, women tend to spend more time in production than men, while Johnson notes that French housewives are noteworthy for the great amount of time they spend working around the home. In effect, they maintain produced goods by performing such tasks as cleaning house and doing laundry.

The study of another people may make some anthropologists more critical of their home society. So it was with Allen Johnson. After spending time with the Machchiguenga, he and his wife became more critical of industrialized cultures such as France and the United States. He notes that, when people produce a lot, they also devote a great deal of time to maintaining and consuming what they have produced. This is why industrialization does not necessarily result in more leisure time. The more people produce, the more they must maintain and consume, and the less time there is for leisure. Time in such cultures thus becomes scarce and, therefore, more valuable—a precondition, perhaps, for the emergence of the slogan "time is money."

One should be cautious with Johnson's remarks, however. First, he does not measure the character of work of the people under study (whether it is hard or easy to accomplish, for example). Second, he speaks only of the Machchiguenga. On the basis of this study (as of the San who have often been mentioned in this book) one cannot say that, in their "undeveloped" condition, the so-called primitives of this world have had an easier (and therefore possibly better) life. Remember the hard-pressed Shoshone, mentioned earlier in Chapter Four, as only one of a number of counterexamples that may be cited. But the suggestion by Johnson that production may shape consumption, as well as the reverse, is a valuable one. In the United States, for example, producers, driven by a profit motive, are constantly pushing consumers to expand their wants. So, a glass of water is replaced by a can—or two cans—of soda pop; and one car is replaced by two or more. But can this kind of thing go on indefinitely? Obviously, there are limits to economic growth. Moreover, as we have just seen, growing economies such as those of the United States and France are not necessarily better ones. Such observations, which undermine the cultural ground on which most of us stand, seem to flow naturally from this particular anthropological investigation.

THE BOTTOM LINE

Every society attempts to satisfy culturally generated wants. The process by which a society does this involves the production of commodities, the transfer of the rights to these, and their utilization. This process constitutes the economy of the society. Economic science, which was traditionally preoccupied with the market-oriented, capitalist economies of the West, has had to expand and adjust in order to take into account not only the command economies of socialism, but also the economies of the peoples traditionally studied by anthropologists. In this chapter, the minimum prerequisites for any economy have been discussed. Seen from the anthropological viewpoint, an economy is an aspect of a way of life of a people, that is, a part of a culture and its setting. Additionally, the anthropologist tends to see an economy as involving flesh-and-blood human beings who create and maintain it and who act in ways that add up to the graphs and charts that have become an intrinsic part of standard economic analysis.

Like all aspects of a culture, economic norms acquire a hold over a people and shape their lives. As a result, they tend to produce, transfer, and consume in patterned ways; and in turn, they are affected by economic arrangements. Vocationally oriented college students probably don't have to be convinced of this, nor would Americans who went through the Great Depression of the 1930s or who are currently the subjects of "pink slips" that result from the downsizing of corporations. But the manner in which economic actions affect other actions, economic or noneconomic, needs to be explored. In anthropology, one encounters many statements about the collective or individual consequences of certain economic arrangements. Thus, wife exchange between different kinship groups has been seen to create a greater feeling of solidarity between them. Or private property is viewed as cutting people off from one another. But if these are accurate statements of the facts, how do these things come about? How do such economic arrangements actually shape or socialize people?

Consider only one aspect of an economy: the work that people do. How does their work shape a people's behavior? One can see this happening through the process of socialization. First, on the job, workers are socialized through direct participation in a particular form of work. Thus, as they perform their duties, American nurses learn to defer to higher-ranking doctors.

Second, there is anticipatory socialization: a worker-to-be is socialized in a way that is consistent with certain jobs. Thus, in some American schools of nursing, student nurses have been schooled in the art of deference to authority figures like doctors and of indirection in getting their way (habits are changing, as nurses are allowed—even expected—to be more assertive). In this respect, the economy may be seen as shaping a person's behavior through its work roles.

In a well-known, cross-cultural study that has stood the test of time, Herbert Barry, III, Irving Child, and Margaret Bacon (in "Relations of Child Training to Subsistence Economy") note that, in over one hundred preindustrial societies around the world, there is an association between mode of subsistence and the way in which children are socialized. Specifically, agricultural and herding people, who have a longer-run investment in food production, tend to put an emphasis on compliance in their socialization practices. On the other hand, hunters, fishers, and gatherers, with shorter-term strategies for producing food, tend to put greater stress on self-assertion. Although there is a dispute about the exact mechanisms involved, it does seem that, for those people studied, the work orientation of adults is being carried through into the socialization of their children.

This tendency has been very apparent to me in my explorations on the Côte d'Or, where the work patterns of the *vigneron* pervade all aspects of family life, and where family members and other workers have acquired the dispositions that go with them. Thus, the nurturing side of the typical homemaker comes to the fore in taking care of her family and permanent workers, the harvesters who show up in late September, and even with small operations on the vines such as suckering (removing small shoots from trunks). Such an association is found also in the much more complex United States where, as Daniel Miller and Guy Swanson have demonstrated (in *The Changing American Parent),* children of bureaucrats who work in large organizations tend to be raised differently than those of entrepreneurs who work in small ones, and the different modes of socialization are consistent with the kind of work involved in each form of productive enterprise. For example, children of entrepreneurs tend to be raised to show more initiative, which is favored in such work.

In simpler, more tradition-bound societies, there should be fewer problems in knowing what work to do and how to do it. That is what Krishna, the Indian charioteer (God in an earthly disguise) tries to tell the warrior Arjuna just before a battle involving kinsmen in *The Bhagavad Gita.* Krishna points out that strictly personal inclinations are irrelevant in such a situation and that Arjuna should do what his caste position requires him to do. Arjuna is of the warrior caste, which means he must fight. In more complex societies such as the United States, where questioning is the order of the day, such advice would seem to be less appropriate. How is one to know what to do in life in a society where the winds of socialization blow from many different directions? Though economic and other forces do act through socialization to constrain their lives, people in complex societies have opportunities for personal choice that do not exist elsewhere. The kind of work one is to do and the person one is to become has to be achieved in confusing and sometimes difficult circumstances. People have to find jobs, which, if they exist, will be more or less compatible with their talents and interests. The fortunate ones will find some productive niche in the economy that suits them. Others will spend their lives looking for something more desirable or be turned out as the result of some corporate restructuring or lack of qualification. Still others may find few opportunities for employment and sink into despair.

If any of these people have read only a little anthropology and kept up on current events, they should have come to understand that an economy, like any aspect of culture, is a human creation that works better or worse for its creators and their descendants. If an economy is to survive, it must successfully answer the economic questions that Oikonomos is said to have dealt with. In keeping with the American expression about the absence of free lunches, one should never expect to find an economy somewhere without problems. For example, the market-driven, capitalist systems that have come to the fore in today's world are not without problems of distribution. In them income inequality is an endemic problem. Of course, poverty has existed among other peoples with other economic arrangements, but for mainstream Americans the problem is compounded because of their expectations to the contrary. Deep down, there is a tendency among these Americans to think that if only people apply themselves they will do better.

A glance over the anthropological record will show that there have been peoples such as the aboriginal San who have pretty much solved the problem of income inequality. But the ways in which they did so, while appropriate to a small-scale, low-tech, hunting and gathering existence, are not for people in the contemporary Western world. Command economies, such as those that existed until recently in communist Eastern Europe and that still exist in a few other places, seem not to have worked. What about continuing capitalist ways, but with more government involvement, such as exist in Scandinavia? There are problems there too, as moderate socialist utopianists have found, perhaps on a visit to one of the Scandinavian countries. Is it possible to do better by decreasing whatever governmental involvement now exists, as some people in the United States are now advocating? Mention of the Great Depression, which occurred after a period of comparatively free economic enterprise, should give one pause in this regard.

But if one is convinced that a society can do better in addressing an economic problem, it would seem advisable to approach it not only with an awareness of the range of economic alternatives available, but also with an understanding of how each alternative has fared in the societies of humankind. From what has been said in this chapter, it should be clear that an economic problem cannot be dealt with on economic grounds alone. After describing the nature and extent of such a problem, the anthropologist would likely want to know about the culture in which the economy operates and its values. For the ancient Greek household mentioned at the beginning of the chapter that would be a comparatively easy job. Going beyond that household, the task would become more difficult. And for a society in today's complex, changing, globalizing world, it would be a very difficult task indeed. It might be best, therefore, to begin with the essentials of any human economy that have been discussed in this chapter.

SELECTED REFERENCES

BARRY, HERBERT, III, IRVING CHILD, and MARGARET BACON, "Relations of Child Training to Subsistence Economy," *American Anthropologist,* 61 (February), 1959, 51–63.

BLANTON, RICHARD, PETER PEREGRINE, DEBORAH WINSLOW, and THOMAS HALL, eds., *Economic Analysis Beyond the Local System.* London and Lanham, MD: University Press of America, 1997.

CHAPUIS, LOUIS, *Vigneron en Bourgogne.* Paris: Éditions Laffont, 1980.

COATES, CLIVE, *Côte d'Or.* Berkeley: University of California Press, 1997.

COOK, SCOTT, *Peasant Capitalist Industry: Piecework and Enterprise in a Southern Mexican Brickyard.* New York: University Press of America, 1985.

GALBRAITH, JOHN, *The Good Society.* Boston: Houghton Mifflin, 1996.

HEILBRONER, ROBERT L., and LESTER C. THUROW, *The Economic Problem,* 7th ed. Englewood Cliffs, NJ: Prentice Hall, 1984.

JOHNSON, ALLEN, "In Search of the Affluent Society," *Human Nature,* 9, (September), 1978, 51–59.

LEE, RICHARD B., *The !Kung San.* Cambridge: Cambridge University Press, 1979.

MAGUBANE, BERNARD, *The Making of a Racist State: British Imperialism and the Union of South Africa, 1875–1910.* Trenton, NJ: Africa World Press, 1996.

MILLER, DANIEL R., and GUY E. SWANSON, *The Changing American Parent.* New York: John Wiley, 1958.

PLATTNER, STUART, ed., *Economic Anthropology.* Stanford, CA: Stanford University Press, 1989.

PRYOR, FREDERICK, *The Origins of the Economy.* New York: Academic Press, 1977.

SAHLINS, MARSHALL, "On the Sociology of Primitive Exchange," in *The Relevance of Models for Social Anthropology,* ed. M. Banton, pp. 139–236. London: Tavistock, 1965.

The Developing World

A PERSONAL TRAGEDY

In *Salvador Witness*, Ana Carrigan describes the American Jean Donovan as a brash but vulnerable young woman. Donovan grew up in Connecticut in the 1950s and 60s, went to college, and found a respectable job in an advertising agency. She had good friends and marriage prospects. Somehow these were not enough, and at the age of twenty-six she put them aside to become a Catholic lay missionary. Sent to El Salvador, she became involved in work with the poor and with the network of Basic Christian Communities there. Archbishop Oscar Romero, an outspoken critic of social injustice and the outrages of the Salvadoran army and its associated death squads, became her idol. The biographer reports that Jean Donovan was transformed by her experience in El Salvador. Originally a naive political conservative, she came to believe that the problems of the Salvadoran poor were somehow tied up with U.S. policies toward that country. She and her mission associates, including lay-workers and nuns, began to be viewed as subversives by some members of the establishment. They lived in an atmosphere of danger. Despite this, and despite pleas by family and friends that she leave El Salvador, Donovan remained. With her associates, she continued to help the victims of a growing civil war and to propagate the faith. Eventually, she and three woman associates were abducted, raped, and murdered. Their bodies were found shortly afterward in a hastily dug grave. Efforts to find and punish those responsible have been only partially successful.

THE SPECIFIC CONTEXT:
EL SALVADOR AND THE UNITED STATES

The personal tragedy of Jean Donovan occurred at a significant point in the history of El Salvador and its relationship with the United States. At the time she entered the country, revolutionaries were beginning to have some success in their drive against the established powers. While countering the guerrillas with aid from the United States, the government had also, at the insistence of North Americans, undertaken some social reforms such as land redistribution. However, El Salvador's problems were so enormous and entrenched interests so resistant that doubts were raised about whether such reforms would proceed fast enough and far enough to mitigate the many social problems that existed.

In the early 1980s, El Salvador was a poor country with an economy based primarily on agriculture (mainly coffee, cotton, and sugar cane). Economic growth, which had been substantial for more than a quarter of a century, had at that time begun to stagnate and even decline. This made the condition of the country's vast mass of poor, who were mostly Indians, even worse. In contrast, the small group of European-derived elites (the so-called "Fourteen Families"), who had accumulated huge fortunes in agriculture and other sectors over the years, suffered only slightly, if at all. A small but growing middle class also suffered, but not to the extent of the poor, who usually bore the brunt of any economic downturn.

El Salvador was ruled by what amounted to an oligarchy, an alliance of large landholders, business interests, and an army that kept the government in line, a not infrequent political arrangement in the developing world. The Roman Catholic Church, which also had been a full-fledged partner in this alliance, had begun to split into factions, one of which became especially concerned with the plight of the poor. The most significant spokesperson for this group was Archbishop Oscar Romero, who was later assassinated. Members of this faction spoke of "structural injustice,"—that is, the exploitation of the poor and weak by the rich and powerful—and they implicated outside powers such as the United States (often seen as supporting the rich and powerful) in this. They worked through Basic Christian Communities, small groups with a great deal of lay participation, in opposing such injustice and working for a more just society.

The United States had been the dominant power in Central American affairs since early in the century, when it had supplanted Great Britain as the principal outside influence. With strategic interests centering on the Panama Canal, and business interests such as those of the United Fruit Company, the

United States was concerned with keeping the area tranquil and secure. To that end, it tended to side with governments in power no matter how repressive or exploitative they were. It intervened directly or indirectly from time to time to maintain these governments and to prevent potentially hostile takeovers. It had toppled one regime in Guatemala, and at the time of the Jean Donovan tragedy the U.S. government was on the way to bringing down the socialist revolutionary government of Nicaragua. For El Salvador, the U.S. government had two goals: social reform and pacification. The guerrillas were to be defeated and their support dried up. Without the accomplishment of these goals, according to one government adviser, it would be impossible for (capitalist) development to proceed normally and for all Salvadorans to benefit. This was the official American view. It was implemented through economic and military aid to the Salvadoran government and its armed forces. American capital was also directly or indirectly involved in various economic undertakings.

But a number of Americans, as well as many Salvadorans, were not happy with what was going on in El Salvador and its neighbors. The country seemed to be a long way from pacification. Indeed, despite a continuing military campaign and other repressions, more and more people joined the rebels who had achieved *de facto* control of important territory and dealt with the government almost as if they were a separate state. The inability of the civilian government to control the military, paramilitary groups, and the police, and the slow pace of social reforms led to the departure of one outspokenly critical American ambassador. Other Catholic missionaries besides Jean Donovan began to share the views of Archbishop Romero that American economic and military intervention, no matter how well intended, was doing more harm than good and was, in fact, contributing to the "sinful" structural injustice in the country. In the United States there were increasing doubts not only about the morality, but also the wisdom of U.S. policies in Central America, which tended to take the form of overt and covert support of the status quo, public condemnation of the excesses of those in power, and what amounted to token support for democratization. For El Salvador, in particular, this policy became more and more unacceptable to Americans, and calls for cutting off all foreign aid to the country were heard more and more frequently.

So rapid is the pace of change in the world today that anthropologists' descriptions of cultures may become outdated even as they write them. Speeded by the decline of the Soviet Union and the drying up of its support for revolutionary movements in developing countries like El Salvador, as well as the emergence of a more pragmatic American policy, a United Nations' brokered compromise between the government and the rebels was reached in January 1992. This compromise, which included significant social and military reforms and eventual internationally monitored elections, seems to have put El Salvador on a new course. In the second election since the agreement, the former rebels more than doubled their representation in the Salvadoran Congress and have achieved virtual parity with the governing party there. With the government of the United States having given its blessing to the election results, one is entitled to the belief that El Salvador is on a new course. Major problems, of course, lie ahead. The "structural injustice" involving various social inequalities that Jean Donovan had worked against has not disappeared. In what may be a mixed blessing, economic aid from the United States has declined dramatically. But the fact that the electoral process in which the former rebels have made significant gains has replaced a vicious civil war and that the United States has given it its full support is news indeed. Other developments in Central America (in Guatemala and Nicaragua, for example) seem to be following the same course.

THE BROADER CONTEXT:
THE DEVELOPING WORLD

El Salvador at the time of the Jean Donovan tragedy could be considered a part of the Developing World (sometimes referred to as the Third World), a world very familiar to anthropologists, who have often "caught" (during their fieldwork) some tribal or peasant society in the grip of rapid developmental change. There are huge cities in some developing countries, such as Kuala Lumpur in Malaysia and Cairo in Egypt, but the typical community still is more likely to be a small one in which direct, personal relationships tend to prevail, and people in the cities, where the use of computers and cellular phones may be widespread, still carry the marks of this kind of community life with them. It is a world of lower productivity, which is often inadequate to meet the needs of populations that are frequently in an alarming rate of expansion and flooding into the cities. The peoples here, of course, have a history of their own making and of contact with each other, but they also share a legacy of imperialist or colonialist domination by powerful industrial nations of Europe and America that goes back to the time of the Great Discoveries by Western explorers.

Most of the countries of this Developing World had attained political independence by the middle of the twentieth century, but they were still likely to be in a state of economic or other dependence (sometimes called neo-colonialism) and to retain the marks of years of Western domination. The governments of these countries had in mind a variety of developmental goals, but one thing they all shared was a desire to increase economic productivity (indicated by, for example, the Gross Domestic Product). There were, however, certain impediments or bottlenecks, among which were inadequate natural resources, low technological skills, struggling public institutions, inadequate demand for their products, lack of capital, and continued foreign exploitation. As they set sail on their various developmental courses, these countries were not in the same situation as those in the West before and during the Industrial Revolution, and they usually wanted to accomplish their goals much more rapidly. Indeed, the pace of change in some of them appears positively frenetic, with many social dislocations involved. As one Indonesian official put it, his country had set sail while the ship was still being built.

Various kinds of outside input could help to reduce bottlenecks and help development. For example, consider a country that lacked capital and technological know-how for an agricultural project. A developed country such as the United States had a surplus of both available, and under the right conditions (perhaps if tax incentives were offered to American companies) it might become involved in this developmental project. According to certain developmentalists, such assistance would eliminate the bottlenecks that stood in the way of development and help it to progress. There were problems, however. Outside assistance often has strings attached, some of which may be discovered only after it is too late.

The ideal scenario from the capitalist point of view would go something like this: The project, aided by outside capital and technical assistance, would not only increase output, but also provide jobs for workers who tend to come cheap in the Developing World. These workers would then have the wages to buy not only what they produced, but also the products of others. Thus, the economic benefits of the project would spread throughout the country by the so-called "trickle-down" (or "ripple") effect. At the same time, new forms of behavior (perhaps even true democracy) appropriate for such projects would be acquired through formal and informal education. So, the general standard of living would be improved and a general modernization of behavior would occur. This rosy, capitalist scenario often was not realized, however. There were notable economic successes in places, as in certain Asian countries, but often economic conditions in a country were no better, and were sometimes even worse after developmental efforts. For those who wanted the trickle-down effect to benefit all of the people, there was the annoying tendency for benefits to flow toward the rich and powerful in and outside of the country. Also, outside forces have had an insidious way of undermining and transforming native cultures in unfortunate directions, as, for example, the promotion of sex for tourists in Thailand, a country that many Western economists once thought was on a favorable developmental course, but is currently in some disarray. Thus, the fruits of development too often have been sour for the peoples of the Third World. In addition, developing countries frequently find themselves more dependent on the outside and less in control of their destinies after assistance than before.

All of this is apparent in tourism development under capitalist auspices in the Caribbean, as John Bryden has shown in *Tourism and Development*. The typical Caribbean country has only limited natural resources, but it does have the plentiful "sun, sea, and sand" that northern tourists seek, especially in wintertime. Tourism development would therefore appear to be something of a bonanza for such a country. But the results rarely have met expectations. It is true that tourism does provide jobs, but for the natives these are mostly low-paying, seasonal jobs such as chambermaids, waiters, janitors, guards, and gardeners. The few higher-level positions—at least at the outset—have tended to go to outsiders or the educated elite. In addition, tourists (and the natives who often attempt to follow their example) require amenities, which usually have to be imported. Frozen foods, modern toilets, automobiles, and television sets are only some of those amenities. So, in addition to the profit that outside tourism agencies such as hotel chains and airlines expect, additional tourist income is paid out to secure these items. The flow of income to the outside (leakage) from such a developmental scheme, therefore, can be considerable. Further, subsistence agriculture and fishing may languish as people take jobs in tourism or related areas and acquire tastes for foreign things. Still more income is now paid out for what amounts to basic necessities.

All of this suggests how a country that becomes dependent on tourism can profit very little, if at all, from this form of development. It suggests how whatever benefits are derived from such development can be unevenly distributed. Such considerations have caused Bryden to argue that a good case can be made *against* those who think that in "sun, sea, and sand" there are to be found sources of overall economic benefits from tourism.

There are reasons for questioning such development on noneconomic grounds as well. Among the "social" costs of tourism development are environmental degradation and social disintegration. Social stresses may be caused when some people profit from tourism while others do not. There may also be a decreasing quality of life, which one scholar has referred to as "Las Vegasization." In addition, there can be an increasingly narrow dependency on tourists and the outside forces that control them, a condition that is all too apparent in the Caribbean area these days. Finally, one may expect the development of a kind of surly commercialism that infuses not only relationships between tourists and hosts, but among the hosts themselves, a development that may be periodically countered by campaigns encouraging a more civil, friendly atmosphere. It is not inevitable that such negative social costs, as well as economic costs, will outweigh the positive benefits of tourism development (host societies are becoming increasingly sophisticated about dealing with the negative side of tourism), but there are enough "bad" examples to make a people proceed with caution in promoting such a scheme. The key here appears to be the ability to control tourism and other development for the host country's own benefit, a not impossible but certainly difficult task. One has to look with interest at Cuba's experiment with tourism development, in which both capitalist and socialist principles are currently mixed. So far, the results there, also appear to be mixed.

And what of the socialist road of development? This path, which only a few years ago was pursued with considerable fervor in the Developing World, now seems to have lost much of its allure. Certainly there are plenty of bad cases to cite here too, as, for example, in socialist Ethiopia, which has been analysed by Alemneh Dejene in *Environment, Famine and Politics in Ethiopia,* or in Soviet Russia's development of its arctic regions, which is referred to by Norman Chance and Elena Andreeva in "Sustainability, Equity, and Natural Resource Development in Northwest Siberia and Arctic Alaska." Of the various socialist developmental efforts, that of the Chinese is particularly striking. Working initially with collective and state ownership, the Chinese, after overthrowing a capitalist-based regime in 1949, sought to increase both agricultural and manufacturing productivity with some success. Still, faced with a stagnating economy, the Chinese have turned increasingly to various incentives that were once associated with the scorned "capitalist road." These have included bonuses for workers in collective and state enterprises and increasing opportunities for people to profit from private enterprise. Indeed, the Chinese have gone so far in this direction that one might be forgiven for taking them at this writing to be a nation that is more capitalistic than socialistic. Their acquisition of Hong Kong in 1997, which China appears willing to maintain as an enclave of capitalism, certainly does nothing to discourage this view. Whatever one calls the economic mix that currently exists in China, it certainly is producing a rapid rate of development. But, as often is the case on the "capitalist road," not everyone is benefiting equally. The gap between the rich and the poor is increasing and unemployment is becoming a real problem.

On the "social" side, the costs of development in China have been even more disquieting. China continues to be a one-party nation, ruled by men who, as the Tiananmen Square massacre in 1989 demonstrated, may resort to killing to curb even nonviolent dissent. And one cannot forget the abuses of the Cultural Revolution from the mid-1960s to the mid-1970s when socialist revolutionary principles were in full flower. Then, Red Guards roamed the streets and countryside pointing out those who they thought were following the capitalist line. Such people were publicly shamed or imprisoned, and millions of city-dwellers were forcibly relocated to the countryside. Earlier, at the outset of the revolution (1949–1955), punishment of deviators took a more extreme form. Not only was there harassment by organized mobs, forcible relocation, and imprisonment, but also widespread executions.

Until recently in developing countries, the infrequent success of the economic side and the considerable costs on the social side of the socialist road of development did not deter convinced revolutionaries. Looking about them, they were likely to see too few instances of widespread benefits under capitalism, noting instead that any benefits were often concentrated among the rich and powerful. This would have been right about the wealthy Cubans

I knew who lolled about the Havana Yacht Club in pre-revolutionary times chatting about this and that, drinking daiquiries and other rum drinks, and giving occasional peremptory orders to the waitstaff. Besides this, if the revolutionaries had some knowledge of the history of the world, they were sensitive to the conditions of colonialism or imperialism in which one country dominates others. As with Jean Donovan and her associates, they may have come to feel that one must look outside in order to fully explain what is happening to developing peoples. They may have come to believe that the interests of multinational corporations and the governments of the industrialized world associated with them are the ultimate sources of their developmental problems. From this point of view, anything would be better than continuing the status quo, and some kind of socialist program still could seem attractive. Despite the demise of communist systems in Russia and the rest of Eastern Europe and despite the well-known troubles of socialist countries such as Cuba, North Korea, and Albania with their development projects, these visionaries (as, for example, the hard-line Sendero Luminoso of Peru and the Khmer Rouge of Cambodia) appeared to think that somehow things could be worked out along a socialist road that would lead to a better life for all.

Rejecting both capitalism and socialism (or any mixture of the two), another road of development, based on various versions of Islam, has opened up in the Middle East and Asia. Here, states like Algeria, Afghanistan, Egypt, and Iran and more radical sect-like movements within them have been trying different tenets of a religion that offers sometimes minute prescriptions for social behavior. One of the most interesting of these lines of development was that taken by the Muslim Brotherhood, which had its origin in Egypt in the late 1920s. This militant, highly organized, utopian religious movement, which may have had as many as a million members in Egypt and neighboring countries in the 1940s, aimed at bringing all aspects of society in line with its leaders' interpretation of Holy Law. Resolutely antiestablishment and anticolonial, it was only one of a number of radical Islamic groups that are continuously being spawned in this part of the world.

Whichever road of development a country chooses, it must make certain changes that will increase its productivity. This usually involves some kind of industrialization and the things that go with it, matters that are dealt with more fully in Chapter Ten. People from the Developing World may say that they don't want to follow slavishly in the footsteps of the advanced industrial societies. Their countries have some room for maneuver, of course (as in, say, increasing and distributing the fruits of productivity), but they will also be constrained by the requirements of industrialization and external economic factors that impinge on them. The pioneers of the ubiquitous process of industrialization, that puts a premium on technological development were countries in Europe and America that are mentioned often in history books in connection with the Industrial Revolution. Even a revolutionary will recognize the primary virtue of industrialization, as indicated by the comments of a patron saint of the Cuban revolution, Che Guevara. Asked by an American correspondent whether there was anything about the United States he liked, Che responded, "Your technology. Period."

ANTHROPOLOGY AND DEVELOPMENT

Development is often narrowly conceived in an economic sense, but the term might also be used more broadly to refer to any form of cultural change leading to desirable goals. Thus, changing methods for increasing food production, decreasing infant death rates, killing more enemies, extracting more energy from the earth, distributing wealth more evenly, or increasing the efficiency of any number of projects could all be called developmental trends. All such trends involve cultural change, which is a process that has fascinated anthropologists over the years.

As Robert Bee has argued in his comprehensive treatment of anthropological approaches to the study of this subject (*Patterns and Processes*), the actual conditions of human existence involve both change and persistence, with one prevailing over the other at any given time. There will always be some mixture of the two, however, as is demonstrated by the phenomenon of culture lag, in which one aspect of a culture changes and others (which formerly may have been better adapted to it) tend to lag behind. In zeroing in on change instead of what persists, therefore, an anthropologist tends to emphasize one side of cultural reality. The questions asked are the usual scientific ones: What is it like? (a question of description), and Why is it like that? (a question of explanation).

Early in the history of anthropology, there were social evolutionists who saw all cultures evolving according to some grand design, as, for example, from savagery to civilization. With views derived from the theory of biological evolution, these scholars saw cultures changing, usually in a Western direction, under the impetus of internal growth mechanisms. Another school of thought saw sociocultural changes following from borrowings or diffusion from culture centers around the world. More recently, anthropological studies of change have become more modest and limited in scope, as, for example, the investigations of various cases of sociocultural change resulting from Western contact with the peoples of the Developing World. Of the many native responses that have received attention, one has come to be known as a revitalization movement.

A revitalization movement is a religiously inspired response to the sociocultural disorganization usually brought about by outside contact. Famous examples have occurred in North America (the Ghost Dance of the Plains Indians or the Peyote Cult in the Southwest, for example), the southwest Pacific (cargo cults), eastern South America (searches for utopias to the east), and the Middle East (where Christianity is sometimes mentioned as a revitalization movement).

The North American Ghost Dance, which is reported on by James Mooney (in *The Ghost Dance Religion and the Sioux Outbreak of 1890*), provides a good illustration of the processes involved in a revitalization movement. In the late nineteenth century, the Indians of the western United States had been subjugated and forced to take up life on reservations where it was difficult, if not impossible, to carry on traditional ways. There, in what one writer has referred to as an atmosphere of "numbing discouragement," they began to receive news from Nevada of the Paiute shaman, Joseph Wovoka, who said that if a certain ritual (the Ghost Dance) was followed, the dead would be resurrected, the bison (on which the Plains Indians had depended) would return, and the whites would disappear. The Ghost Dance complex soon spread among the Indians of the western United States and figured in the tragedy at Wounded Knee where a Sioux Ghost Dance was forcibly disrupted by the U.S. Army with many resulting casualties.

The perspective that anthropologists tend to share in looking at a culture (recall Chapter Two) also will serve as a framework for this brief excursion into the problems of describing and explaining a revitalization movement or any other kind of sociocultural change. First, any established culture has a historical dimension that gives it a certain impetus and direction. It also has an internal order. Although the degree of integration sometimes has been overestimated, its essential aspects (economy, government, etc.) are likely to be related in some way. Thus, like an organism, a culture's growth or change is limited to some extent by its nature. One has to be careful with this biological analogy, however. Cultural limitations on change are certainly less restrictive than biological ones. Finally, there is the setting of a culture—its natural and social environment—from which borrowing or diffusion may take place; it also operates selectively (through the process of adaptation) on cultural elements. All of these parameters of a culture must be considered in accounting for the way in which a culture changes.

The role that setting or context plays in culture change has been especially noticeable under Western colonialism or imperialism. Around 1930, more than 80 percent of the globe was under the control of the big, industrial, capitalist nations of the West. Anthropologists, who have done most of their studies in this part of the world, could not help but be struck by the apparent consequences of this domination for culture change among the people they studied. Sometimes the effect seemed simply shattering, as when native people were decimated by a disease introduced from the West. Sometimes a people would survive, but their traditional way of life would be destroyed by, say, an incautious logging program that led to deforestation. Sometimes the change would be subtler, as when a traditional ceremony was turned into a tourist commodity. True, there were changes for what most people would consider the better, as when modern medicine was brought to bear on some intractable native disease or when a colonial government managed to impose some order on native warring factions. In most cases involving imperial or colonial domination, however, the changes originated from without, with the native population having comparatively little say in the matter. People who led movements that opposed such domination were often better educated and more Westernized. Gandhi and Nehru, who led the Indian movement for independence from Britain, are examples.

After World War II, Western colonial (governmental) domination of what one anthropologist has called "the little peoples of the world" all but disappeared, but other forms of domination continued, some of which may be as large-scale and as organized as the British empire once was. The most important continuing form has been economic, as when a country must follow economic guidelines set down by the International Monetary Fund in order to qualify for American or European loans or adhere to the work rules of some multinational corporation. Increasingly sophisticated peoples in what were once Western colonies are aware of this and other kinds of domination, including that which can be found in anthropological work. In the old days, anthropologists tended to feel that they were entitled to study any people that interested them and, after coping with the usual problems of fieldwork, to report on their culture without consultation. Nowadays, anthropologists may have to discuss a project with the people involved and take their views into account before writing and publishing a report.

The emerging assertiveness and increasingly critical attitude of native peoples toward anthropological work (most of which continues to be practiced by Westerners) seem to have played a role in raising anthropological consciousness and sensitizing investigators to the value stands that they take in studying change under conditions of colonial or postcolonial domination. While some anthropologists have been accused of serving colonial masters, many have been more or less opposed to Western domination of native peoples. Their opposition has varied from total rejection, as with those who side with revolutionary independence movements, to what one anthropologist has called "elegiac regret," as in the case of the French anthropologist-missionary, Maurice Leenhardt. Despite witnessing all of the cruelties and exploitation associated with French colonialism in New Caledonia in the southwest Pacific, Leenhardt remained convinced that the best long-term possibilities for New Caledonian development lay with the French, a view that has been vigorously contradicted by native factions seeking independence.

The attitudes that anthropologists have taken toward colonial or postcolonial domination have influenced their views of culture and culture change as well. Consider a well-known problem encountered in most developing situations: the fact that the people are "multiplying like rabbits" and that this "eats up" whatever increased productivity there is. Some Western anthropologists (perhaps including those working for an agency bent on population control) might look on this as maladaptive. But others might view the high birthrate as adaptive in the usual developing situation where the infantile death rate is high, where social security in old age is provided by kinship groups, and where more hands increase the productivity and, therefore, the welfare of the extended family. Which of these views is correct? Depending on the overall point of view taken, both may be. It is important, therefore, to figure out the vantage point from which the developmental process is being viewed in evaluating an anthropologist's conclusions.

Although anthropologists cannot legislate points of view (a variety of which can be scientifically desirable), they do have to grapple with the problem of what ethical and political stance they ought to take in their work. This problem has become more acute as the state of the world in which anthropolological work is concentrated has increasingly become an ethical mine field. It has been especially the case with applied anthropology where studies are oriented toward practical ends. The variety of projects that applied anthropologists have assisted range from systems of food delivery in American fast-food restaurants to health care in Sri Lanka. Considering anthropologists' extensive involvement in the Developing World, it is not surprising that much of their applied work has been done in the area of development. In Vicos, Peru, for example, a project jointly sponsored by Cornell University and the Peruvian Institute of Indigenous Affairs, sought to identify the sociocultural consequences of introducing a form of participatory democracy into the developmental process. This project eventually ran into vested interests seeking to maintain the traditional authoritarian way of life (and system of privilege) in peasant areas, a problem often encountered by aid projects. As a result, the anthropologists involved were forced to take sides. They chose to side with what they took to be the commitment of the Vicosinos to the new participatory way of doing things.

A more sticky ethical problem arose in connection with an ill-fated U.S. Army study called Project Camelot. Originally designed to identify the conditions leading to revolution in the Developing World and the ways in which a government might act to defuse the potential for revolution, the study needed to enlist social scientists (including anthropologists) who would carry out on-the-spot investigations. This project, which focused initially on Latin America, eventually died from public exposure, but it had significant repercussions in the anthropological community. Here was an instance where anthropologists were being enlisted to find out ways of promoting stability and order, a condition that might not (as in El Salvador) satisfy many native people. At the same time, rumors of other "counterinsurgency" projects were being heard, and the general public outcry undoubtedly had something to do with the adoption by the American Anthropological Association of a statement of the problems of anthropological research and ethics ("Principles of Professional Responsibility"). This statement in its various revisions has continued to stress the importance of anthropologists' responsibilities to science and to the people they study, whoever they may be (See Fluehr-Lobban 1991).

Finally, there is the issue of sustainable development, which has rapidly become a kind of mantra for "good" development. This notion, which has received the imprimatur of a United Nations special report (*Our Common Future* by the U.N Commission on Environment and Development), includes sustaining the environment in the face of change, as, for example, preventing growing numbers of scuba divers from ruining coral reefs in Bali; but it also often refers to social goals involving, for example, the distribution of wealth or making a living, and may concern itself with issues of cultural integrity or authenticity. There is so much support for the notion of sustainable development that it is easy to lose sight of the fact that some sustainable goals may be contradictory, as when people must cut down forests in order to live in their accustomed way. Further, people who are in favor of sustainable development in principle may back off when confronted with the hard facts of a particular case. In doing applied work on sustainable development or any other kind of development, an anthropologist needs to have in hand all the basic understandings concerning sociocultural change as well as the specific problems associated with whatever practical application is involved.

CASE STUDIES

Here, I would like to summarize two studies of the developmental process as it has been taking place in different areas of the Developing World. The societies involved came under Western colonial control some time ago and have experienced the various vicissitudes of this encounter. In both cases, the anthropologists studying the development process were particularly concerned with a people's ability to maintain an acceptable degree of cultural integrity in the face of powerful outside forces. In other words, they were working within a framework of what can be seen as sustainable development. Both studies are concerned with the sometimes complex give-and-take between the various parties active in particular developmental processes, and though they attend to basic scientific considerations, they also consider important practical concerns of the native peoples involved.

The first study was done by Mark Mansperger as a young doctoral candidate in anthropology, who had become interested in the effects of tourism on small-scale societies. Mansperger did his fieldwork on Yap, a small cluster of islands in Micronesia in the western Pacific, an area that became famous during World War II when American assaults against Japanese redoubts in the western Pacific, such as Iwo Jima and Tarawa, were very much in the headlines. Since the time of its discovery by Europeans in the sixteenth century, Yap had been involved in American, European, and Asian trade and under the political domination of various colonial masters (Spain, Germany, Japan, and finally the United States) and so subject to these powerful outside influences. Though considerable acculturation had taken place as a result, the Yapese have acquired a reputation for hanging on to their traditional ways. Mark Mansperger considers this issue, particularly as it relates to tourism development, in "Tourism and Culture Change in Small-Scale Societies."

The other study—or series of studies—was carried out on the Eskimo or Iñupiat of northern Alaska over a period of about thirty years by Norman Chance, an anthropologist and colleague of mine at the University of Connecticut. An authority on development, Chance first came to know the Iñupiat in the late 1950s, when he began fieldwork in Kaktovik, a village on the shore of the Arctic Ocean. His aim was to study the ways in which the people there were affected by powerful outside influences, such as energy extraction (oil) and military activities (radar installations), as well as normal colonial operations of local and national governments. Following his report on the study (see, for example, *The Eskimo of North Alaska*) and several decades of research on the Chinese revolution, Chance returned to the arctic to continue his account of the Iñupiat, this time seen from a broader perspective that includes the Russian and Canadian arctic as well as the relevant seats of power in the industrialized world (see *The Iñupiat of Arctic Alaska: An Ethnography of Development*).

Mansperger on Tourism Development on Yap

At the time of their discovery by Europeans, there may have been as many as 30,000 people living on the Yap islands, a figure that would be reduced by migration, disease, and violence to approximately 7,500 by 1990, when Mark Mansperger began his study. This dramatic decline in population, as well as the historical accounts of Yapese suffering and the brutal practices of some colonial masters, do not suggest that these people would manage to keep their old ways to the extent that they have. Mansperger's account makes it clear that though there have been many acculturative changes, some practices continue that correspond to those reported in historical accounts. For example, the old ranked system of land tenure involving a hierarchical system of control over horticultural practices remains in place, paternalistic social arrangements continue and huge pieces of circular limestone money, once used as a means of exchange, still can be found throughout the islands. However, many instances of sociocultural change are evident, a number of which seem to be associated with Yap's recent "Compact of Free Association" with the United States that has involved the acquisition of American social and political forms, the most important being a growing U.S.-styled governmental bureaucracy that is the largest single employer on the islands.

This and various entrepreneurial endeavors have taken many Yapese away from agriculture and fishing and made the islands increasingly dependent on imports for subsistance. Because the traditional ways of earning a living have tended to disappear and because the Yapese have "bought" heavily into an international consumer culture, the Yapese at the time of Mansperger's study had acquired a huge trade deficit that they have coped with largely through American aid. They also have begun some cash-earning projects of their own, one of which is small-scale tourism development. Mark Mansperger wanted to find out how this development has affected the Yapese.

Mansperger's dissertation research took an applied turn when he received an invitation from the Yap government to assess the impact of tourism and make recommendations for a sustainable course of tourism development on their islands. Though still comparatively few in number (about three thousand young adventurers visited Yap in 1990), tourist arrivals are increasing. Along with agricultural and fishing development, tourism offers the Yapese (who worry about the possible termination of American aid) an opportunity to begin correcting their trade deficit. It should be noted, however, that an alternative course of development that would have involved reducing imports was considered politically impracticable by Yapese leaders (perhaps because of the growing dependence on Western consumer goods) and was hardly mentioned by them or Mansperger.

Tourism on Yap has involved scuba diving in waters inhabited by huge manta rays, visits to a museum village, and cultural shows or picnics, during which guests eat Yapese food and witness traditional dances. All tourist enterprises (including lodging which totals no more than a hundred rooms) are owned and run by Yapese. So one can say that some people of Yap have been the almost exclusive beneficiaries of the small, but increasing income from tourism. (Mansperger, however, does not deal with the issue of leakage to the outside of this income by way of, for example, imports necessary to provide Western amenities for tourists.)

In response to questions about tourism on Yap, native informants have had some minor gripes about tourists' insensitivity to their customs, and some think that tourism is contributing to social conflict and a decline in their tradition of sharing, which still is an important component of Yapese culture. But the general attitude toward tourism on Yap is favorable. Mansperger concludes that the effects of tourism on village peacefulness, on sharing, and on traditional disciplines and tastes are minor and that it has so far brought economic benefits and few social costs to this society.

An important reason for this, Mansperger believes, is that tourism has so far remained a small-scale operation and not yet become a large-scale, foreign-based enterprise. The Yapese have resisted the proposals of resort representatives from the United States and Japan to build large-scale facilities that include golf courses and beach developments. Were the Yapese to go along with such a proposal, according to Mansperger, tourism would take on an entirely different quality and become unmanageable and unsustainable in Yapese terms. In writing his recommendations, therefore, Mansperger, though aware that the Yapese, driven by financial necessity, may be forced to accept it, stresses the importance of avoiding large-scale, externally based tourism development.

Here is a "bad" scenario for tourism development that Mark Mansperger thinks is a real possibility: Following the passage of a law of eminent domain (pending at the time of the anthropologist's report), outside developers would persuade chiefs and their loyal relatives and friends to *lease* land to them (the sale of land to foreigners being against the law) for large sums of money. Others, not fully aware of the implications of the deal, might be tricked into selling their land to other Yapese who would, in turn, lease it to the developers. Still others might be pressured to go along. All of this would lead to the lease by outsiders of enough land for the construction of one or more large-scale Western-style resorts.

This scenario, the anthropologist points out, would result in major changes in Yapese culture and its environment, including a modification of the system of land tenure, which he takes to be a key component of the culture. The best that the Yapese could hope for along this developmental road would be to obtain the best possible income and maintain as much control as possible over the development and operation of the resorts. Even so, the income from tourism (and presumably other developmental efforts) might not be great enough to cover the costs of a lifestyle to which the Yapese are becoming accustomed. Then, because of the tourism-induced disintegration of their culture, these people would not have a "cultural support system" involving the traditional system of land tenure to fall back on.

It would be better, according to the anthropologist, to gradually develop environmentally and socially friendly tourism on a small scale, which would involve expanding diving operations and "village tourism" in which visitors live in Yapese homes and interact with their hosts in a relaxed and intimate way. Further income might be generated by tours in glass-bottomed boats and traditional canoes (the museum village and cultural picnic would, presumably, continue in operation at a somewhat higher level). At the same time, in order to minimize whatever friction exists between the Yapese and tourists, brochures on Yapese etiquette could be made available to visitors and the Yapese would make an effort to clean up trash and increase the supply of fresh water, both of which were subjects of complaint by visitors. All of this is in line with the policy recommendations adopted at a seminar convened in the late 1970s by the World Bank and UNESCO to consider tourism development in developing countries (see de Kadt, *Tourism: Passport to Development?*). It appears that the Yapese so far have generally tended to follow this developmental alternative, though Mansperger continues to be ignorant of the impact of his recommendations on them.

Chance on Development among the Alaskan Iñupiat

Norman Chance is a long-time friend of the Alaskan Iñupiat and sympathetic to their active role in a developmental process that he traces back thousands of years. He is especially interested, however, in the period since the days of the first Western (Russian) contact in the eighteenth century, and more recently, in the period of American hegemony. In Chance's view, the principal external forces that have shaped the development of these people in recent times stem from industrial capitalism and federal and state control. He concentrates on how the Iñupiat have dealt with these forces.

Norman Chance refers to historical and archeological materials to construct a picture of the aboriginal condition of Iñupiat culture, traces of which were still evident during his first fieldwork at Kaktovik in the late 1950s and continue still. For example, the existence of extended family ties, a key element of aboriginal social organization, was suggested by the networks of electrical wires linking the wooden huts of composite nuclear families. Chance uses the term *extended family* loosely to embrace related cooperating groups of as large as fifty people under the leadership of an older male who had limited political power. It was customary for the larger of these families and their whaling associates to have a meeting place in which they "played games, told stories, danced, and participated in various rituals." Several of these meeting places (*qargis*) could exist in a single settlement. Commitment to one's family was deep and long-lasting, less so to the settlement or band, beyond which was hostile territory where (unless one could bring up some kinship or trading connection) the threat to limb and life could be serious. Warfare also was a regular aspect of interterritorial relations, but its manifestation was mitigated by the requirements of trade.

Closely related to kinship connectedness in this culture was the custom of sharing which tended to take the form of generalized reciprocity, that is, involving the return of roughly equivalent value. This was brought home to Chance when he was confronted by fellow hunters with the problem of what to do with the carcass of a seal he had killed on a hunting expedition. He indicates that his decision to give it to the woman of the household with which he was most involved did a great deal to further his acceptance in Kaktovik. Many other examples of sharing are given including the routine cutting up and distribution of whale carcasses on the shore. Especially in his later work on these people, Chance shows great respect for the custom of sharing, particularly in contrasting it with the developing competitive-individualistic practices encouraged by capitalistic wage labor.

This anthropologist also stresses that the aboriginal Iñupiat tended to think of themselves as a part of nature and contrasts this with the sharp distinction between nature and human life that tends to prevail in Western culture (where nature often is thought of as something apart, to be controlled or subdued for human ends). Following a subsistence-oriented way of life, they lived on close terms with the natural environment and (considering their primitive technology) achieved a remarkable adaptation to it; but they also were keenly aware of nature's vicissitudes and that it was filled with hostile powers over which they had little control. These people took from the sea (walrus, whales, seals, fish) and land (reindeer, caribou, smaller animals, birds, berries, and various vegetables) by hunting, fishing, trapping, and gathering, but usually not more than could be naturally replenished. Like the aboriginal San, they lived lightly on their environment. The sustainability of their way of life, therefore, was hardly the issue it would become with the advent of Western-generated demands on their resources.

Norman Chance uses the hunting of whales as one example of the emergence of such demands. In aboriginal times, whales were taken by boat crews using harpoons, lines, and floats in a system that might require that the animal be followed for a long time before it expired. The advent in the nineteenth century of rifles and harpoons with more killing power, as well as other technology, increased the efficiency of this operation and made possible the taking of more of these animals. The demand for whales, however, was comparatively low until the discovery in the nineteenth century by Western mariners of the huge whaling grounds in the arctic. With a growing demand for whale oil and bone at home, it did not take long for a sizeable whaling industry (that included Iñupiat hunters) to emerge in the area. Indeed, so many whales were taken that questions were raised about their survival. Later, in the twentieth century, the U.S. government, having noted a growing scarcity of whales, would establish a quota system, negotiations over which only partially restored the Iñupiat right to take whales when and where they wished (The issue continues to be debated in international conferences today.)

The development of whaling and associated trading, of course, involved the acquisition of new (Western) ways of doing things among the Iñupiat, which have continued to the present day in workplaces such as those pertaining to radar installation and operation during the Cold War between Russia and the United States, and (more recently) the extraction of oil, both of which have had a special impact in and near Kaktovik and its surroundings. The discovery of an enormous oil field at nearby Prudhoe Bay resulted in a massive influx of oil-drilling equipment and associated personnel, and the construction of a radar installation forced the villagers to relocate twice. Chance uses interviews with white employers to illustrate the prejudice and discimination against these natives and suggests that it has contributed to a lessening of Iñupiat autonomy and sense of self-worth while at the same time justifying white mistrust of native labor.

Other Westernizing pressures have come from the U.S. government, which acquired rights over Alaska in a colonial deal with the Russians in 1867. Made with no reference to the status and rights of the aborigines, this understanding simply stated that they would be subject to the laws and regulations of the United States. Out of this there emerged governing arrangements based on a policy of assimilating the natives. In their schooling in government schools, for example, native children were taught only in English and sometimes punished for speaking in their native language. In addition, no special consideration was given to native history and traditions. The activities of missionaries and newly established Christian churches also appear to have had an assimilationist thrust. But prejudice and discrimination in the workplace and elsewhere ran counter to assimilation. The resulting contradiction, according to Chance, tended to favor the production of the kind of underclass that often has been associated with colonialism.

But as Chance sees it, the Iñupiat have not been passive pawns in a developmental setting that has involved a number of more or less powerful parties, among which have been commercial interests including an oil industry that spans the globe; the American military, which during the days of the Cold War with Russia, saw Alaska as a part of the first line of defense against potential Soviet attacks on the U.S. homeland; various federal organs such as the U.S. Congress, the Department of the Interior, and the Bureau of Indian Affairs in Washington, DC, and departments of what would become the State of Alaska; and an array of native associations including the Alaskan Federation of Natives, the Arctic Slope Regional Corporation, and various native communities like the North Slope Borough that extend along the arctic rim of Alaska. Each of the parties in this developmental process is seen by Chance to be pursuing its own interests that both conflict and coincide with others depending on the issue involved.

The paramount issue that has emerged in this process of development, as seen by Norman Chance, has to do with the maintenance of tribal rights, particularly those pertaining to the natural environment, on which so much of native aboriginal life depended. Do the land and sea "belong" to the Iñupiat in a way that suits their understanding of their native prerogatives (which is to ask whether they are able to control these aspects of the environment for their own benefit)? An affirmation of such an understanding of tribal rights would mean that the Iñupiat could tax oil taken from their land, hunt and fish without restriction, and curb policies that would lead to serious destruction of their environment. Such an affirmation is found in the Alaska National Interest Lands Conservation Act, passed by the U.S. Congress in 1980, in which the right to hunt and fish, as well as other rights on federal lands, were explicitly recognized. But earlier in 1971, in the Alaska Native Claims Settlement Act, the native population had given up tribal rights to land in favor of ownership by regional corporations that would function as northern extensions of industrial capitalism. The present arrangement, proposed by the Alaska Federation of Natives and passed by the U.S. Congress in 1988, is a mix that attends to both tribal and corporate authority.

In it, according to Chance, though tribal sovereignty is not recognized, "native lands in Alaska are relatively well protected within the context of State and Federal law."

Considering the comparatively weak and restricted forms of political organization (bands of hunters, fishers, and gatherers) in their tradition, the Iñupiat have demonstrated a remarkable ability to further their own developmental interests in the contemporary world and to maintain core elements of their aboriginal culture. Though Chance makes it clear that these natives do not all speak with one voice and that outsiders often have greater power in determining what course their development will take, native views have sometimes prevailed, as in the 1988 proposal of the Alaska Federation of Natives. Certainly, their power is much greater than it was in the early days of colonialism, and it appears to be much greater than that of the pastoral-nomadic people in the Russian north, whose petro-chemical-linked development has also been studied by Chance and Russian colleagues. And one sees that the Iñupiat are continuing to strengthen their political hand by involving themselves in activist groups that extend well beyond northern Alaska to the entire arctic rim. How a people, who in their aboriginal state had such weak and localized political organization, could come to operate with such assurance in the wider political world is an interesting question that Chance does not really address.

For Norman Chance all questions about development in this region eventually return to the industrial or post-industrial societies that want to control and utilize the resources of the arctic. It is these increasingly business and consumer-oriented societies that raise greater and greater demands for northern resources, such as petroleum and gas, and that offer a powerful model of a new way of life to native people. Though the Iñupiat have become more powerful in directing their own development, though they have managed to maintain some traditions (for example, in what Chance refers to as their subsistence economy,) and though some tribal rights remain intact, they have moved farther and farther away from the sharing and subsistence-oriented practices that once constituted the core of a culture to which they now (even if the oil gives out) can never return. While recognizing this, Chance cannot help but reveal a sense of loss for the old communal practices that once prevailed among these natives and criticism of the increasingly internationalized system that has taken it away from them. This is an attitude that one often encounters in anthropological studies of development.

Norman Chance's "ethnography of development" stresses the complex give-and-take that has gone on in one particular developmental setting. As in Mark Mansperger's study, changes in native culture and problems involved in developmental change are noted; but the focus is extended to include the political processes involved in that change. Here, natives are seen to play (or be capable of playing) a part in a setting that is ultimately controlled by various powers in a "world system." It is to the seats of power in this system, according to Chance, that we must eventually trace the violations of sustainability (for example, damage to the environment and various social injustices) that are all too evident among the Iñupiat and throughout the Developing World. We still have much to learn, however, about how this all works out in specific developing situations.

The summaries of the studies conducted by Mark Mansperger and Norman Chance, which are only two of thousands of development studies done by anthropologists, are inevitably inadequate. This is not only because they are summaries, however. They are inadequate also because no single study can embrace the entire developmental process, which, in reality, has as many aspects as does a culture. Considering this, and considering all of the developing societies of the world, it would seem to be very difficult to make generalizations about them. However, there are certain things that societies in the Developing World tend to share. First, these societies have a recent history of colonial domination by the industrial nations of the West, such as Great Britain, the Netherlands, and the United States, and carry with them marks of that domination today. Because of this and because they have had relations with each other in the past, it is incorrect to see them as having developed out of some kind of "traditional" culture entirely of their own making. Second, though these societies have become formally independent of their colonizing masters, they have developed new relationships with the increasingly internationalized Developed World that often continue their former position of subordination. Mark Mansperger's scenario of the possible large-scale tourism development on Yap and his mention of an Americanized governmental bureaucracy are examples of this. A key issue in the developmental process these days is the ability of the Developing Societies to maintain autonomy or control in their relationships with outside powers. Using the summary of Chance's study of Iñupiat development, what grade should we give them in this regard? Third, these societies are in the grip of a sometimes dizzying rate of change, which has brought some of them to the point where a superficial observer (say of Malaysia, Taiwan, or South Korea) might take them to be a part of the Developed World. Further observation might reveal, however, that there are many aspects of their culture that indicate their less developed status and many problems of integrating the old and the new. There are also many developing countries such as El Salvador where the use of the term *underdevelopment* would not be out of place.

THE SIN OF THE FIRST WORLD?

Jean Donovan came to believe that the social injustice that prevailed in El Salvador was literally sinful and that the United States, in particular, and the Developed World, generally, were implicated in that sin. From this brief overview of the issues of development, it is now possible to evaluate her beliefs, not only as they apply to El Salvador, but to the rest of the Developing World as well. Since the time of the Great Discoveries, Western Europe, and later the United States and the Soviet Union, attained power over this part of the globe. As a glance at today's headlines will reveal, the present condition of the peoples of the Developing World is not entirely of their own doing, but is (at least in part) due to this dominance. Consider, for example, how many leaders of Developing countries owe their existence to the kind of support from the Developed World that the United States gives to Egypt (nearly a quarter of the entire U.S. foreign aid budget). Now, to the extent that it is associated with moral responsibility, the Developed World can be seen to be morally involved in their developing fate. Most anthropologists would likely share this view.

Although anthropologists may be on the side of the underdogs of the world and interested in helping them, their primary mission is to understand; and it is clear now that a proper understanding of the Developing World involves unraveling complex networks that can extend into the boardrooms of multinational corporations and the highest councils of governments in the Developed World. Such studies by anthropologists have barely begun. An especially interesting project that would have significant ethical and political implications would consider those "assembly industries," such as Nike, a maker of sport shoes, that locate many of their operations in the Developing World where labor tends to come cheap.

And how might all of this go down for someone who is just being introduced to anthropology? They may be surprised, first of all, to learn that there is a world out there full of legitimate others who are not like them or the people around them. Most of these others are a part of the Developing World, which is largely a world of have-nots. The fact that twenty-nine countries in sub-Saharan Africa are poorer now than they were in 1960, that Middle Eastern terrorism has become a cause of steadily increasing concern, or that the United States, the current center of power in the Developed World, is considered in some developing countries as a kind of public enemy (and referred to by some Iranians as "The Great Satan") can no longer be attributed entirely to the inadequacies or irrationalities of distant strangers. Indeed, because of shared colonial and postcolonial histories, these others are more like political neighbors.

This knowledge would seem to be a necessary basis not only for practical actions in an increasingly internationalized world, but also for whatever moral outlook a person chooses to adopt concerning the Developing World. No longer can these peoples be viewed as simply interesting or exotic—those who have invented intriguing cultural variations on human themes. Rather, through the anthropological study of development, they come to appear as struggling human beings with whom the Developed World has been, and continues to be, involved in important ways. In fact, these others may have become indispensable in helping people in the Western world to maintain their way of life. This knowledge, as it did with Jean Donovan, can transform a person.

SELECTED REFERENCES

BEE, ROBERT L., *Patterns and Processes*. New York: Free Press, 1974.

BERGER, PETER L., *Pyramids of Sacrifice*. Garden City, NY: Anchor Books, 1976.

BRYDEN, JOHN, *Tourism and Development: A Case Study of the Commonwealth Caribbean*. Cambridge: Cambridge University Press, 1973.

CARRIGAN, ANA, *Salvador Witness*. New York: Simon and Schuster, 1984.

CHANCE, NORMAN A., *The Eskimo of North Alaska*. New York: Holt, Rinehart and Winston, 1966.

———, *The Iñupiat of Arctic Alaska: An Ethnography of Development*. Fort Worth, TX: Holt, Rinehart and Winston, 1990.

CHANCE, NORMAN A., and ELENA N. ANDREEVA, "Sustainability, Equity, and Natural Resource Development in Northwest Siberia and Arctic Alaska," *Human Ecology*, 23 (2) 1995, 217–40.

CHASE-DUNN, CHRISTOPHER, *Global Formation: Structures of the World Economy*. London: Basil Blackwell, 1989.

DEJENE, ALEMNEH, *Environment, Famine and Politics in Ethiopia*. Boulder, CO: Lynne Rienner, 1990.

EICKELMAN, DALE, *The Middle East and Central Asia: An Anthropological Approach*. Upper Saddle River, NJ: Prentice Hall, 1998.

FLUEHR-LOBBAN, CAROLYN, ed., *Ethics and the Profession of Anthropology*. Philadelphia: University of Pennsylvania Press, 1991.

GILSENEN, MICHAEL, *Recognizing Islam: Religion and Society in the Modern World*. New York: Pantheon Books, 1982.

MANSPERGER, MARK, "Tourism and Culture Change in Small-Scale Societies," *Human Organization*, 54, (Spring) 1995, 87–94.

MOONEY, JAMES, *The Ghost Dance Religion and the Sioux Outbreak of 1890*. Chicago: University of Chicago Press, 1965.

RUSSELL, PHILIP, *El Salvador in Crisis*. Austin, TX: Colorado River Press, 1984.

U.N. COMMISSION ON ENVIRONMENT AND DEVELOPMENT, *Our Common Future*. Oxford and New York: Oxford University Press, 1987.

WALLERSTEIN, IMMANUEL, *The Modern World System*. New York: Academic Press, 1974.

WOLF, ERIC R., *Europe and the People without History*. Berkeley: University of California Press, 1982.

WORSLEY, PETER, *The Three Worlds*. Chicago: University of Chicago Press, 1984.

ZUNZ, OLIVIER, ed., *Reliving the Past*. Chapel Hill: University of North Carolina Press, 1985.

Industrialism
and Beyond

A MORNING ROUTINE

Consider an average American homemaker getting up one winter morning. She gradually makes her way from bedroom to bathroom to kitchen. During this process, she turns on several lights, turns up the heat, switches on a radio, opens the refrigerator, and turns on the stove. Various gadgets are made to do their work. Water will have been flowing in toilets, washbasins, sinks, and a dishwasher by the time she and her family have finished breakfast.

You know how it is on a winter morning. People act in an almost automatic, unconscious way. It takes a while before they really begin to think about what they are doing. But an anthropologist, scribbling furiously, could have been following most of these early morning actions or gathering information from daily diaries. What would they report in this instance? First, they probably would comment on the ritualistic, taken-for-granted quality of the early-morning actions. Next, they might emphasize the central role the body plays in these actions: cleaning it (washing, shaving), getting rid of its waste (defecation, urination), feeding it, dressing it. Finally, they would probably refer to the use of machines all along the way—machines that are activated by turning a knob or flicking a switch, often in an unconscious manner.

If a machine is taken to be some kind of inanimate object that does work, then the average American family seems to be dependent on quite a few of them in its morning routine. The light bulbs, radio, stove, oil burner, hot water heater, and refrigerator all turn electricity into useful work. So, too, do the machines that pump water for this household. In turn, electricity is produced and distributed by an elaborate network of devices. Needless to say, a group of hunters and gatherers like the aboriginal San have a morning routine that is hardly dependent on machines, and their way of life is quite different as a result. An anthropologist doing fieldwork among them would see them stirring up their fires and using only a few simple implements as they get into the day. If they were deprived of these implements for a few hours, there would be nothing like the consternation of the average American family when the power goes off.

THE INDUSTRIAL WAY OF LIFE

In an industrial society, machines play an important role in its way of life. Though they enter into all areas of activity, it is usually to the productive, and more specifically, the manufacturing sector that one refers in thinking about an industrial society. Furthermore, it is the factory that constitutes the model for the industrial way of life. What is the nature of this model? Consider a modern automobile assembly plant as an example.

Such a plant is a large-scale enterprise that is organized around the various machines that do its work. Each apparatus is designed to do a specific task in a reliable and effective way. There may be computer-directed robots that weld body seams. They work in conjunction with other robots that smooth out the welds afterward and numbers of people who handle the computers and do various more or less specialized operations by hand. As new knowledge becomes available, the design of machines and their arrangement is changed in order to improve performance.

As for the workers themselves, the timing and sequence of their activities are regulated by the machines of the plant. Depending on the job, individuals may have more or less control, but the general tenor of the manufacturing operation is established by the machines themselves. It would be fair to say that, as far as the relationship between the machines and the employees of the plant is concerned, the burden of adaptation is on the employees. Though human factors are taken into account in a general way, the overall manufacturing plan of the plant does not include many provisions for how individual workers feel at a given time about the job they are doing or the people they are working with. Whatever feelings a person has should either be put aside or controlled in order to promote a machine-like way of acting.

Workers should be hired and promoted on the basis of merit. Personal connections, though they do operate on an informal level, are not supposed to play a role in personnel decisions. Workers are selected and trained for specific tasks or a limited array of tasks. Unlike the small dairy farm on which I once worked, there are no jacks-of-all trades here. The ideal is to maximize competence by limiting the range of activity. In contrast to the work of the small farmer who does almost everything, each job involves specific requirements that a worker must have the competence to perform. In contrast to the work of the typical *vigneron* of the Côte d'Or, mentioned in Chapter Eight, industrial work tends to engage a smaller part of the whole person. Relationships with other workers on the job and with machines may have an emotional tone only if they contribute to the work at hand. The average worker is a long way from the finished product that he or she has helped to make. Whatever alienation people feel as a result of all of these formal requirements can only be made up by informal arrangements on and off the job. The American coffee break puts people into personal contact with others. The Japanese have company outings that accomplish the same thing.

Governance of the automobile assembly plant is accomplished through a series of pyramid-like systems of authority in which there may be more or less input from below. In a Swedish plant there will be quite a lot of input, in a Spanish plant, less. Americans may be amazed at the numbers of Japanese factory members who must be consulted before a decision is made and the extent and depth of their agreement afterward, but both Americans and Japanese would agree that there must be a chain of command that functions on the basis of precise rules that apply to specific areas of work. The areas of responsibility of bosses and their range of authority is carefully specified. Directives are phrased in terms of more or less specific rules that deal with categories or types. For example, installers of engines will be told that a new procedure is to be employed in tightening certain bolts. People with authority are not supposed to act on the basis of personal whim, but according to the rulebook. There are ways of getting around this, of course (using family connections or "covering" for fellow workers on the job, for example), but that is not how the system is supposed to operate.

Besides power differences, there are differences of income and prestige based on the type of job done. These differences may be more muted in some cultures, but they exist in any industrial system. A worker can receive more pay through seniority or doing a job better, but also by taking a job higher up on the pay scale. It is possible to move up in this system by learning different kinds of work. Or, as in the United States, individuals may join another firm that offers better opportunities. Thus, individual mobility through job changes is an intrinsic part of this or any industrial operation.

The automobile assembly plant that has been considered here uses resources that come from outside. On the human side, it must attract a work force from a surrounding hinterland and help to maintain that work force close by. It also depends on finished or unfinished materials that have been produced elsewhere. For example, the steel that is fabricated into some automobile body parts has been produced from ores and coal that have been mined and then combined at a high temperature before being transported to the plant. This industrial operation uses large amounts of raw materials, including those for producing power for its own manufacturing operations, in transport, and (indirectly) in the extraction and production of the materials it employs. By drawing on resources from outside, the plant affects the setting in which it is located. Compared with preindustrial productive operations, that effect is tremendous. In addition, there is an effect on the world outside through what it produces. Waste from its power and from its various material operations is disposed of, and the vehicles it produces are distributed to affect the environment in a variety of ways, good and bad.

From the anthropological point of view, the automobile assembly plant has a recognizable subculture that, because it is organized around the large-scale, concentrated use of machines, is clearly an industrial one. Though there may be variations from society to society (between capitalist and socialist societies, for example) and according to the nature and technological level of the operation, there are certain features that all industrial operations have in common. These features are clearly evident in the automobile assembly plant, which is a large-scale, concentrated productive arrangement of machines and the people associated with them. Because of the machines, it tends to be a capital-intensive, rather than a labor-intensive, operation. Everything in it should, ideally, work in a machine-like way, that is, according to the logic of machinery and mechanical processes. That logic involves, first of all, great precision and reliability of operation. Second, it involves a specialized task, and everything that is not directly relevant to assembling automobiles is, ideally, ruled out. Third, its parts and functions are clearly set off from one another. People have specific areas of responsibility or authority, which may be more or less specialized. Fourth, it is hierarchically organized. Regardless of the amount of worker input from below, it can never be a totally egalitarian operation. Fifth, everything has, ideally, been calculated to work in a certain way. Nothing is supposed to be left to chance, personal whim, or feelings. People and machines are designed or trained, selected, changed, and discarded on a rational basis. Sixth, through what it uses and produces, directly and indirectly, the plant goes heavy on its environment. And finally, the entire operation involves a supreme commitment to machine technology, which becomes something of a god of the industrial way. Obviously, this is very far from a San type of productive operation.

If there is an automobile assembly plant, of course, there have to be other manufacturing operations in the society. The culture of industry pervades them all. The agricultural and service sectors, as well as other areas of life, begin to exhibit many of the same features. The growth of larger-scale, complex social groupings (cities, for example) will reinforce these developments. Thus, it would not be inappropriate to say that the society has an industrial way of life.

Something like an industrial culture, though not always conceived of as centering on factories and their operation, has preoccupied social scientists over the years. Termed "modern" or "industrial," and contrasted with its polar opposite, "traditional" or "preindustrial" culture, it was thought to have been emerging all over the world. Modern peoples were said to be more rational than traditional peoples because they put a greater emphasis on calculating how to do things. Their societies had larger-scaled social units, such as large corporations and cities, and were more differentiated and complex as a result. They were also more impersonal, more open to outside influences and to change, more achievement oriented (with a greater possibility for individuals to change their station in life), as well as increasingly committed to higher levels of technology and the specialization of labor that goes with it.

There are a number of aspects of this scheme that can raise questions among present-day anthropologists. First, the notion of "modern" or "industrial" has sometimes been ethnocentrically biased toward the culture of the capitalist, industrial powers of Europe and America. Second, there seems to lurk in the scheme the notion of some inevitable evolution all over the world toward the type of culture that characterizes these powers. Third, there is a curious omission of economic, political, and other developments, which as Chapter Nine on the Developing World makes clear, can play crucial roles in sociocultural change. Fourth, there seems to be a mistaken view that all the hunter and gatherer, agrarian, and pastoral peoples of the world have had basically the same traditional, confined, unchanged way of life that extends back into antiquity. And finally, there lurks in this scheme the idea that something like industrialism or modernism is the end point of all culture change, which may not be the case.

In writing this revision of *A Little Anthropology*, I find it hard to dispute the notion that an evolving Western way of life is exercising a powerful influence on all development in the world, but the nature of that way of life is being variously conceived by social scientists. One group of scholars refers to the emergence of "post-industrialism" which they see to be most apparent in places like California's Silicon Valley (see *Post-Industrial Lives* by Jerald Hage and Charles Powers). In this culture, there appear to be less specialization of labor, less power distance between managers and workers, a greater opportunity for personal expression, and greater flexibility all around. It also is more capital intensive than labor intensive, has a greater concern with the creation and processing of information than with the handling of materials, and tends to change more rapidly. But the "god" of this allegedly new society continues to be a machine—in this case, the computer, a knowledge machine that continues the stress on precision and reliability and the massive use of energy. This suggests to me that though there are, indeed, changes in the wind, they are basically a furthering of the industrialization that has increasingly gripped the world in the recent past.

So, though we should keep the various criticisms of the overall developmental scheme in mind, it seems to me that there indeed appears to be more than a germ of truth in it. Looked at from the very general perspective that includes all of humankind over the entire course of its existence, there does seem to be a general trend toward higher technological levels, larger and more complex social units, etc. At one time or another, different aspects of culture seem to have taken on the role of prime mover of change, but as people's lives have become increasingly linked to more sophisticated machines, as Americans now are, machine technology has come to exercise a greater influence on the character of the world's cultures and on the way in which they change.

INDUSTRIALIZATION

That the world has been becoming more industrialized should be evident to everyone. Take the frightening development of military hardware as an example of industrial production. Though at this writing important steps have been taken by the great powers to reduce their arsenals, they still are developing new weaponry. At the same time, the governors of developing societies and others continue to show an appetite for more destructive armaments, most of which flow to them from the Developed World. This recent line of technological development is only one example of how industrialization has spread around the world. It is the latest phase of a historical progression in which people's lives have been increasingly bound up with machines. That process began long ago.

The first human use of machines probably occurred in the food-getting quest. Carrying devices, tools, and weapons were material aids that enhanced human powers and aided human adaption. The archaeological record shows the development of tool and weapon technologies. They became more specialized, refined, and efficient. This record also reveals the emergence and development of other machines that enhanced human powers: agricultural implements such as the plow, for example, or means of transport like boats and carts. Our understanding of how all of these devices worked is enhanced by observations of contemporary peoples' use of similar implements. The record shows that the rate of technological innovation was at first quite slow, but it began to pick up from the time people first began to practice agriculture twelve thousand or so years ago. Viewed from a general historical perspective, the rate has been increasing ever since. Sometimes one society has led the way, sometimes another. Inventions diffused from one society to another and were adapted by them. The emergence and spread of machine technology thus became a hallmark of human development.

Through the early historic period, the technological pace continued to quicken with the lead first taken by peoples in the Middle East and Asia. They now seem to have been responsible for the invention of such important devices as the cart, the canal lock, the kiln, the loom, the ship, and gunpowder. Europe, the cradle of the so-called Industrial Revolution, which many people identify with industrialization, appears to have been a relatively late starter in the technological race, and it was not until the fifteenth century that it began to surpass other regions of the world in its technological inventiveness.

The Industrial Revolution itself can be traced back to eighteenth-century capitalist England when the factory, which had been in existence since at least Roman times in the West, was filled with clockwork-like machines powered by water and then steam. The first of these factories produced cotton, silk, and pottery, and it is with the factory-based production of cotton products that the Industrial Revolution usually is associated.

Why did it emerge in this place at this time? Certain features of English culture appear to have been conducive. First, there were an array of relevant technologies such as the dam, waterwheel, spinning and weaving machines, and steam engine, as well as the engineering and scientific interests that would contribute to their ever-increasing productivity. Second, the various private companies that in this capitalist society would undertake this new form of production had available to them adequate capital to finance their endeavors. Third, an expanding market ensured the increased demand for more productive arrangements. Fourth, there were adequate resources (coal, cotton, running water, wood, iron, stone, etc.) to support a higher rate of production. Finally (and this is debatable), it may have been more profitable (for profit-seeking capitalists) to substitute machines for human labor in an area having fewer people. Surely, other reasons for the onset of the Industrial Revolution in eighteenth-century England can be advanced, but whatever they are, they all would reaffirm the anthropological view that any culture (and its setting) is a system with interrelated parts and that technological or other innovations and elaborations do not occur in a vacuum.

If one uses the term "revolution" to mean drastic and widespread change, then the Industrial Revolution was aptly named. Not only was there a rapidly increasing commitment to the use of machines in the productive sector, but in other areas of English life as well. The development of the railroad is an example. It combined the use of new steam engines with the increasing demand for transport of goods and people. The advance of technology also affected other aspects of the culture, such as the urbanized living that came to be associated with large factory complexes. Such developments were not confined to England, however. One by one, other countries followed Britain's example, and the revolution spread. In the newly independent United States, for example, English ideas were adopted as a part of an increasing commitment to technological development and the machine way of life.

If one assumes that there is a rough equivalence between technological level and energy use, an overview of the general trend of industrialization described in this section can be offered. All peoples make use of energy that comes indirectly or directly from the sun, but hunters and gatherers use relatively little (from plants and animals, water, and firewood) while highly industrialized peoples use a great deal (mainly from various nonrenewable natural resources like coal, oil, and natural gas). Now, if the entire history of humankind can be seen as falling in a rough chronological sequence, from hunting and gathering through lower and higher levels of agriculture, and recently, into various stages of industrialism, it is clear that there has generally been an increase in energy usage and technological level among the world's peoples from past to present. Of course, not all peoples have passed through these stages and in this sequence. As we saw in the last chapter, hunters and gatherers like the Iñupiat have been drawn directly into modern, industrial ways of life, so their development has often involved a giant leap forward. But the general trend in the world from past to present can be seen as a step-by-step progression toward higher levels of technology and energy usage.

However, as Earl Cook points out in "The Flow of Energy in an Industrial Society," this general trend has been exponential rather than linear. In other words, it involves an increasing rate of increase toward the present, and the rate has increased most dramatically since the Industrial Revolution. Therefore, if England just prior to that revolution can be taken as an example of an advanced agricultural society, and if the United States today can be seen as the most advanced industrial society, then in the three centuries or so since the Industrial Revolution there has been a greater increase in energy usage per capita than in the previous twenty thousand or so centuries of human development.

The energy that humans have used in recent years has come mostly from nonrenewable sources, which, in contrast to the apparent expectations of most people these days, are ultimately of limited supply. So, unless there are changes made in the pattern of energy usage, this latest spurt of industrialization cannot be open-ended. The day when the nonrenewable fuels will be used up is being pushed back by various energy conservation strategies and new discoveries, but ultimately, if humans continue to elaborate their modern industrial ways, renewable energy resources (direct sunlight, wind, water, plants, the earth) will have to be tapped. The best estimates now predict the *necessary* changeover for some time in the twenty-first century. However, critics of this strategy argue that it should be done as soon as possible, not only because the nonrenewable sources will eventually run out, but also because of the dangers associated with the use of nonrenewable fuels. One possible danger is the so-called "greenhouse effect"—which is now generally accepted as valid by the world's scientific community—in which the climate of the world warms up and becomes more volatile as a result of increased levels of carbon dioxide in the atmosphere. Other dangers include various maladies associated with the pollution of land, water, and air; environmental destruction, as in the case of acid rain; and the enormous threat of radiation and nuclear explosive damage that has become all too evident.

And this is not the whole story. Industrial operations require not only energy, but other natural resources that are also limited. Humans can use other resources (plastic instead of metal for automobiles, for example) or reuse (recycle) the ones they now use, but it is still unlikely that the earth can sustain the rate of industrial growth that humans now pursue. This means that, barring some unlikely breakthrough, future generations will have to learn how to live with a reduced level of industrial operations, which is to say that there will have to be a dramatic change in their culture. It will not be easy for people who are committed to industry-based economic growth to do that.

From an anthropological perspective, it appears that humans are now at an important juncture in their existence. In order to survive, they will have to change the industrial ways of doing things that have produced many benefits and on which they have come to rely. Will they have to be dragged toward some new, more adaptive arrangement and thus reconfirm the old saying "necessity is the mother of invention," or will they use their famed foresight and flexibility to prepare for and bring about the necessary changes? There is always the possibility, of course, that some of the machines humans have created will, by accident or intention, produce some catastrophic destruction. It has been estimated, for example, that there still are more than enough nuclear devices in the world to cause a "nuclear winter," which would threaten all life on this planet. In that event, there might not be much of a twenty-first century.

CASE STUDY

Wallace on Industrialization In Rockdale, PA

As has been customary in this book, let me once again bring a discussion down to earth by referring to a specific case involving recognizable human beings. The broad sweep of industrialization has been viewed here as beginning with the earliest humans and continuing up to the present. Generally, it has involved an increasing commitment to, and development of machine technology by the peoples of the world over a course of more than two million years. Whatever one thinks about industrialism today, it is evident that this way of doing things has brought many benefits to human beings from the time of the first tools and weapons. However, as with any other aspect of culture where issues of adaptation are concerned, technology has had its good and bad points.

This is the way industrialization looks to anthropologists when they consider the entire history of humankind. That history is a kind of summing up of thousands of specific cultural histories. In each one of these, industrialism is a part of an entire way of life, and it is the job of the anthropologist to comprehend it. What kind of picture emerges when an anthropologist puts on culture-specific glasses and looks at industrialization as a part of a whole way of life or culture?

Consider Anthony Wallace's study (in *Rockdale*) of the industrialization of a small community in early nineteenth-century Pennsylvania, one of many communities in the United States that followed the same developmental course. It was during this period that the two thousand or so people of this community became involved in the water-power based factory system of cotton production. Because all potential informants had died, this community had to be studied through the use of personal documents and various other historical sources. The anthropologist, Anthony F. C. Wallace, whose name is associated with a long list of psychological and religious studies involving, among others, the Iroquois Indians of North America, happened to live near Rockdale and became fascinated with the past of this little community. He decided to bring his anthropological expertise to bear on it.

Wallace sees Rockdale as a symbol of the early phase of the Industrial Revolution in America where, in contrast to more industrialized England with its huge, steam-powered, urban factories, manufacturing was more likely (but not exclusively) to take place in small towns and villages situated along watercourses. Rockdale, which always has had a rural character, consisted in the early nineteenth century of seven hamlets situated along a three-mile stretch of Chester Creek in the lower Delaware Valley of southeastern Pennsylvania. At the time of the study, each of these hamlets came to be organized around a water-powered cotton mill that owed its existence to the comparatively steep drop of the stream bed over a three-mile stretch, which provided a renewable source of power. Wallace shows how the natural features of the land and the necessities of a specific form of manufacturing influenced the layout of each hamlet. He points out that the roads had to run "just so" and that the housing for workers had to be situated as close to the mill as possible. Higher up and farther away were the homes of the managerial personnel and the manufacturer or owner-manufacturer.

The people responsible for the industrial development were the men who had bought the various mill properties (usually leftovers from previous water-powered operations). Sometimes, the owner of the mill site was also the manufacturer, but the owner usually leased the plant site and associated structures to a manufacturer who had accumulated enough capital to pay the lease, purchase the necessary equipment, hire managers and workers, and pay for the raw materials and transport to and from the mill. Wallace's study centers on the manufacturers (in some cases owner-manufacturers) who were the owners of the means of production and the ruling spirits of the hamlets of Rockdale.

These men were capitalists of an entrepreneurial sort, that is, they were willing to take considerable risks in seeking a profit from a small-scale enterprise. Risks were considerable because of the ups and downs of the cotton market, an often weak capital base, and competition from other cotton manufacturers in Rockdale, the rest of the United States, and abroad. Besides an entrepreneurial spirit, the personal qualities that contributed to success in small-scale cotton manufacturing at that time were, according to Wallace, an ability to inspire trust and confidence in personal relations (with the kinsmen and friends who provided capital, business contacts, employees, and even competitors), the patience necessary to start small and grow slowly, a good business sense, and the technical know-how needed to recognize and implement useful innovations that would keep a factory up-to-date and competitive. The men did not need to be machine technicians themselves, but they had to be capable of drawing on knowledge about cotton manufacturing, which in the early part of the nineteenth century was changing rapidly.

The manufacturers, according to Wallace, played a major role in shaping the culture of their hamlet. People who came to work in the mills were dependent on them for jobs (more or less according to their capacity to fall back on agricultural ways of making a living), and employees' way of life was influenced not only by the work he provided, but also by their general authority in community affairs. This was a system of more or less benign paternalism, and though workers did on occasion band together and even strike, and though there were those who flirted with more socialistic or communally based forms, the authority of the manufacturers to run their hamlets as they saw fit was never seriously challenged.

The manufacturers, as well as all of the other people of a hamlet, were creatures of a culture that involved small-scale capitalist enterprise and a factory system of production that could only develop so far, that is, it was limited by the potential for water-powered operations in this area. Wallace devotes considerable attention to the nature of the machines involved and to the people who created and dealt with them (the machine technicians, managers, and especially the manufacturers). One gets from him an intimate sense of a workplace filled with picking and drawing machines and the throstle, mule, and loom, all of these turned by a complex series of belts, shafts, and gears, as well as the human routines involved in working with them. Workers (usually several from each family in the hamlet, including children) were subject to rules designed to promote a general orderliness and precision of operation. These emphasized cleanliness, punctuality, no smoking, no drinking of alcohol, no fighting, and no fooling around between the sexes. The division of labor is seen to be affected by the machines and their arrangement, which were constantly being upgraded and displacing workers associated with them.

What kind of meaning did the people of Rockdale attach to their work? What to them was the point of their productive activity? Max Weber argued that certain kinds of Protestants in Europe and the United States during the industrial era worked in their jobs (callings) in order to save themselves in the afterlife. This and other versions of the belief in "salvation by works," that is, saving oneself in the afterlife by one's earthly activities, were to be found among the leaders of Rockdale. Referred to as Evangelicals by Wallace, these Protestants believed that it was possible simultaneously to pursue economic gain, help one's fellow humans, and accomplish personal salvation. Indeed, they felt obliged to do all three and to try to get others to do the same. Wallace views the development of Rockdale in part as a struggle of these Evangelicals to make their views prevail among the nonbelievers and weakly spiritual in the community and outside. In short, they were missionaries (hence "Evangelicals").

So, the idea world of this community—or at least of the dominant people in the community—had a religious component that supported its industrial way of life. It was thought that some divine plan enjoined individuals to work out their own salvation not only by hard work, saving, and felicitous investments, but also by honesty in public dealing, church activity, and public service. Wallace quotes from personal documents to show how strongly some people in the community believed in this form of salvation by works. And because the people of higher rank appear to have had a strong sense of responsibility to convert others to the gospel as they saw it, their views, besides justifying a developing capitalist-industrial way of life, also appear to have provided support for a growing American imperialism in the world.

But what is there about Wallace's study of Rockdale that is specifically anthropological? Couldn't it be considered a historical work, for example? Of course it could. Anthropologists, like other social scientists, "trespass" on the preserves of other disciplines (and vice versa). Regardless of method and subject matter, however, they have a special intellectual heritage that others have only recently discovered. That heritage involves the concept of culture and the necessity of comprehending it wherever it occurs. Using personal documents and other historical materials, this is what Wallace does in his study of Rockdale. As a result, the reader gets a realistic picture of these people who are "just down the road," as he puts it. The emerging species of social historian would have accomplished much the same thing.

The picture that Wallace presents does not involve huge factories spewing smoke and other forms of pollution and dominating human beings in and around them. Here, with the small-scale use of a clean, renewable resource, something like a balanced equilibrium prevailed. Families, many of whom had earlier been farmers, tended to remain intact; and though there were social abuses (child labor and sometimes difficult working conditions, for example), most people appear to have gone along with what usually was a fairly benevolent, paternalistic social arrangement.

One problem with Wallace's study is the slight attention he gives to the social setting of this industrializing community. Where does Rockdale fit into the overall picture of industrialization in the United States? Wallace makes only vague references to many other communities similar to Rockdale in the developing United States and to larger communities, such as Lowell, Massachusetts, with big cotton-based industrial establishments. Where does the comparatively simple industrialism of Rockdale stand in relation to later, more expansive developments that involved widespread abuse of people and environment and significant conflict between management and labor? And what of the shadowy market that determined the ups and downs of production, the industrial competitors in Europe and America, and the cotton producers who provided the raw materials? All of these presumably played some role in the industrialization of Rockdale and could have been brought into the picture.

Wallace also encounters a frequent problem with historical sources. Often, they concern people of higher social rank. Here, they tend to favor what Wallace refers to as the "managerial class." The letters of the manufacturers and their wives give us the best impression of real people in the book. Such people were the ones who, in this paternalistic community, had the most to do with shaping its culture, but one wonders about the humbler people of Rockdale who may have come and gone more frequently. What were they like, and how did they view things in and outside of the mill? How did they respond, for example, to the efforts of some managers' wives to convert them? Information about such people has been obtained from live informants in some historical studies of industry, but in this case, the time frame was beyond the reach of this method.

These criticisms aside, Wallace's study does what any study of a culture should do. It reveals a way of life "in the round," that is, industrialism is seen to be a part of a whole way of life lived by a group of people. By showing how industrialization occurred in a specific case, Wallace is able to get a grip on a more general, but limited theory of culture change, one that involves the notion of a series of revolutionary inventions, each of which is elaborated over a period of time.

INDUSTRIALIZATION AND THE INDIVIDUAL

What does industrialization do to the individual? Earlier, it was pointed out that social scientists have associated certain sociocultural trends with industrialization. I say "associated" because I do not want to get hung up on the question of causation here. What is mainly responsible for these trends? Is it technological development, urbanization, an increase in the scale of a variety of social tasks, or a particular kind of economic system? Obviously, these are interrelated, but in the contemporary world, technology has come to assume a position of paramount importance. So, regardless of the nature of a culture (whether it tends toward socialism or capitalism, for example), as the scale and complexity of the technological task increase, so too will the social organization. Consider, for example, the Russian and American space programs with their gargantuan technological tasks. Both have spawned enormous, complex organizations to run them. In such instances, there is a greater specialization of the functions necessary to accomplish the organization's goals, as well as a more complex system of authority that is needed to coordinate them.

What are the consequences of this for the individuals in and around them? It means that they must deal with a greater variety of others, each of whom has a somewhat different point of view. Now, following from the increasingly various roles they must play and the social identities associated with them, people ought to be driven back on their heels, so to speak, and rely more and more on themselves for direction. That this is, in fact, the case for contemporary America is demonstrated in a nationwide investigation by Carmi Schooler ("Social Antecedents of Adult Psychological Functioning"), which shows that employed American men who were raised in a more "complex, multifaceted environment" (for example, in the Pacific states or in a city), tend to be more individuated, if intolerance of external constraints, subjectivism, and the development of intellectual capacities are taken to indicate this. The hypothesis also receives support from Geert Hofstede's cross-cultural study (*Culture's Consequences*) of the work-related attitudes of employees of a large multinational corporation, which shows a significant correlation between the general level of industrialism of an employee's country and his or her individualism. Hofstede barely touches on socialist countries in his study, but impressionistic observations suggest that the advance of the technological order in more collectively oriented countries has also been associated with a growing individuation.

What about the specific qualities of the increasingly individuated people required by the advancing industrial order? A number of more or less impressionistic suggestions come to mind. One way of making coherent sense out of all of these issues is to continue with the machine model that has dominated this discussion. If a society is heavily committed to the machine way of life, then its people ought to be more machine-like in their natures. Where assembly lines prevail, the people on them will reflect their position in a system of production that amounts to being a cog in a machine. Alex Inkeles and David Smith, in their cross-cultural study of developing peoples (*Becoming Modern*), show that, among other things, this type of factory experience does indeed tend to inculcate these qualities. And with the emergence of computer-directed robots, it is the computer and its requirements that takes hold of its operators. In each case, it is the machine and its program that establishes the basic routine of the job. This suggests that bodily functions, for example, which tend to have routines of their own, will have to give way to machine-dictated routines and it accounts for the fact that in a series of preliminary investigations, I have found evidence that more "developed" Americans tend to be more alienated from their bodies (presumably through the psychological processes of repression or suppression) than people from less developed countries.

The transformation of the individual by industrialization is, of course, never so clear-cut as these hypotheses suggest. In the first place, it is difficult to find adequate cross-cultural data on the subject. Imagine, for example, trying to construct a cross-cultural instrument that would get at individualism, as Hofstede did. Second, there is evidence to indicate countervailing tendencies or throw-backs to earlier epochs in any industrial arrangement. There may be, for example, a vigorous informal culture in a modern factory or bureaucracy that is based on individual feelings and personal relations. The American coffee breaks and the Japanese outings referred to earlier are examples of this. In addition, family ties and feelings that are not supposed to enter into full-scale industrial operations can persist and even be incorporated into them, as Wallace's study of Rockdale and Tamara Haraven's study of the mills of Manchester, New Hampshire (*Family Time and Industrial Time*), amply show. Finally, if we are indeed moving in what has been called a post-industrial direction where more complex minds and creative selves are in demand, there may be an opportunity for greater freedom on the job. All of this suggests that though the effects of industrialization on the individual can be considerable, even as people can never be completely socialized, they can only partially take on the character of machines.

CODA

It is all well and good for a more individuated person from an advanced industrial society to say (perhaps with some relief) that people cannot be made into machines (or, for that matter, into creatures of the state or some other social institution). But this possibly comforting idea is not the only conclusion that an anthropologically trained person should draw from this discussion. Looked at in anthropological terms, the culture of a highly industrialized people has both good and bad points. At the moment, however, some of the bad points are pretty disturbing. When all life on earth becomes threatened by certain cultural developments, one has to be concerned. Yet people may not want to think about it, or if they do think about it, they may feel there is little that can be done.

A little anthropological reflection would show that this is the way a culture comes to dominate the people who have created it. But as soon as one begins to think about the machine way of life and how dependent people can become on it, one begins to loosen the hold of industrialism. The anthropologically trained person would see, as a matter of course, not only the dependence of individuals on machines, but also how their operation pervades all areas of industrial life, and the consequences of this for the environment. An awareness of other cultures not so dependent on machines and an understanding of the process of adaptation that all cultures must address would help this person to sort out the harmful and beneficial consequences of machine-based practices, and therefore figure out how "necessary" they are.

Having loosened the hold of culture by some anthropological consciousness raising, people now have a greater opportunity to choose. Surely, an important choice is whether to rule or be ruled by machines. Cultures, as we have seen, are created by humans and maintained by them. Cultural ways can therefore be given up or changed. If, as seems likely, people decide that machines and the things that go with them are too good to be given up completely, the question becomes how to control them in order to maximize human benefits now and in the future. Environmentally and socially friendly practices might be real alternatives. Ventures in "appropriate technology," in which the scale and complexity of machines and their operation are adjusted to the ends that people want to achieve, are examples of this. Thus, simple, small, wind-driven pumps, instead of electrically driven machines that depend on some huge (possibly dirty) nonrenewable power complex, might be used in small irrigation projects. Or, household enterprises could function along with factories to accomplish certain forms of production.

Finally, there is the question of how to implement the choices one makes about machines and their use. In some cases, it will appear that little can be done. There is not enough money, some people with heavy investments in certain ways of doing things are too powerful, or the changes might have too many nasty side effects. Consider, for example, a project to reduce American dependence on private automobiles and increase the use of more energy-efficient public transportation by busses and trains, with which I am involved. This is a desirable project from my point of view inasmuch as the car is a great polluter of the atmosphere and a great consumer of refined oil that comes increasingly from sometimes politically unstable developing countries. It is obvious, also, that the aged, the crippled, and the poor who cannot afford automobiles will benefit. But this project violates one of the supreme American values (a car or two for every home) and entrenched economic interests such as auto and energy industries, state highway departments, and so on. Even here, however, some progress can be made. Cities are increasingly feeling the crunch of traffic and their parking facilities are being used up. The installation of a system of penalties and incentives against commuter use of motorcars and for the use of public transportation has proved to be not out of the question; and a turn to the increased production of such transport may become a real possibility. It would help, of course, if as much money were spent on advertising this alternative as is currently spent on promoting motorcars. With an awareness of how the culture operates, and of the principles of culture change, informed people can act more effectively to push for more sustainable cultural practices such as this.

It is not only machine technology, but all culture traits that can be questioned and acted on in this way. People who have studied anthropology know that though everyone becomes to some extent a creature of their culture, they are also capable of shaping it to better fulfill their own and collective needs. If she had read a little anthropology, the average American homemaker mentioned at the outset of this chapter might be aware of this— even early on a winter morning.

SELECTED REFERENCES

ARON, RAYMOND, *The Industrial Society*. New York: Praeger, 1967.

ASHER, ROBERT, *Connecticut Workers and Technological Change*. Storrs: University of Connecticut, Center for Oral History, 1983.

COOK, EARL, "The Flow of Energy in an Industrial Society," *Scientific American*, 225, (September) 1971, 134–44.

HAGE, JERALD, and CHARLES POWERS, *Post-Industrial Lives*. Newbury Park, CA: Sage Publications, 1992.

HARAVEN, TAMARA, *Family Time and Industrial Time*. Cambridge, England: Cambridge University Press, 1982.

HOFSTEDE, GEERT, *Culture's Consequences*. Beverly Hills, CA: Sage Publications, 1980.

HOSELITZ, BERT, and WILBERT MOORE, *Industrialization and Society*. Paris: UNESCO-Mouton, 1963.

INKELES, ALEX, and DAVID SMITH, *Becoming Modern*. Cambridge, MA: Harvard University Press, 1974.

SCHOOLER, CARMI, "Social Antecedents of Adult Psychological Functioning," *American Journal of Sociology*, 78 (September), 1972, 229-332.

SPIER, ROBERT, *From the Hand of Man: Primitive and Preindustrial Technologies*. Boston: Houghton Mifflin, 1970.

WALLACE, ANTHONY F. C., *Rockdale*. New York: Alfred A. Knopf, 1978.

WHITE, LESLIE, *The Evolution of Culture*. New York: McGraw-Hill, 1959.

American Culture

The Individual to the Fore

THE PROBLEM

It is a challenge to try to comprehend American culture (or the culture of any large, complex society) in a single, brief chapter. Consider some of the obstacles. First, there are always problems with studying one's own society. Earlier in this book it was pointed out that one takes a good deal of one's own culture for granted. As a result, the questioning attitude so necessary in any anthropological investigation may be lacking. Second, the United States is a big, complex, highly differentiated country. There is not one "city on a hill," to quote a phrase used by former President Ronald Reagan, but many "cities" with different ways of life. There is considerable variation according to wealth, region, ethnic and racial background, gender, and sexual preference, to mention only some of the differentiating factors, a fact that students at American colleges and universities are becoming aware of through the increasing stress on diversity in and outside of the curriculum. General statements about American culture with its highly differentiated way of life, therefore, are difficult to make. Third, American culture, like any culture, is multifaceted. Many different kinds of behavior make up a way of life, and they are changing more or less rapidly. In America this is especially the case, making it more difficult to find any internal coherence in its culture. Finally, any American knows that the ways in which things are done in this society are changing rapidly. To get at something that abides for more than a generation is not easy.

Despite such problems, and despite the fact that they have been primarily concerned with the non-Western world in their studies, American anthropologists have been looking into American culture for some time. This has mostly involved, however, the study of fringe elements such as the poor, the downtrodden, or strange religious sects with which they seem to have a special affinity. But anthropologists have begun to join sociologists and other scientists to investigate more central aspects of the society. All of this work provides the basis for the present chapter, which is informed by the anthropological perspective cultivated in this book. Here, I consider Americans as another one of all the peoples it is the anthropologist's privilege to study. Americans, like all of the others, are seen to have a culture that has a history and fits into some social and natural setting. From what we already know about it, this particular culture appears to be a very complex system of highly differentiated, changing parts, which will make it extremely difficult to propose rules or norms that apply to all—or most—Americans. Generalizations may soon begin to founder in the melange of subcultural variability that is clearly evident. Is there *anything* that these obviously various Americans have in common?

One thing that many Americans seem to share is what might be referred to as their "middle-classness," and it is in the ideals of the American middle class that I propose to look for the key elements of American culture. Over and over again in public surveys, despite a considerable (and recently growing) disparity of income, the vast majority of Americans (more than eight in ten, according to recent surveys) have assigned themselves to an amorphous category that they call the middle class. This is no surprise, considering the stress on equality that many scholars of the American scene, beginning, perhaps, with Alexis de Tocqueville (in *Democracy in America*), have found in American life, as well as the current facts at our disposal. It is the members of the middle class, many of whom are in the process of leaving their ethnic identities behind, who establish the dominant tone of American culture.

This is not to say that Native American Indians, recently arrived immigrants, or the considerable number of more or less deprived African Americans are unimportant. But these individuals tend to be something of the nature of outsiders, whose lives tend to revolve loosely around the predominantly white middle class. There are also the various power-wielding elites—the board members of big corporations, the owners of expensive homes in Palm Beach or Palm Springs, the big donors to presidential campaigns and charity fund-raisers, and the newly rich of this or that burgeoning industry—who, while undoubtedly accepting the perquisites of elite status, are nevertheless cautious about putting themselves too far above the great middling category. For them, even, the pull of middle-classness continues strong. In America, it is difficult to escape the influence of this middle ground.

George and Louise Spindler offer a similar view in *The American Cultural Dialogue and Its Transmission.* They see various groups in American society carrying on a dialogue, the reference point of which continues to be the ways of a somewhat WASPish middle class. Some groups, such as upper middle-class whites whose ancestors came from Northwestern Europe, have fully internalized these values, while others such as lower middle-class African Americans are struggling to come to terms with them. The same kind of struggle characterizes the American women's movement in its attempts to gain full equality for women in a society that has not yet eliminated racism or male domination. According to this view, which may at times overemphasize the consensual aspect of American culture, even those groups such as countercultural New Age people or the erstwhile "hippies" still may be taking mainstream values into account in working out their adaptation. Some may be lukewarm about them, others may be in revolt, but most take them as a point of orientation.

What are these mainstream values and how widely are they shared? Despite all of the current talk about diversity, national samples of Americans' opinions reveal a considerable consensus on certain points. Using a number of such samples of American adults questioned in the 1970s and 1980s, Alex Inkeles (in "National Character Revisited") has constructed an "American Ethos" consisting of an array of values on which three out of four Americans demonstrate agreement. These values have to do with a number of different aspects of culture such as governance, the economy, and the person. In looking over the list one is immediately struck with Americans' preoccupation with the person, or more specifically, the autonomous person. Looked at from Inkeles' data, Americans appear to be highly individuated and to think of themselves as detached, self-governing people.

Something of the nature of this concept of person or self was intimated in Chapter Three where comparisons were made between Americans and Japanese. It is important to keep in mind that the person we are considering here is culturally structured or constituted and is a distillation from a range of tendencies that can be observed not only in individual citizens' responses to polls, but also in the various idea worlds of the culture. In Inkeles' analysis, as well as in the advertisements, movies, songs, agendas of the educational and therapeutic establishments, and slogans of the business world and politicians, it is possible to discern an ideal of personal autonomy that appears to be a central feature of American culture. However, as Melford Spiro emphasizes in "Is the Western Conception of the Self 'Peculiar' within the Context of World Cultures?" it is important to keep in mind here that we are considering a *cultural ideal* and not individual Americans' conceptions of themselves, which may vary from this ideal.

Many observers, beginning perhaps with the Frenchman, Alexis de Tocqueville, who visited America in the early days of the Republic, have noted the emphasis on individualism among Americans. To cite a more recent example, Geert Hofstede, in his cross-cultural study of job-related attitudes among employees of the great multinational corporation, which has been referred to at various other points in this book, notes that American employees are the most individualistic of the forty different nationalities that he tested. American individualism has been conceived and evaluated in different ways, but it is the rare observer of the American scene who has not been struck by it. Of course, Americans are not the only individuated people in the world and they certainly have not given up on social involvement, but this quality stands out among them.

Where does this individualism come from? What are its determinants? Here, I will mention only some of the many explanations that have been suggested. Certainly, American individuation is at least partially derived from English individualism, which in *The Origins of English Individualism* Alan MacFarlane traces back to the Middle Ages. Industrialism also seems to have contributed to it. As was pointed out in Chapter Ten, individuation is everywhere associated with industrialization, and America is perhaps the most industrialized nation of the world. Many observers refer to the American version of a competitive, private enterprise economy, that is, capitalism, as a cause. Protestantism, with its emphasis on the individual's direct relation to God (as opposed, say, to the Catholic use of intermediaries such as priests and saints) also has been implicated. Some authors suggest that the European-derived current of political ideas that flowed through the pens of the American founding fathers was responsible, while others point to the wide-open spaces of the American frontier. Whatever the reason or reasons, they seem to have conspired to make Americans one of the most individuated peoples of today's world. In the United States, the person tends to be thought of as separate from the setting in which they must function. Americans stand increasingly alone, and despite rising collective pressures from the big public and private bureaucracies and mass media, which Americans use to organize their increasingly complex social life, the value of the autonomous person still persists. What is its specific nature?

THE AUTONOMOUS IDEAL

"I've Gotta Be Me" goes a popular song. Frank Sinatra, the singer who made it famous, seems to have taken the songwriter's advice. The cowboy heroes played by a couple of generations of movie stars have been superseded by various private eyes, police officers, and lawyers who fill American movie and television screens. These are mostly people who manage to be true to themselves in an often uncooperative world. Many Americans would like to be like them. What is the nature of this ideal self that is thought to go with such a character?

First, the ideal American self tends to be separate or distinct from others. There are clear boundaries between it (and the things associated with it) and what belongs to it and the rest of the world. Second, it tends to be thought of as located within the individual and not, for example, in his or her relationships with others. Third, this self is supposed to be the result of one's own choosing. Though responsive to social considerations, the individual tends to be thought of as someone who ultimately makes up his or her mind about who to be and how to act. And finally, even though socially aware and involved, this self (when push comes to shove) is considered to be more important than any other. These generalizations refer to an American ideal, of course, which, as it turns out, many Americans fall short of realizing. The struggle to come to terms with this ideal, which is the main theme of the modern existential novel, often is in fact the story of a typical American's life. Born into a society where who one is to be is not laid out early in life, and faced with the difficult task of making sense out of the definitional input from a complex society in flux, Americans tend to be in a position of weakness when it comes to making up their mind about who they are. There are plenty of outside others who tell them who they are or who they should be, but these others generally do not have the force of personal persuasion that one sees in a smaller, simpler, more tradition-bound society.

That Americans have a tendency to think of themselves as separate and distinct from others is suggested by an exploratory study by Richard Shweder and Edmund Bourne ("Does the Concept of Person Vary Cross-Culturally?"), in which small groups of people from Chicago, Illinois, and the state of Orissa in India (no national samples were involved) were asked to describe close acquaintances. Responses were categorized and compared statistically. Shweder and Bourne found that the American respondents were more likely to use abstract, context-independent terms in their descriptions; for example, an American might say that an acquaintance was "stubborn," "friendly," or "difficult." Though the Indians used terms like these, they were more likely to say something like "He shouts curses at his neighbors" or "He jokes with his friends." This indicated to the authors that the notion of person held by the Orissans in the study tends to be more concrete and context-dependent and that the Chicago Americans are more likely to think of themselves as separate and distinct from others. Obviously, this small study is a far cry from one employing representative national samples and, therefore, should be taken with a grain of salt, but the differences noted seem to be in tune with what we know about Americans from other sources.

The American self discovered by Shweder and Bourne in their study and evident from other sources would seem to have its uses in a society where individual mobility is high. Tending to define themselves as detached individuals, Americans could more readily cut ties to specific people or situations and move on and up. Inkeles reports that 98 percent of the Americans in his samples agreed that "everyone in America should have equal opportunities to get ahead." The self-realization project of the typical American, therefore, would involve freeing oneself from ascribing influences, such as family, relatives, and community, and succeeding in the world. College students who go away from home are involved in this process, and they may experience some of its difficulties, one of which is trying to make sense of a shifting, ambiguous world. In contrast to many other peoples (excepting those who have been subject to catastrophic social changes), Americans encounter greater confusion in their life courses, a confusion that seems to be steadily increasing. They find fewer tried-and-true recipes for defining themselves in a way that enables them to act with assurance. Ultimately, they are supposed to make up their minds about this, but many find this hard to do. For assistance, Americans may look to culturally emphasized areas that, depending on how they are used, can provide either support or fulfillment. One can see this in different areas of life, for example, the worlds of work, material objects, and other persons.

Although there is a growing underclass for whom working in a meaningful job is only a remote possibility, most Americans find work to be a particularly important aspect of their lives. Work is the area *par excellence* of what Robert Bellah and his associates refer to in *Habits of the Heart* as utilitarian individualism. To know what an American *does*—more specifically, the kind of work he or she does—is to get a preliminary idea about who that person is. At the beginning of the usual public opinion survey is a question about the respondent's occupation. Americans answer the question with "salesman," "machinist," "engineer," "homemakers," and so on, and in so doing, they begin to define themselves.

The importance of the job for Americans is particularly apparent at times of layoffs, which were numerous during the Great Depression and which continue to worry workers these days as corporations downsize in the interest of their "bottom lines." In addition to sometimes severe economic pressure and associated anxiety, layoffs can be a threat to the American individual's identity; at such times an American may begin to creep about in an apologetic way and sink into depression. The jobs Americans hold should also have prospects for the future. These people like to think of themselves as being on their way up to higher levels of income, power, or prestige. Women of a previous generation were more likely to depend on their husbands for their identity, and accordingly, referred to their spouse's achievements in the world when defining themselves. Now, they are more apt to pursue self-realization on their own, and they also entertain American visions of success. But for men and women alike, success, like happiness, is a goal with a quicksilver quality about it.

A part of the *doing* orientation that many observers have attributed to these people, work now seems somewhat less important than it once was in this culture. Indeed, Max Weber's view of religiously driven workers seems less and less applicable. American college students, for example, may be told by parents or professors of an older generation that they don't know the meaning of work. There is probably some truth in this. They do not seem to feel the same pull of work the way the older generation did, which may be responsible for the rise in importance of institutions that cater to what Bellah and his associates refer to as expressive individualism. The vacation is increasingly an end in itself rather than a time to renew oneself for work. Leisure industry stocks are good bets for growth on the New York Stock Exchange. Retirement communities are multiplying, especially in southern regions. In these, more and more older Americans are exploring activities that open up new, more expressive areas of themselves. And for Americans who have trouble finding satisfaction with such things as games, hobbies, and pure sociability, there are trips to faraway places and any number of therapists or counselors who will try to help them express their feelings and gain satisfaction from *being* rather than *doing*.

Although this trend is well under way, it would seem to be a mistake to say that expressivity has supplanted the utilitarian attitude as the dominant orientation of American individualism. Reversing a well-established trend, the working hours of the average American have even increased recently, and in a typical middle-class family it is more likely that the wife/mother will be working to add to its income. So work continues to be a cornerstone of the American culture. Indeed, 83 percent of Americans in Inkeles' study argued that they would continue to work even if well fixed for the rest of their life.

A second area in which Americans can gain self-support or fulfillment is in the realm of the material world. The pursuit of wealth (a material symbol) is an overriding concern. If not making money, the typical American tends to feel some sense of inadequacy. All of the things that Americans identify with can be partially or wholly reduced (in their minds) to money. Consider their world of material objects. In an earlier era, the things that people produced such as a bridge, a railroad locomotive, or a loaf of bread probably played a more important part in Americans' conception of self than they do now. As alienation of workers from the finished product has advanced, as the service sector has expanded, and as knowledge-based skills have become ends in themselves, it has become more difficult for Americans to think of themselves as producers of some material product. Instead, the realm of consumer goods is increasingly the point of existence. People buy houses and begin to think of them as their own. Or they believe the diet faddist who claims that "you are what you eat." People accumulate material possessions that become more or less tied up with themselves.

Take, for example, the car, an archetypical prop for the American male identity that enables Americans to be quickly and easily mobile, but that is a cause of so much environmental degradation. A young fellow may believe that he should have a high-powered machine that gives him a head start at the stoplight. Later on in life, he may move toward more sedate models. The purchase of a new car adds something to the self, but that something has to be renewed periodically. So the American, urged on by a crescendo of advertising (for example, "We build driving excitement") is in the market for a new car more and more frequently. He may even purchase more than one to express different aspects of himself or provide for different members of his family. Even toward the end of life when he may become a threat to others with his driving, he wants to hang on to his car as, perhaps, a last vestige of his manhood.

On the female side, clothes tend to function in the same way. American women also get involved with cars, but (more than men) they tend to think of themselves in terms of the clothes they wear. One must have on the correct dress for the occasion or time. Women renew themselves through the endless cycles of fashion, which are watched with radar-like sensitivity. (A "house-mother," I knew asked about the major problem among her young college women, said "What to wear.") In the workplace, American women worry about wearing the correct "uniform" and thus about presenting themselves properly. On a night out they may want to exhibit a greater uniqueness, which David Riesman in *The Lonely Crowd* calls "marginal differentiation." American women, of course, are not alone in such preoccupations. Clothing and fashion seem to be important to women in other cultures as well (for example, in France).

Material accumulation is a fact of life in American society. Unlike the aboriginal San, wandering hunters and gatherers for whom the accumulation of possessions amounts to excess baggage, Americans live in a culture where the desire for material things is supposed to expand continually. *In Culture Against Man*, Jules Henry traces the connections between an ever-expanding productivity and the character of different kinds of Americans. He points out that, in contrast to a primitive society where (if all goes well) production rises to meet wants, American wants *must* rise to meet production. So, there have to be homemakers who feel a threat to their identity if they do not have the latest kitchen utensil, young people who feel deprived without the latest stereo gimmick, and generals who experience fear if America is not in the vanguard of arms technology. In a fascinating study of material possessions in contemporary American life, *The Meaning of Things*, Mihali Csikszentmihalyi and Eugene Rochberg-Hilton point out that Americans have carried material accumulation so far that they have now entered a phase of "terminal materialism," that is, a period when material possessions begin to be acquired for their own sake.

I have saved for last what may be the most interesting area for American identity—work, that is, the world of other persons. Though an ideal of untrammeled individuation continues to be attractive to some Americans, as indicated by the popularity of writers like Ayn Rand or some of the discourses of people in conservative religious groups, most Americans are, in fact, importantly involved with others. The weakly autonomous may depend on others to tell them who they are, while the strong may find in others a path to fulfillment. Whether they begin from strength or weakness, most Americans are enthusiastic participants in social life. It would seem that they, indeed, need others almost as much as they need to stand alone. Many Americans are constantly "on the make," with their renowned openness and friendliness, to get others to respond to them in a way that tells them they are accepted—even loved—and that, therefore, each of them is *somebody*. How important this is for their self-conceptions is quickly apparent when strategies that have proven routinely effective at home do not work, as in a Vietnamese prisoner-of-war camp or with Frenchmen for whom friendships tend to be longstanding affairs and not so easy to acquire.

How do Americans think of the other persons in their world? There are two general classes of such beings: those who play by the same rules (and who are, therefore, entitled to a fair shake) and those who do not. Ideally, every American is considered to have an equal right to exercise his or her self-interest provided that others' self-interest is not violated. Competition can be fierce in America and many competitors fall by the wayside, but the competition ideally ought to be carried on according to the principle of fair play. This is why Joe Paterno, the highly successful Penn State football coach, has so much contempt for cheaters. They do not live up to the American ideal. Those who fail should not do so because others cheat, but because of some fault of their own. Thus, 77 percent of Inkeles' Americans feel that what happens to them is their own doing. This is partially fiction because not all Americans are prepared to compete on equal terms. One has only to watch a class where people from an urban ghetto are being trained to get on the job trail to see how much they have to learn to make themselves presentable to an employer. Paterno, for example, has had all those sons and grandsons of coal miners and steel workers living nearby who could be turned into linebackers and an established reputation that brings elite quarterbacks and running backs to his door. An American may be aware of the fiction involved here, but usually not enough to give it up as a guiding principle. A visit to a developing country, where people who get an advantage over others are expected to use it and where life is a continual round of dominance and submission, would show a sceptical American how important this principle is for him or her.

Let us resort to an American metaphor: the ballpark. Outside of this ballpark are others who play by different or opposing rules. These people, who vary according to current American preoccupations, can be used as negative points of reference in defining the self. For a former generation, it was the fascists, especially Nazi Germans. Since World War II, there has been the communist threat, which can be magnified by Americans' intense fear of socialism (82 percent of the people in Inkeles' sample think that communism, if adopted by the United States, would make things worse for most Americans). Today there are terrorists spilling out of the Middle East and criminal elements spawned in big city ghettoes. "People who won't work," who collect welfare checks for a living, or who fail to take advantage of the opportunities provided have long been targets of American strivers. And for fundamentalists, that great abstraction of all evils, Satan and all that he stands for, provides the supreme negative point of reference.

On the positive side, that is, inside one's own ballpark, there is considerable room for maneuver. Here are one's equals of the moment or better-than-equals who one would like to emulate. They include advertising models who are manipulated to generate more desire (and therefore consumption), the people in one's own profession, the so-called Joneses who Americans try to keep up with, and so on. In contrast to peoples living in simpler, more tradition-bound societies, Americans have more of a choice about who they will "play" with. Jules Henry's acute analysis of American adolescents is an appropriate way of introducing the problems they face. On their way to adulthood, he points out, American adolescents are confronted with the challenge of leaving their families' orbit and getting involved in new personal communities. In order to do this they must make themselves appealing to others. Henry, using the adolescents' discussions of their own problems, demonstrates how unsure of themselves these young people are and how much anxiety they feel in their social life. This anxiety would seem to be bound up with the problem of self-definition. American adolescents are bent on finding themselves through the responses of others, and most of them spend a good deal of their time presenting themselves in ways they hope will give them the kind of response they need. Of course, as Bernard Lefkowitz makes clear in his book, *Our Guys*, which deals with the darker side of an American suburb, things go a lot easier for the handsome jocks among them.

One of Arthur Miller's characters, Willie Loman (in *Death of a Salesman*), is an overgrown adolescent who, permanently unsure of himself, failing in his job, and past middle age, has dreams of being loved in Scarsdale, Providence, and other towns on his round. This, for him, is the primary measure of success. Loman, is, of course, a fictitious character, but Miller seems to have put his finger on a principal preoccupation of many Americans for whom achievement and the self-realization that goes with it are measured in terms of the acceptance, recognition, and even love they manage to wring from others.

The tragedy of Willie Loman illustrates the dangers of a context-dependent self in this society. Here is a man whom the world (of the traveling salesman) has passed by; and because he is dependent on that world for a sense of self, he succumbs. Whether it is through work or leisure, the material realm, or others that one finds self-definition, the context-dependent option can have only limited success in America. This is so because, in contrast to Orissa, India, where a more stable social world provides the long-term, consistent feedback that is necessary for a firm sense of self, Americans live in a world of flux that offers conflicting and confusing signals about who they should be. For this reason, it would seem that a context-independent strategy of self-realization would be the more adaptive course in this society. That this course is being followed by some Americans (how many?) is suggested by the study of Shweder and Bourne mentioned earlier.

That this option has also been accompanied with steps toward true autonomy has been confirmed by a nationwide investigation by Carmi Schooler, which was mentioned in the Chapter Ten. And, in a rebuttal to those critics who argue that this development spells trouble for individual Americans, Schooler notes that people with a more autonomous self have a greater feeling of self-worth. What was earlier regarded as a utopian goal for Americans and other advanced industrialized peoples by David Riesman and his associates, that is, the development of individuals with more assured, autonomous selves who carry out their lives on the basis of personal choice rather than external dictation—may be on the way to realization, in which case the American cultural ideal will be fulfilled. Considering the vast social forces that are arrayed against individuals in this society, however, this realization can never be accomplished easily, and it is likely that many Americans will adopt some kind of compromise similar to what Michael Moffatt reports finding among Rutgers University students (in *Coming of Age in New Jersey*). That compromise involves offering a series of agreeable, mask-like presentations of self in the style of the person conceived by Erving Goffman in *The Presentation of Self in Everyday Life*. But, according to Moffatt, there is a different, truer self behind these masks, which permits the individual to follow the American ideal of the autonomous self even while appearing to be one of the boys or girls, so to speak.

THE CULTURE OF THERAPY: AMERICAN STYLE

In a Woody Allen movie, almost everyone seems to have a shrink. This is an exaggeration—even for Manhattan—but there are certainly many Americans who, struggling with problems of self-definition, are resorting to psychotherapy of one sort or another. In the Hollywood area I once asked a psychiatrist how business was. His response: "Are you kidding?" The American therapeutic establishment is flourishing as more and more clients, dissatisfied with the way their lives are turning out, beat a path to its doors.

This establishment consists of psychiatrists, counselors, psychologists, social workers, religious practitioners, and the like who adhere to a variety of therapeutic systems. Some of these people deal with psychotics and use drugs and hospitalization as principal methods of treatment, but even these people are likely to treat neuroses and behavior disorders for which some kind of psychotherapy is indicated. It is with these latter kinds of disorders and their treatment that I am mainly concerned here. The treatment is carried out by therapists who appear to have a subculture of their own. Using the information gathered by Robert Bellah and his associates as a principal source, I want to lay out some of the essential elements of this subculture and show how it is connected to what has been taken here to be a key fact of American culture, the self.

These days it is considered more and more acceptable for a troubled American to seek professional help from some kind of therapy. The therapist may work one-on-one, with couples, or with larger groups. Medication may be prescribed, but ideally the form of treatment involves people talking to each other. In orthodox psychoanalytic therapy the patient does almost all of the talking, and other therapies also try to keep the interventions of the therapist to a minimum.

The more or less asymmetrical relationship between patient and therapist in secular psychotherapy is contractual, that is, the patient usually pays for the service of listening, with some intervention occurring now and then. This relationship is also segmental, in that it represents only a part of the participant's current life; it is ideally profound on the part of the patient in that strong feelings and significant changes can result; and finally, it is (hopefully) of short duration. The patient usually follows a fixed routine: regular sessions with the therapist and perhaps others and routinized procedures. Eventually, he or she is expected to leave the relationship and go it alone. Experts are uncertain about how much improvement is accomplished by this "talking cure," as one of Freud's patients called it, but its effectiveness is not at issue here. One might also raise questions about the prevailing custom in upper-class England a century or more ago of going to the French Riviera to cure bronchial ailments. But criticism of the effectiveness of a system of therapy need not invalidate its influence over peoples' behavior.

What are the reigning beliefs of the American therapeutic establishment? Bellah and his colleagues got at some of these by interviewing practitioners, clients, and bystanders who share (more or less) the views of the first two. Indeed, they found that the beliefs of the establishment permeate the society and are selectively adopted in the workplace, the political arena, and the church, for example. The first of these beliefs (which Bellah and his co-workers seem to have assumed) is that if conditions are right, some form of healing will take place. The establishment tends to be upbeat about its effectiveness. The prevailing view seems to be that if experience made the problem, other experience can unmake it. They, like the American educational establishment, may recognize that the possibilities for change are not limitless, but they certainly feel that the potential for change is considerable. Second, they believe that a large part of therapeutic progress is up to the patient who must take an active role in the treatment. Third, they believe that during the course of therapy the patient must gain greater insight into, and acceptance of the forces that move him or her. If there has been, for example, repression or selective forgetting of anger toward the opposite sex, it must be recognized and accepted, which enables the patient to gain a degree of control over the once hidden force that has been troubling him or her. Finally, it is desirable for patients to give up their sense of unreasonable obligation to others, as in neurotic guilt, for example. Ideally, they should come to realize that they do not owe others anything and that they should take responsibility only for their own actions. Others may be important to them, but they should act not for the sake of others, but for what others mean to (or do for) them. This means that people will do less running after others to define themselves. The American therapeutic ideal (in contrast to that of the Japanese mentioned in Chapter Three) promotes an individual who knows who he or she is without a lot of feedback from outside and who accepts this knowledge, whatever it amounts to. The individual, thus, is guided by his or her own personal standards and is truly autonomous. One American New Age spiritualist is reported by Michael Brown (in *The Channeling Zone: American Spirituality in an Anxious Age*) to have gone so far as to suggest that human beings are, in essence, gods.

Bellah and his associates, were concerned about the social consequences of this "radical individualism," and they vigorously questioned some of their respondents to see how far they would take it. Asked if she would ever accept responsibility for another, one respondent said no. Was she responsible for her husband? No. And what about her children? Were they responsible for their own acts? Though hedging a bit, she nevertheless answered in the affirmative. So, in the end one is responsible only to oneself. People should know themselves and know how others fit into their life. In their relationship with others they do have a responsibility to be open and aboveboard, but that is all. They should act in terms of enlightened self-interest, and if a relationship no longer satisfies that self-interest it should end. It may be argued that this extremely individualistic response came from a skewed sample of the American public (research on American therapy was carried out in "a southern city" and "the San Francisco area"), but there are good grounds for arguing that this response is not too far out of line with contemporary mainstream values.

All of this illustrates how different elements of a culture or subculture tend to go together. In this case a therapeutic institution has arisen to deal with problems of the key element of a culture, the self. In America the process of individuation is far advanced, which means that people are very much on their own when it comes to establishing an identity. They have their problems, however. Attempts to define oneself by reference to the external world (the context-dependent option) do not work as well in America as in a simpler and more stable preindustrial setting such as Orissa. But the alternative strategy of developing a more context-independent self that will permit one to move with assurance in a shifting, impersonal world is not so easy in this society. Many people need help. Some of this is provided by a burgeoning institution of psychotherapy that aims to produce the truly autonomous selves that are the American ideal.

However effective American therapists are in helping people solve their personal problems, they cannot solve all of them. Intrapsychic conflict can never be eliminated, and problems of the individual with others and in society will continue. American psychotherapists, for example, cannot guarantee that a successfully treated person will find the long-term, intimate relationship he or she has been encouraged to look for. And it would be difficult to give most Americans the feeling that their own affairs and those of the dominant institutions of their society are closely intertwined. American society itself also has its problems, which would appear to be beyond the reach of individual-oriented therapies. What, for example, can the American practice of psychotherapy do about the growing gap between rich and poor in America and the world? What is the answer to the many problems of an environmental nature, booms and busts in the economy, or the threat of nuclear holocaust? There are the homeless, urban adolescent "wolfpacks," various "militias"and many people with AIDS. And what of the sense of national community that American presidents from time to time refer to? It is clear that even if all Americans do realize themselves perfectly, this realization cannot be a panacea for them or for other peoples. Freud, the father of psychotherapy, was aware of all of this, but many American psychotherapists and like-minded others, who have taken on the effort-optimism orientation of this culture, may tend to forget.

THE AMERICAN SELF IN ACTION

Despite problems with a world that seems to be getting more and more out of control, many domestic difficulties, and personal problems, most Americans remain comparatively optimistic about their life and the possibility of making it better. Constantly on the move toward some future goal or other, they often are impatient with past practices and with history. There is routine, of course, but in this culture routines are made to be broken. Americans often seem to feel best when they are on their way somewhere or planning something new. In their various projects they like to take the most efficient course. "Time is money," they say, and it always seems to be "a-wasting." Speedy accomplishment (as with a computer, for example) is desirable, and the resulting frenetic pace of American life has been remarked upon by many observers. But Americans' speed is supposed to be highly controlled and focused. They set goals for themselves and move forward step by step to reach them. If there is a particularly large job to be done, such as trying to put someone on the moon, it is divided up into a series of rationally organized, manageable problems. In working on a problem they find it desirable to rule out all extraneous matters, which contrasts with the less task-specific behavior of people in less industrialized countries. Americans would find the behavior of a group of pot-making gypsies I once encountered rather bizarre. There they sat, those gypsies, chatting with each other and enjoying the give-and-take. Every now and again, one or another would give a few whacks to a pot they were making. Their production moved forward slowly and unsystematically, it seemed to me, and I, being an American, was acutely frustrated by the irrationality of it all. I thought of my father's saying, "When you work, work, and when you play, play," and my mother's, "Get a move on," and I wondered why these people could not see the self-evident truth of such propositions. Other overseas Americans such as Peace Corps representatives and medical technicians who are trying to get their less industrialized hosts to adopt more efficient procedures are similarly frustrated.

In going about their various projects in life, Americans still like to think that they have, or ought to have, their destinies pretty much in their own hands. They are supposed to live in the "land of the free" where everyone has the right to say what they think (97 percent of Inkeles' sample believed in freedom of speech). This ticket to apparent anarchy, or what has been called the war of each against all, does not in fact produce such dire consequences because Americans' freedom is necessarily limited. They have freedom, true, but they also recognize that others are entitled to a similar freedom that has to be respected. In addition, there is the need to be liked, which was discussed earlier. Finally, there are the growing bureaucracies, which increasingly organize the lives of individual Americans, and the mass media, which influence their thinking. The result of this is considerable conformity mixed with individuality. Florence Kluckhohn and Fred Strodtbeck were not quite correct when they said, "In America one is free to be like everyone else," but it is obvious that Americans tend to exaggerate the freedom they have (or would like to have) to be themselves.

Sometimes peoples' projects get tangled up with one another. Then, it is considered appropriate for the individual to confront the other directly and not beat about the bush. Nurses still may have trouble doing this with doctors, but assertiveness training courses are now helping them to do what others are supposed to do when really pressed. Problems between individuals and groups are thought to have some rationally based solution if only everyone will declare themselves openly and give a little. This is the way their democratic society is supposed to operate. The fact that it does not always do so, and that legal and governmental remedies are necessary, does not invalidate the moving power of this point of view. Despite evident contradictions here, as indicated by the increasing numbers of people who resort to these remedies (America has been called a litigious society), there remains a strong belief that with proper individual initiative things can be worked out. There still is a can-do attitude and an essential optimism that this, combined with American know-how and effort, can solve most problems. This is especially the case when it comes to huge technological accomplishments such as space flight or to the development of a worldwide organizational structure such as IBM. People everywhere have marveled at these great feats of engineering and social engineering that seem to be getting harder and harder to accomplish for one reason or another.

Americans, themselves, take satisfaction in the grand scale of their accomplishments, but their identification with them tends to be superficial. Consider how often Americans use "they" rather than "we" in referring to the powerful others—such as the Pentagon, Union Carbide, and the government—that can have important influences on their lives. Instead, they prefer to look to more intimate groups such as the family, the small community, clubs, religious groups, or small friendship groupings on and off the job for support and fulfillment. In these circles they are on terms of at least passing intimacy with others. However, in contrast to smaller, more intimate societies, getting to know and understand others in America is not so easy. The comings and goings of people, the numbers involved, and the existence of special interests prevent it. Bellah and his associates suggest that what has emerged is a kind of contractual intimacy in social relationships that can be ended according to the changing interests of those involved, a condition that was mentioned in the discussion of ascription and achievement in Chapter Four.

Americans are coming to know that there are a lot of problems in this world that they cannot solve, yet they continue to have great faith in the person and his or her ability to accomplish things, as well as in the system that gives this person the necessary freedom to accomplish them. A visit to a gathering of salespeople or real estate developers, a political convention, or a backyard cookout in suburbia will convince even the most hardened cynic about this. Even in periods of economic downturn, Americans seem more upbeat than other industrial peoples under similar circumstances. It is not hard to see, therefore, why so many writers stress the effort-optimism orientation of American culture. But there is another side of these Americans that comes out, say, during a visit to the Vietnam Veterans Memorial in Washington, at a time when someone has had too much to drink, on hearing the latest disquieting news from around the world, or possibly on awakening in the dark of night. Then there are the fears, the most important of which, in this society so dedicated to achievement and success, is the fear of failure. These people may fear that they won't amount to much, that others won't have a good opinion of them, that the results of their individual efforts may not measure up to someone's expectations, or that all of their efforts and the efforts of like-minded others will be defeated by a fanatic with an atomic bomb, a madman in the Middle East, or an uncontrollable disease coming out of Africa. And finally, there is the ultimate fear of all: that the self they prize so highly and that they have struggled so hard to realize will, like all other living things, eventually die.

SELECTED REFERENCES

BELLAH, ROBERT N., RICHARD MADSEN, WILLIAM SULLIVAN, ANN SWIDLER, and STEVEN TIPTON, *Habits of the Heart: Individualism and Commitment in Family Life*. Berkeley: University of California Press, 1985.

BROWN, MICHAEL, *The Channeling Zone: American Spirituality in an Anxious Age*. Cambridge, MA: Harvard University Press, 1997.

CSIKSZENTMIHALYI, MIHALI, and EUGENE ROCHBERG-HILTON, *The Meaning of Things*. Cambridge: Cambridge University Press, 1981.

GOFFMAN, ERVING, *The Presentation of Self in Everyday Life*. Garden City, NY: Doubleday / Anchor Books, 1959.

HALLOWELL, A. IRVING, *Culture and Experience*. Philadelphia: University of Pennsylvania Press, 1955.

HENRY, JULES, *Culture against Man*. New York: Random House, 1965.

HOFSTEDE, GEERT, *Culture's Consequences*. San Francisco: Sage Publications, 1980.

INKELES, ALEX, "National Character Revisited," *Tocqueville Review*, 12, 1990–1991, 83–117.

KLUCKHOHN, FLORENCE, and FRED STRODTBECK, *Variations in Value Orientations*. New York: Row, Peterson, 1961.

LEFKOWITZ, BERNARD, *Our Guys: The Secret Life of the Perfect Suburb*. Berkeley: University of California Press, 1997.

LUKES, STEPHEN, *Individualism*. New York: Harper and Row, 1973.

MACFARLANE, ALAN, *The Origins of English Individualism*. New York: Cambridge University Press, 1979.

MEAD, MARGARET, *And Keep Your Powder Dry*. New York: William Morrow, 1965.

MOFFATT, MICHAEL, *Coming of Age in New Jersey*. New Brunswick, NJ: Rutgers University Press. 1989.

RIESMAN, DAVID, with N. GLAZER and R. DENNEY, *The Lonely Crowd*. New Haven, CT: Yale University Press, 1965.

SHWEDER, RICHARD, and EDMUND BOURNE, "Does the Concept of Person Vary Cross-Culturally? " in *Culture Theory: Essays, in Mind, Self, and Emotion*, ed. Richard Shweder and Robert Levine, pp. 158–99. New York: Cambridge University Press, 1984.

SPINDLER, GEORGE, and LOUISE SPINDLER, *The American Cultural Dialogue and its Transmission*. London, New York, and Philadelphia: Falmer Press, 1990.

STEWART, EDWARD, and MILTON BENNETT, *American Cultural Patterns: A Cross-Cultural Perspective*, 2nd ed. Yarmouth, ME: Intercultural Press, 1991.

TOCQUEVILLE, ALEXIS DE, *Democracy in America*. New York: Shocken, 1961 (1835).

WOLF, ALAN, *One Nation After All*. New York: Viking, 1998.

THE END?

This little venture into the domain of (sociocultural) anthropology now is finished. In it, the reader has been introduced to cultural ways that peoples of the earth have created and by which they live. Compared with other animals, humans have a great capacity to adapt to the circumstances in which they live; but the adaptations of groups of people, once created, tend to solidify into social heritages that take on a momentum of their own. Persistence and change in these heritages or cultures is limited by their history and the setting in which they exist. Of course all human beings share a biological heritage given by evolution that is responsible for many of the similarities among them, but there also is an enormous variety in the ways in which humans act. Because people must live in groups and participate in their cultures in order to survive, a good deal of their behavior is culturally dictated. One of the benefits of anthropological study is that it reveals the sometimes hidden nature of a culture's control over people and the possibilities for individual freedom.

A good deal of anthropological work aims to explore particular cultures in depth, to find out if and how different aspects of a people's way of life hang together, and to work out the manner in which individuals fit into them. But anthropologists are also inveterate comparers. They like to discover out the ways in which cultures differ from one another as well as the things they have in common. The peoples of the earth have developed an immense cornucopia of cultural ways, and any good library is filled with reports on hundreds—even thousands—of them. In this little book, the reader has been exposed to a number of cultures from different parts of the world and has been given the opportunity to compare them. One comparison that people like to make is between their own and other cultures. So it was with Samantha Smith, a young American, who once made a visit to Russia at the invitation of the Soviet government. After her little bit of "fieldwork," Samantha Smith said that "down deep, they are just like us." There are those who would disagree with her assessment, but whatever its validity, it illustrates a mental process that often follows a person's exposure to another culture, a process that has been developed to a high art in anthropology. Needless to say, a lot may hinge on particular comparisons of cultures, and they sometimes had best not be left to initial impressions of amateurs.

In addition to having been exposed to different cultures and guided in making comparisons between them, readers of this book have been introduced to the ways in which anthropologists explain why cultures, or particular aspects of cultures, are as they are. Why do the Tiv often purchase wives? Why are they patrilineal? Why don't the headmen of the little Basseri bands have power to make decisions on their own? Why do the Japanese tend to be more collectively oriented than Americans? These are the kinds of questions that begin to nag at us even as we begin to explore other cultures. Anthropologists have created a number of explanatory schemes, but all of them must take into account the fact that any culture trait is created and maintained by people who are subject to certain biologically dictated constraints. It also is a part of a whole culture or group way of life that has a history and that fits into some particular setting. Some of the ways in which anthropologists have worked out explanations have been touched on in this book.

In the foregoing, I have tried to suggest that readers who have finished reading *A Little Anthropology* have only begun to explore the human condition or conditions. If the book is, in fact, a genuine introduction, many readers will not want to stop here, but will seek to continue on their own or in formal coursework. Perhaps they will take a crash course on the eve of some overseas assignment or begin a little "fieldwork" after they get there. For them, then, the anthropological quest will have only just begun. It will not end here.

The study of anthropology usually is not just an intellectual exercise, however. It can also contribute to a person's definition of self. In this encounter with other peoples, we are drawn out of ourselves into the world of others. We try on these others' roles in the same way as we have tried on the roles of fathers, mothers, and other significant others in our lives. Like new clothes, we may reject them, covet them, or accept them with alterations, but we are always asking, "Is this me?" Ethnographic reports, persuasively presented, provide a fertile field for self-realization. Such reports may add to the crisis of identity that affects people, especially young people in complex, rapidly changing societies like the United States, but they can also spark creative solutions to identity problems.

As with former university students who give up more adventurous ways when they take a job and start a family, some individuals may tend to close out their search for identity early in life. For them, further exposure to new and different others can be disquieting, and they may try to hang on to whomever they already are. On the other hand, other individuals may tend to be more open to new experiences of the kind that can come from travel or further study of anthropology. When they have finished *A Little Anthropology*, therefore, they will not have closed the book on self-realization. It will not end here, but may continue to the end of their lives.

Another kind of awareness that can be promoted by the study of anthropology has to do with the links we have with our fellow humans. However cut off from others we may be, anthropology makes us aware that we are part of larger wholes. First, we are a part of some society, and second, of humanity. In a world where the give-and-take between peoples has become an unremarkable fact of life, the poet's observation that "no man is an island" is more relevant than ever. Anthropologists have taken the lead in publicizing the condition of peoples in the less developed world, whose welfare, and even survival, may be dependent on forces emanating from the Developed World. A journal, *Cultural Survival Quarterly*, makes the point repeatedly that there are many peoples whose environment and way of life are threatened by outside forces beyond their control. What will happen to the Mbuti Pygmies when the forest on which they depend for so much is all cut down? And what is to be the fate of all the "little people" of the world who happen to live in areas where big power interests are being played out?

It seems, though, that the problem of survival is no longer confined to the little peoples of the world. It has become a problem for us all. Now, at the end of the twentieth century, ones worries may extend to the future of all of humanity. Beside the natural catastrophes that have, in the past, been responsible for the extinction of more than 99 percent of all the species that have ever existed and which continue to beset us, there is an alarming growth of human-made catastrophes that affect us and other living things. On the one hand are the problems with a poisoned environment that derive from industrialization and its by-products, on the other, the increased scale and destructiveness of human conflict, which, considering the size and extent of nuclear and germ warfare arsenals, have the power to wipe us out many times over.

The words of warning of modern-day prophets about the future of humankind, which may be forgotten until the next crisis arises, ought to fall on fertile ground among the anthropologically trained, that is, those who have considered the entire human enterprise, formed some notion of its value, and become aware of the increasingly fragile nature of its existence. It would seem that they bear a larger share of responsibility for the future of humanity because they have a better idea of what is at stake. So, for the readers of *A Little Anthropology*, one final question: Is there, indeed, a future for the human enterprise which you have just begun to comprehend here? If so, what is that future to be? Or is it all to end?

Index